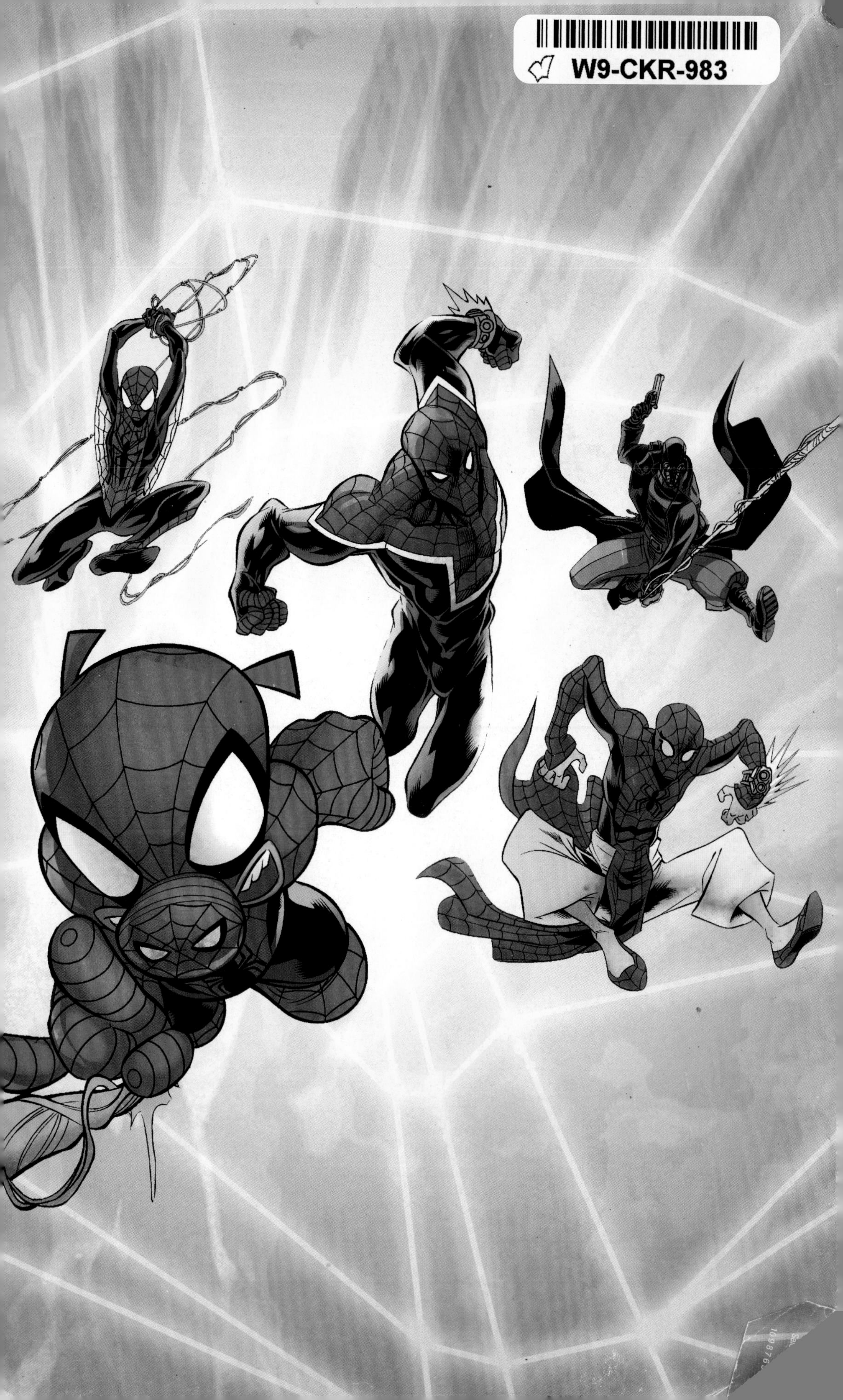

collection editor SARAH BRUNSTAD
associate managing editor ALEX STARBUCK
editors, special projects JENNIFER GRÜNWALD & MARK D. BEAZLEY
vp, production & special projects JEFF YOUNGQUIST
svp print, sales & marketing DAVID GABRIEL
book designer ADAM DEL RE

editor in chief AXEL ALONSO
chief creative officer JOE QUESADA
publisher DAN BUCKLEY
executive producer ALAN FINE

WEB WARRIORS OF THE SPIDER-VERSE VOL. 1: ELECTROVERSE. Contains material originally published in magazine form as WEB WARRIORS #1-5 and AMAZING SPIDER-MAN #1. First printing 2016. ISBN# 978-0-7851-9672-3. Published by MARVEL WORLDWIDE, INC., a subsidiary of MARVEL ENTERTAINMENT, LLC. OFFICE OF PUBLICATION: 135 West 50th Street, New York, NY 10020. Copyright © 2016 MARVEL. No similarity between any of the names, characters, persons, and/or institutions in this magazine with those of any living or dead person or institution is intended, and any such similarity which may exist is purely coincidental. Printed in Canada. ALAN FINE, President, Marvel Entertainment; DAN BUCKLEY, President, TV, Publishing & Brand Management; JOE QUESADA, Chief Creative Officer; TOM BREVOORT, SVP of Publishing; DAVID BOGART, SVP of Business Affairs & Operations, Publishing & Partnership; C.B. CEBULSKI, VP of Brand Management & Development, Asia; DAVID GABRIEL, SVP of Sales & Marketing, Publishing; JEFF YOUNGQUIST, VP of Production & Special Projects; DAN CARR, Executive Director of Publishing Technology; ALEX MORALES, Director of Publishing Operations; SUSAN CRESPI, Production Manager; STAN LEE, Chairman Emeritus. For information regarding advertising in Marvel Comics or on Marvel.com, please contact Vit DeBellis, Integrated Manager, at vdebellis@marvel.com. For Marvel subscription inquiries, please call 888-511-5480. Manufactured between 3/18/2016 and 4/25/2016 by SOLISCO PRINTERS, SCOTT, QC, CANADA.

WHEN A DANGEROUS FAMILY OF INTERDIMENSIONAL VAMPIRES STARTED HUNTING SPIDERS, THE SPIDER-MEN AND WOMEN FROM ACROSS THE MULTIVERSE HAD TO BAND TOGETHER FOR THEIR OWN SURVIVAL. MANY FELL IN THE CONFLICT, AND NOW A SMALL TEAM OF THOSE WHO SURVIVED USE THEIR POWERS TO SHOULDER THE RESPONSIBILITIES OF THE FALLEN AS THE...

PROTECTORS OF THE SPIDER-VERSE
WEB-WARRIORS
ELECTROVERSE

writer
MIKE COSTA

penciler
DAVID BALDEON

inkers
SCOTT HANNA (#1-2)
with **LIVESAY** (#2); and
WALDEN WONG (#3-5) with
VICTOR OLAZABA (#3), **LIVESAY** (#3)
& **ROBERTO POGGI** (#5)

colorists
JASON KEITH (#1-5) with
ANDREW CROSSLEY (#3),
MATT YACKEY (#4),
WIL QUINTANA (#4) &
ANTONIO FABELA (#4)

letterer
VC's JOE CARAMAGNA

"STEAMPUNK'D"
(Web Warriors #1)
writer **ROBBIE THOMPSON**
artist **DENIS MEDRI**
colorist **ANDREW CROSSLEY**
letterer **TRAVIS LANHAM**

"WEB OF LIFE AND
DESTINY" spread
(Web Warriors #1)
writer **MIKE COSTA**
artist **DAVID BALDEON**
colorist **RACHELLE ROSENBERG**
letterer **TRAVIS LANHAM**

"Church and
Quantum State"
(Amazing Spider-Man [2015] #1)
writer **MIKE COSTA**
artist **DAVID BALDEON**
colorist **JASON KEITH**
letterer **VC's JOE CARAMAGNA**

cover art
JULIAN TOTINO TEDESCO (#1-5) and
ALEX ROSS (Amazing Spider-Man [2015] #1)

editor **DEVIN LEWIS**
senior editor **NICK LOWE**

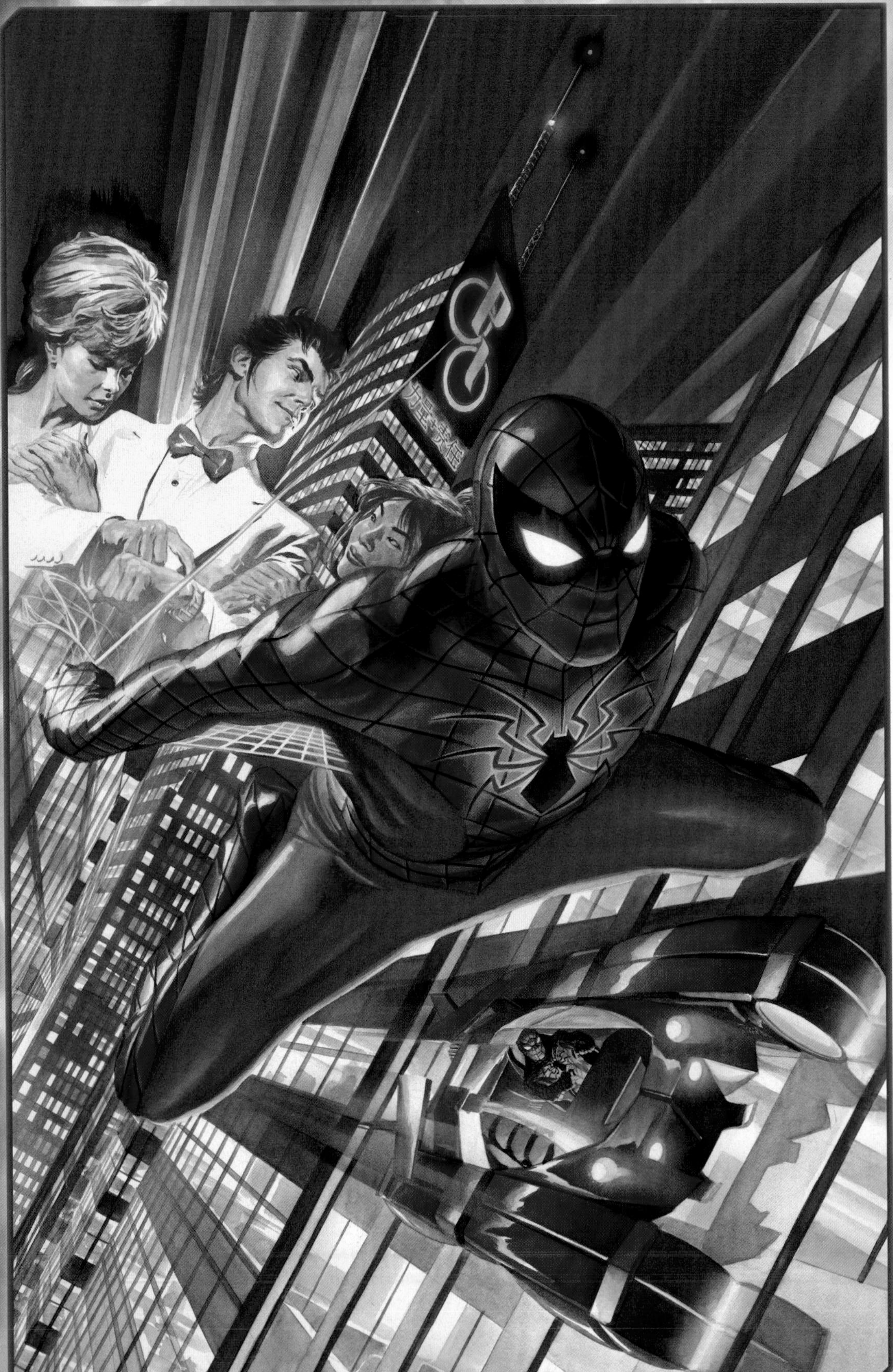

AMAZING SPIDER-MAN (2015) #1

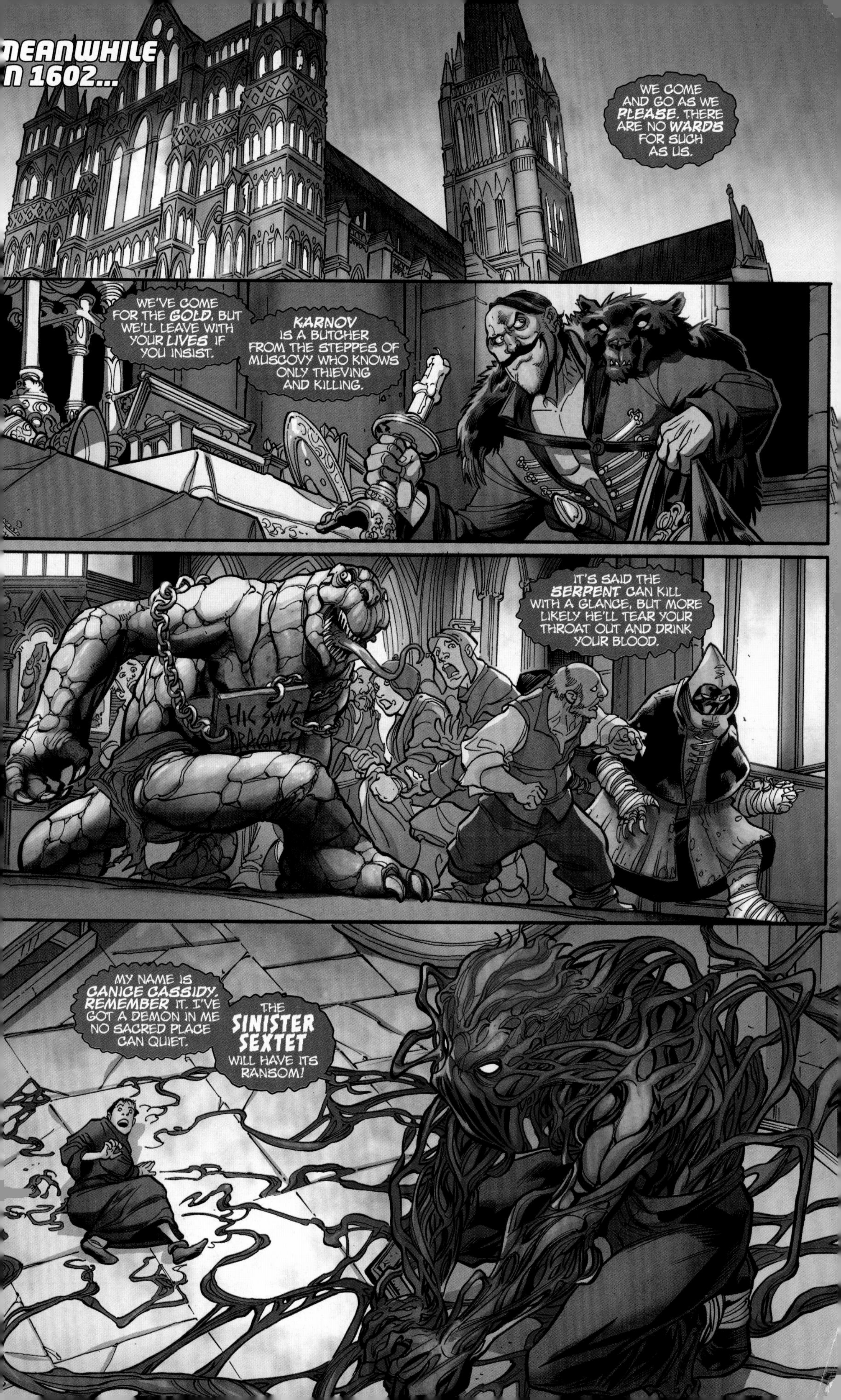

NEANWHILE
N 1602...
WE COME AND GO AS WE PLEASE. THERE ARE NO WARDS FOR SUCH AS US.
WE'VE COME FOR THE GOLD, BUT WE'LL LEAVE WITH YOUR LIVES IF YOU INSIST.
KARNOV IS A BUTCHER FROM THE STEPPES OF MUSCOVY WHO KNOWS ONLY THIEVING AND KILLING.
IT'S SAID THE SERPENT CAN KILL WITH A GLANCE, BUT MORE LIKELY HE'LL TEAR YOUR THROAT OUT AND DRINK YOUR BLOOD.
MY NAME IS CANICE CASSIDY. REMEMBER IT. I'VE GOT A DEMON IN ME NO SACRED PLACE CAN QUIET.
THE SINISTER SEXTET WILL HAVE ITS RANSOM!

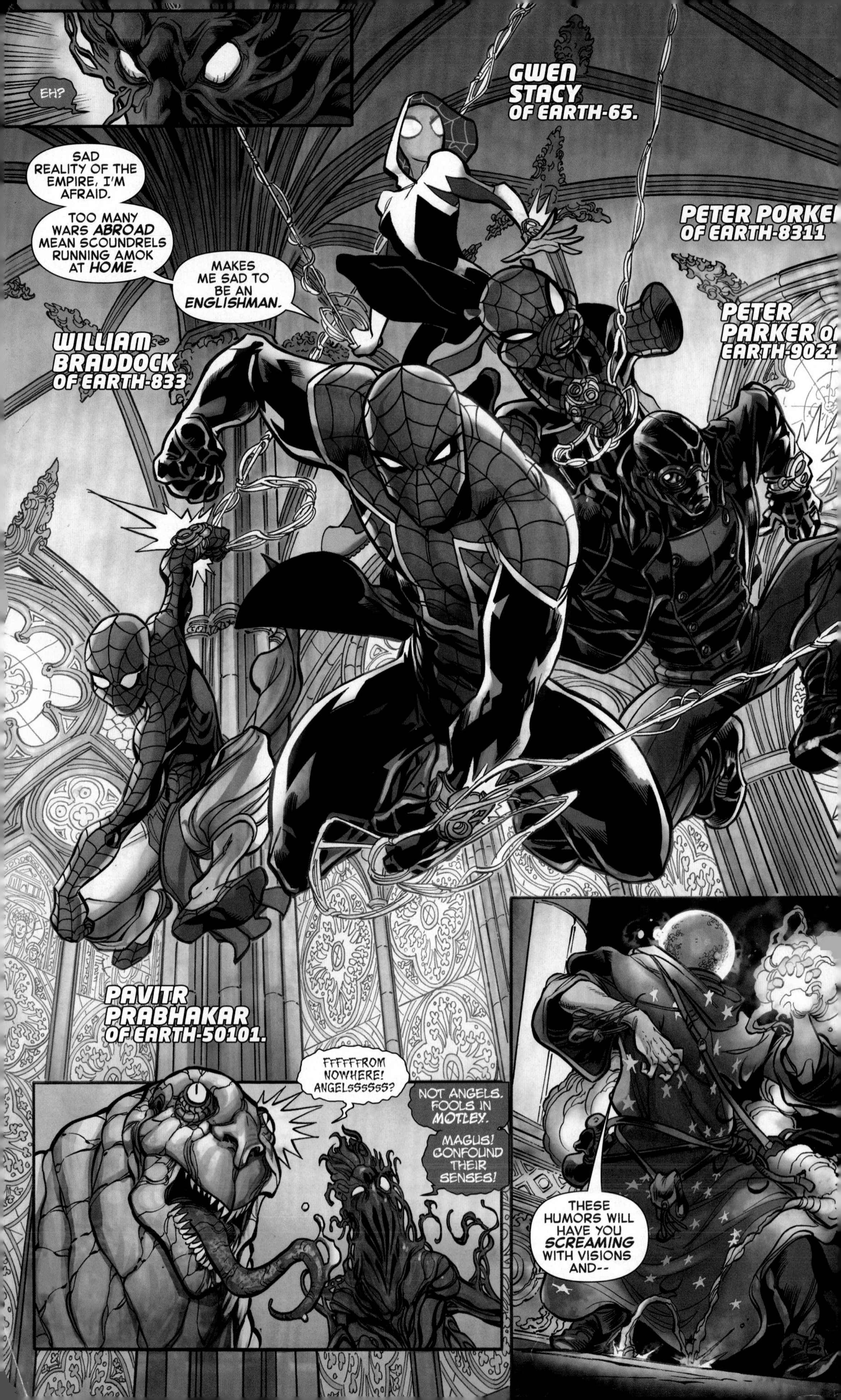
EH?
SAD REALITY OF THE EMPIRE, I'M AFRAID.
TOO MANY WARS ABROAD MEAN SCOUNDRELS RUNNING AMOK AT HOME.
MAKES ME SAD TO BE AN ENGLISHMAN.
GWEN STACY OF EARTH-65.
PETER PORKE OF EARTH-8311
PETER PARKER O EARTH-9021
WILLIAM BRADDOCK OF EARTH-833
PAVITR PRABHAKAR OF EARTH-50101.
FFFFFFROM NOWHERE! ANGELSSSSSS?
NOT ANGELS. FOOLS IN MOTLEY.
MAGUS! CONFOUND THEIR SENSES!
THESE HUMORS WILL HAVE YOU SCREAMING WITH VISIONS AND--

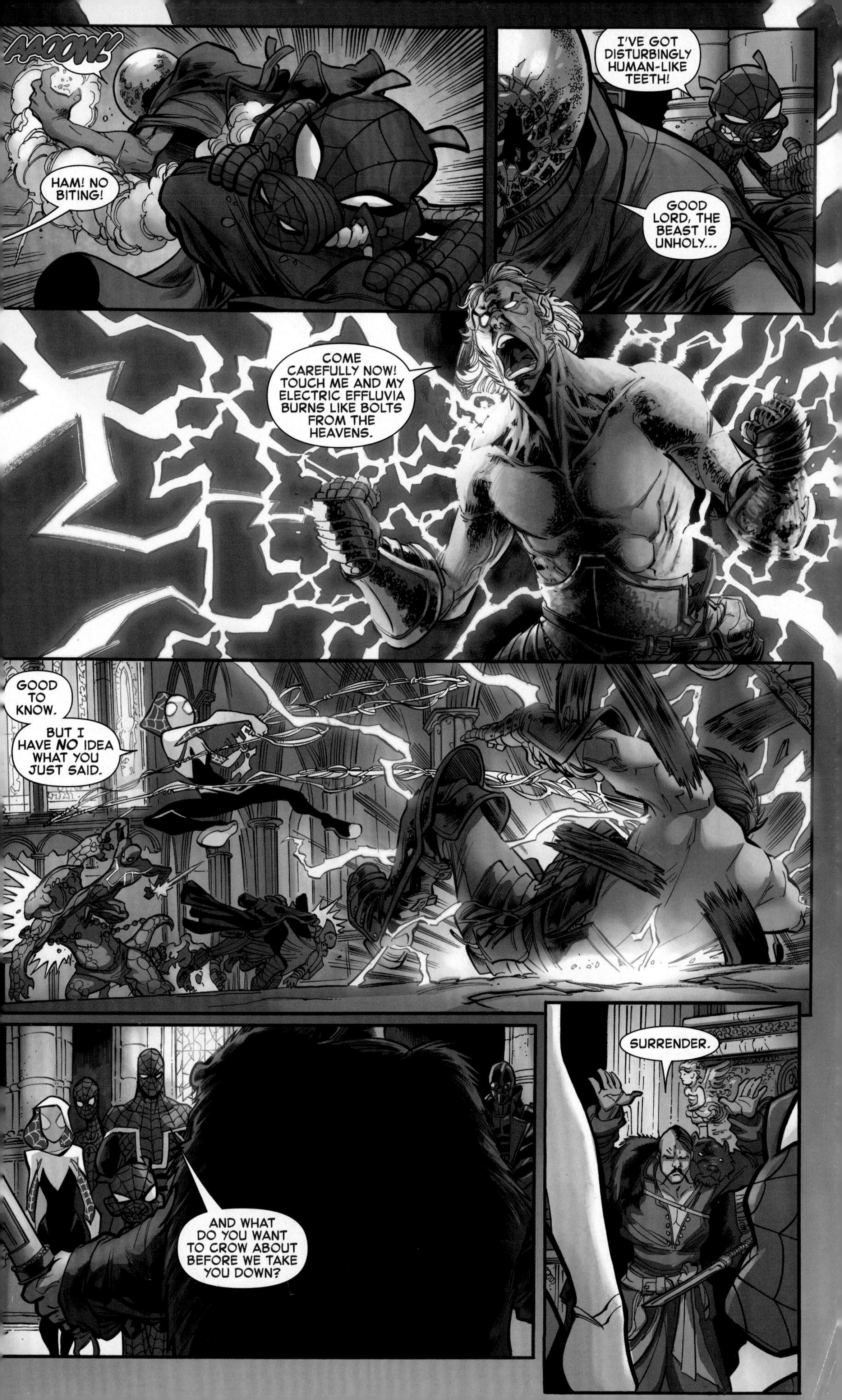
AAOOW!
HAM! NO BITING!
I'VE GOT DISTURBINGLY HUMAN-LIKE TEETH!
GOOD LORD, THE BEAST IS UNHOLY...
COME CAREFULLY NOW! TOUCH ME AND MY ELECTRIC EFFLUVIA BURNS LIKE BOLTS FROM THE HEAVENS.
GOOD TO KNOW.
BUT I HAVE NO IDEA WHAT YOU JUST SAID.
AND WHAT DO YOU WANT TO CROW ABOUT BEFORE WE TAKE YOU DOWN?
SURRENDER.

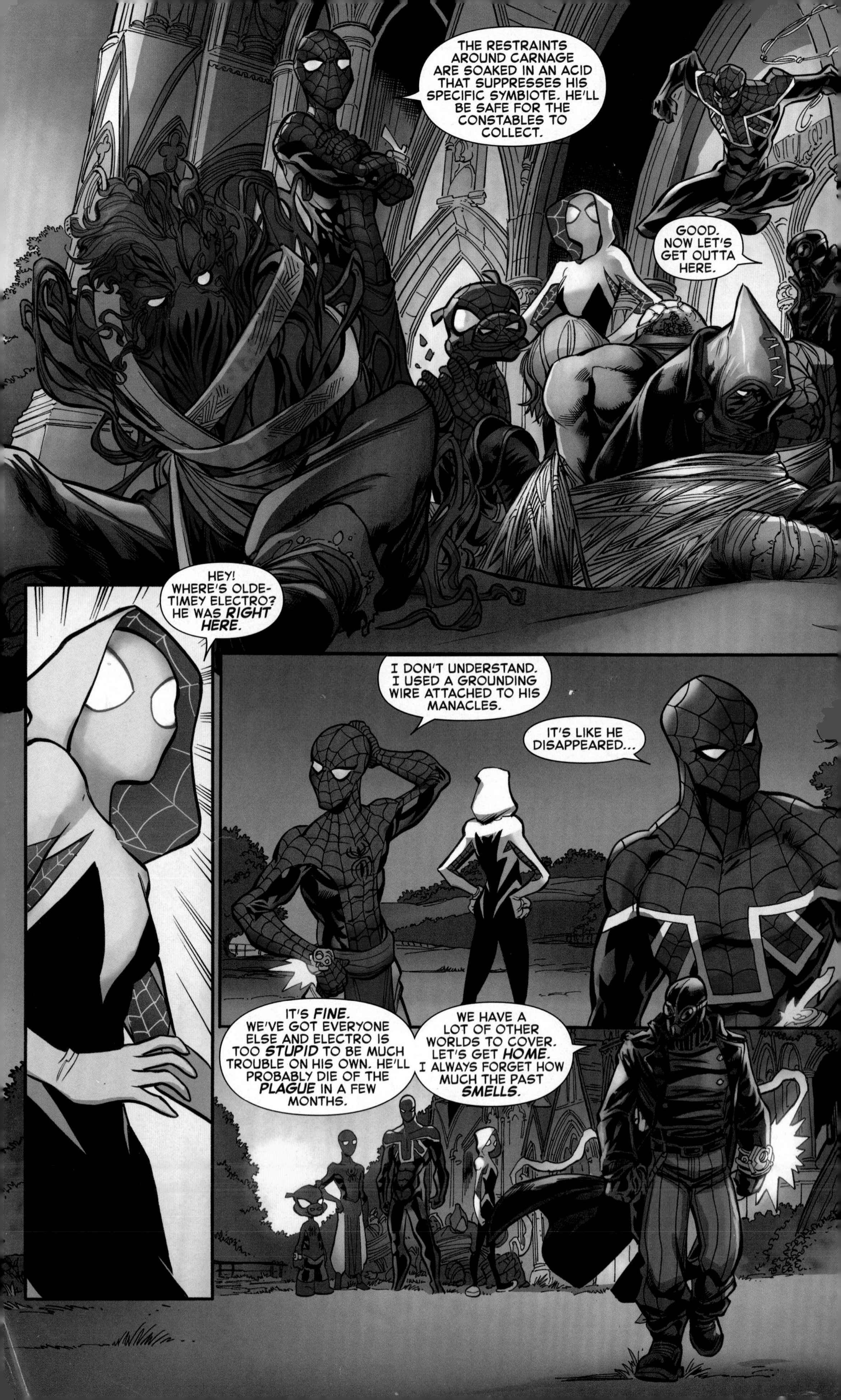
THE RESTRAINTS AROUND CARNAGE ARE SOAKED IN AN ACID THAT SUPPRESSES HIS SPECIFIC SYMBIOTE. HE'LL BE SAFE FOR THE CONSTABLES TO COLLECT.
GOOD. NOW LET'S GET OUTTA HERE.
HEY! WHERE'S OLDE-TIMEY ELECTRO? HE WAS *RIGHT HERE*.
I DON'T UNDERSTAND. I USED A GROUNDING WIRE ATTACHED TO HIS MANACLES.
IT'S LIKE HE DISAPPEARED...
IT'S *FINE*. WE'VE GOT EVERYONE ELSE AND ELECTRO IS TOO *STUPID* TO BE MUCH TROUBLE ON HIS OWN. HE'LL PROBABLY DIE OF THE *PLAGUE* IN A FEW MONTHS.
WE HAVE A LOT OF OTHER WORLDS TO COVER. LET'S GET *HOME*. I ALWAYS FORGET HOW MUCH THE PAST *SMELLS*.

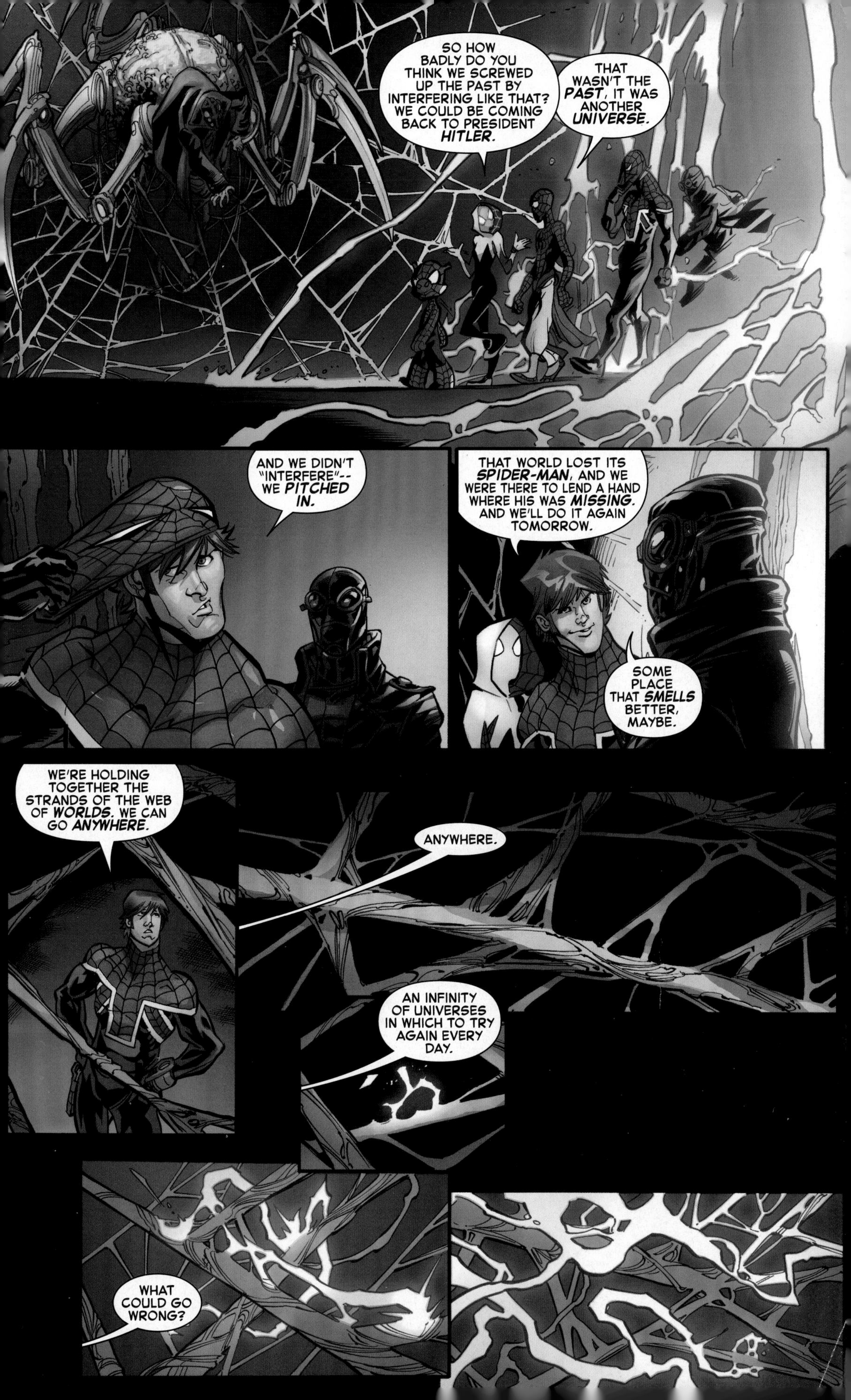
SO HOW BADLY DO YOU THINK WE SCREWED UP THE PAST BY INTERFERING LIKE THAT? WE COULD BE COMING BACK TO PRESIDENT HITLER.
THAT WASN'T THE PAST, IT WAS ANOTHER UNIVERSE.
AND WE DIDN'T "INTERFERE"-- WE PITCHED IN.
THAT WORLD LOST ITS SPIDER-MAN, AND WE WERE THERE TO LEND A HAND WHERE HIS WAS MISSING. AND WE'LL DO IT AGAIN TOMORROW.
SOME PLACE THAT SMELLS BETTER, MAYBE.
WE'RE HOLDING TOGETHER THE STRANDS OF THE WEB OF WORLDS. WE CAN GO ANYWHERE.
ANYWHERE.
AN INFINITY OF UNIVERSES IN WHICH TO TRY AGAIN EVERY DAY.
WHAT COULD GO WRONG?

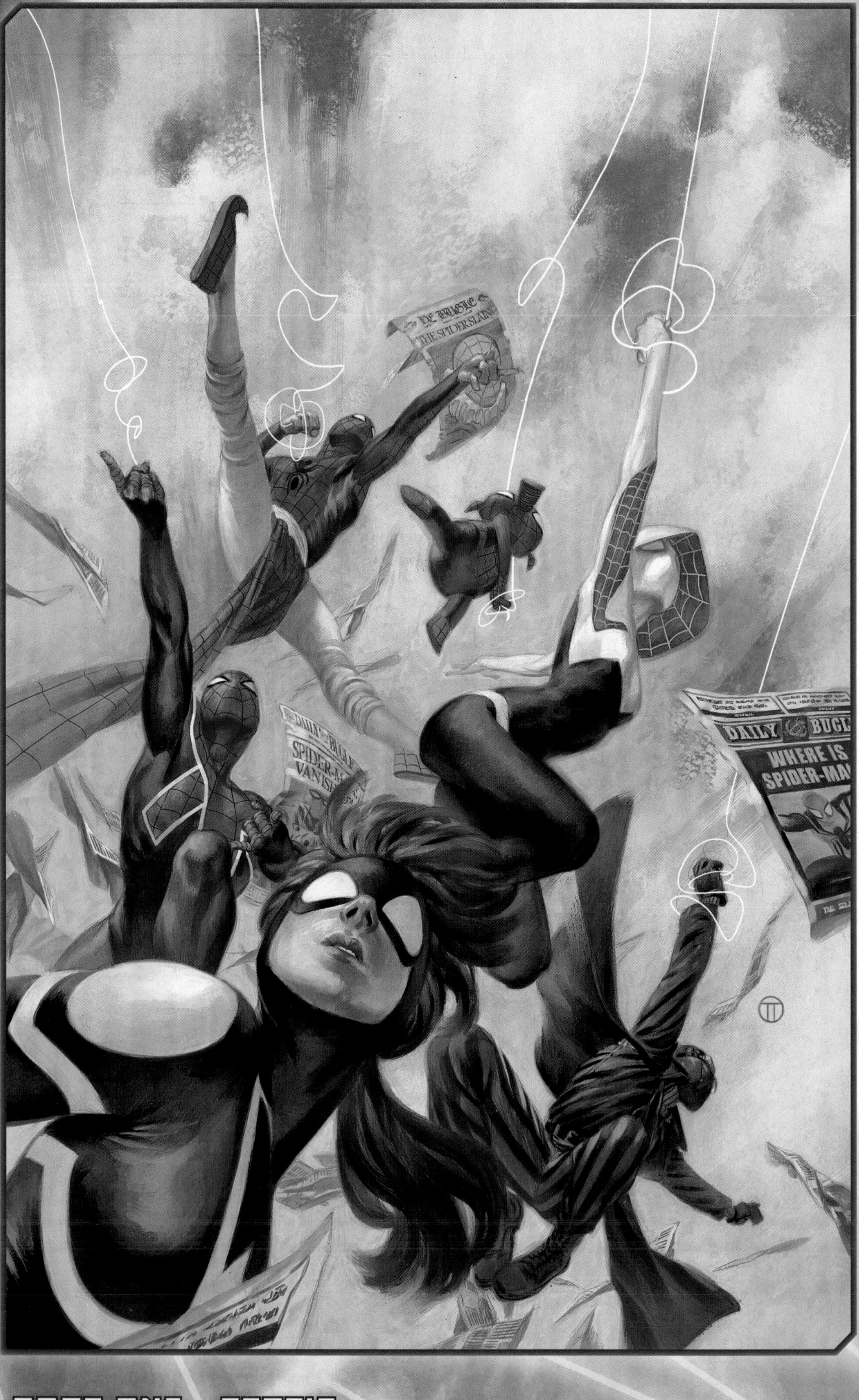
THE SPIDER SLAIN
DAILY
WHERE IS

PART ONE : STATIC

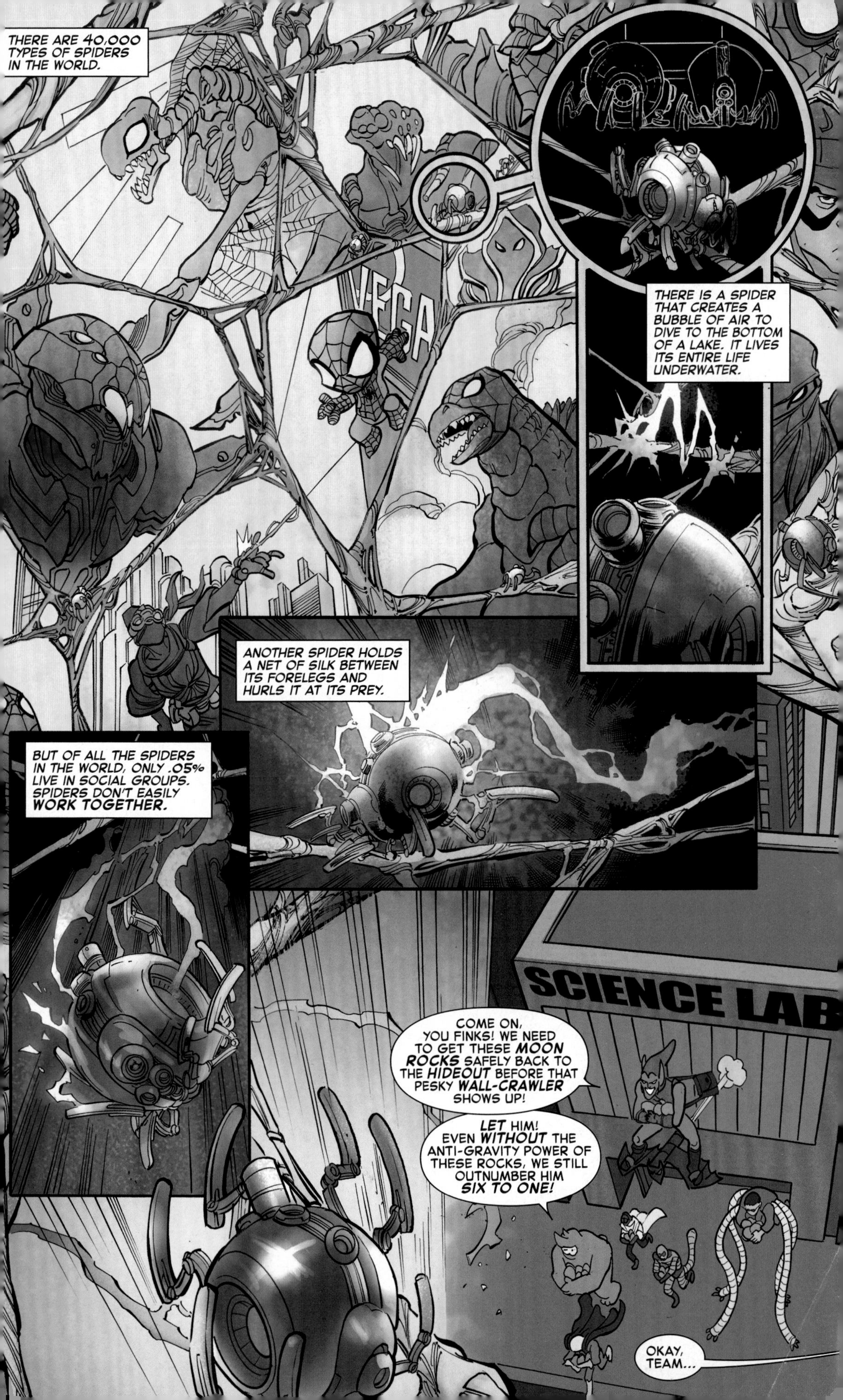
THERE ARE 40,000 TYPES OF SPIDERS IN THE WORLD.
VEGA
THERE IS A SPIDER THAT CREATES A BUBBLE OF AIR TO DIVE TO THE BOTTOM OF A LAKE. IT LIVES ITS ENTIRE LIFE UNDERWATER.
ANOTHER SPIDER HOLDS A NET OF SILK BETWEEN ITS FORELEGS AND HURLS IT AT ITS PREY.
BUT OF ALL THE SPIDERS IN THE WORLD, ONLY .05% LIVE IN SOCIAL GROUPS. SPIDERS DON'T EASILY WORK TOGETHER.
SCIENCE LAB
COME ON, YOU FINKS! WE NEED TO GET THESE MOON ROCKS SAFELY BACK TO THE HIDEOUT BEFORE THAT PESKY WALL-CRAWLER SHOWS UP!
LET HIM! EVEN WITHOUT THE ANTI-GRAVITY POWER OF THESE ROCKS, WE STILL OUTNUMBER HIM SIX TO ONE!
OKAY, TEAM...

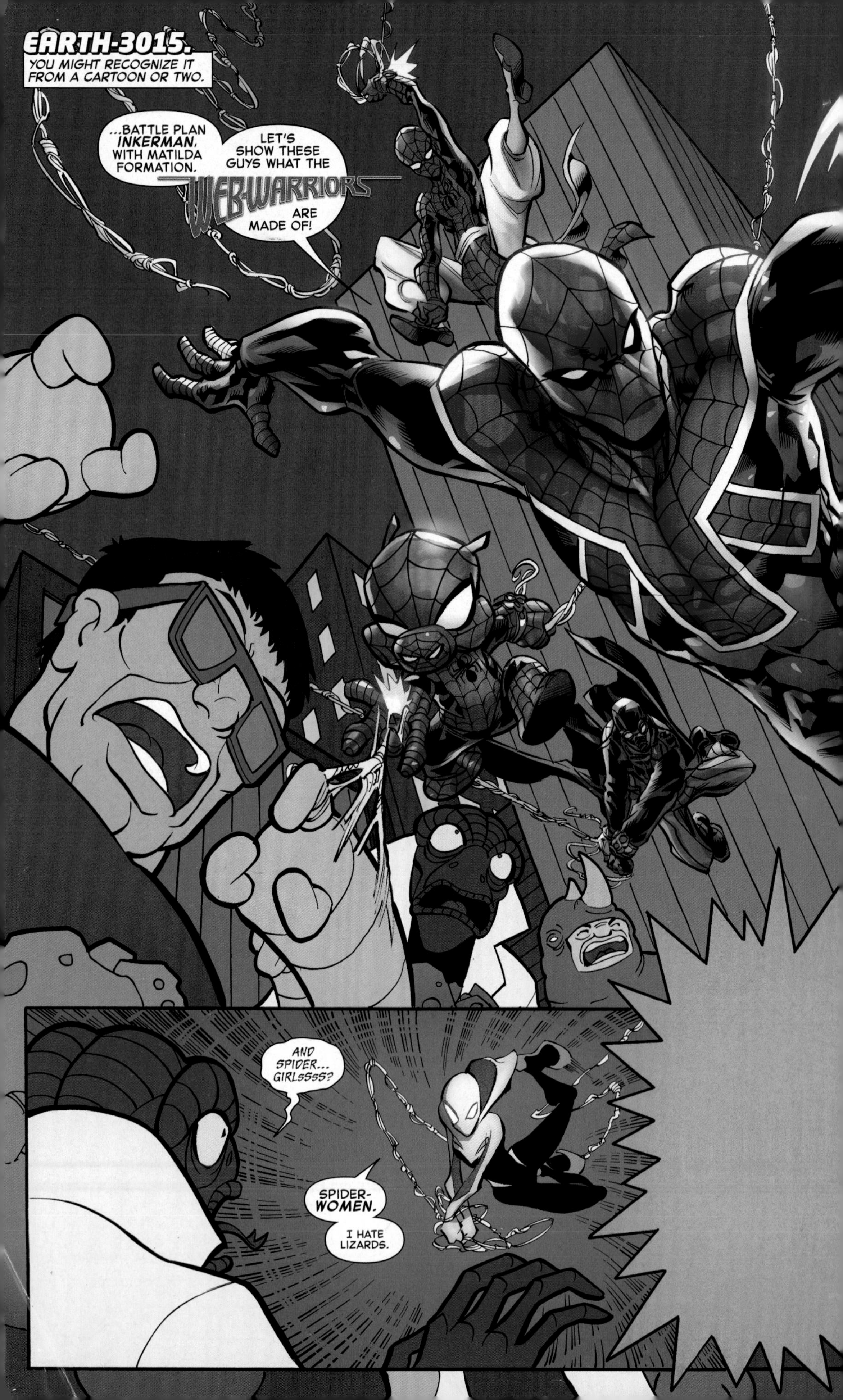
EARTH-3015.
YOU MIGHT RECOGNIZE IT FROM A CARTOON OR TWO.
...BATTLE PLAN INKERMAN, WITH MATILDA FORMATION.
LET'S SHOW THESE GUYS WHAT THE WEB-WARRIORS ARE MADE OF!
AND SPIDER... GIRLSSSS?
SPIDER-WOMEN.
I HATE LIZARDS.

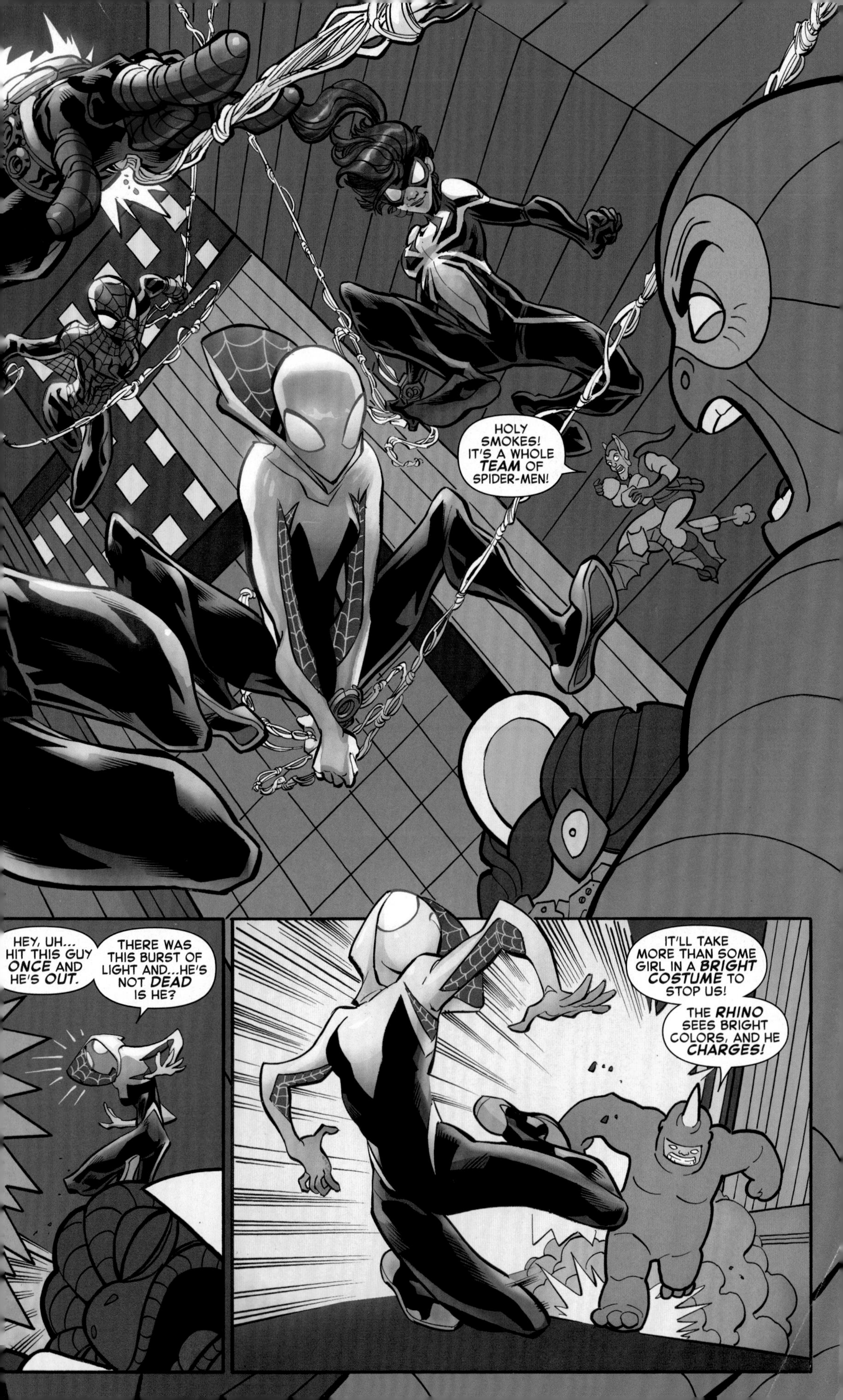
HOLY SMOKES! IT'S A WHOLE TEAM OF SPIDER-MEN!
HEY, UH... HIT THIS GUY ONCE AND HE'S OUT.
THERE WAS THIS BURST OF LIGHT AND...HE'S NOT DEAD IS HE?
IT'LL TAKE MORE THAN SOME GIRL IN A BRIGHT COSTUME TO STOP US!
THE RHINO SEES BRIGHT COLORS, AND HE CHARGES!

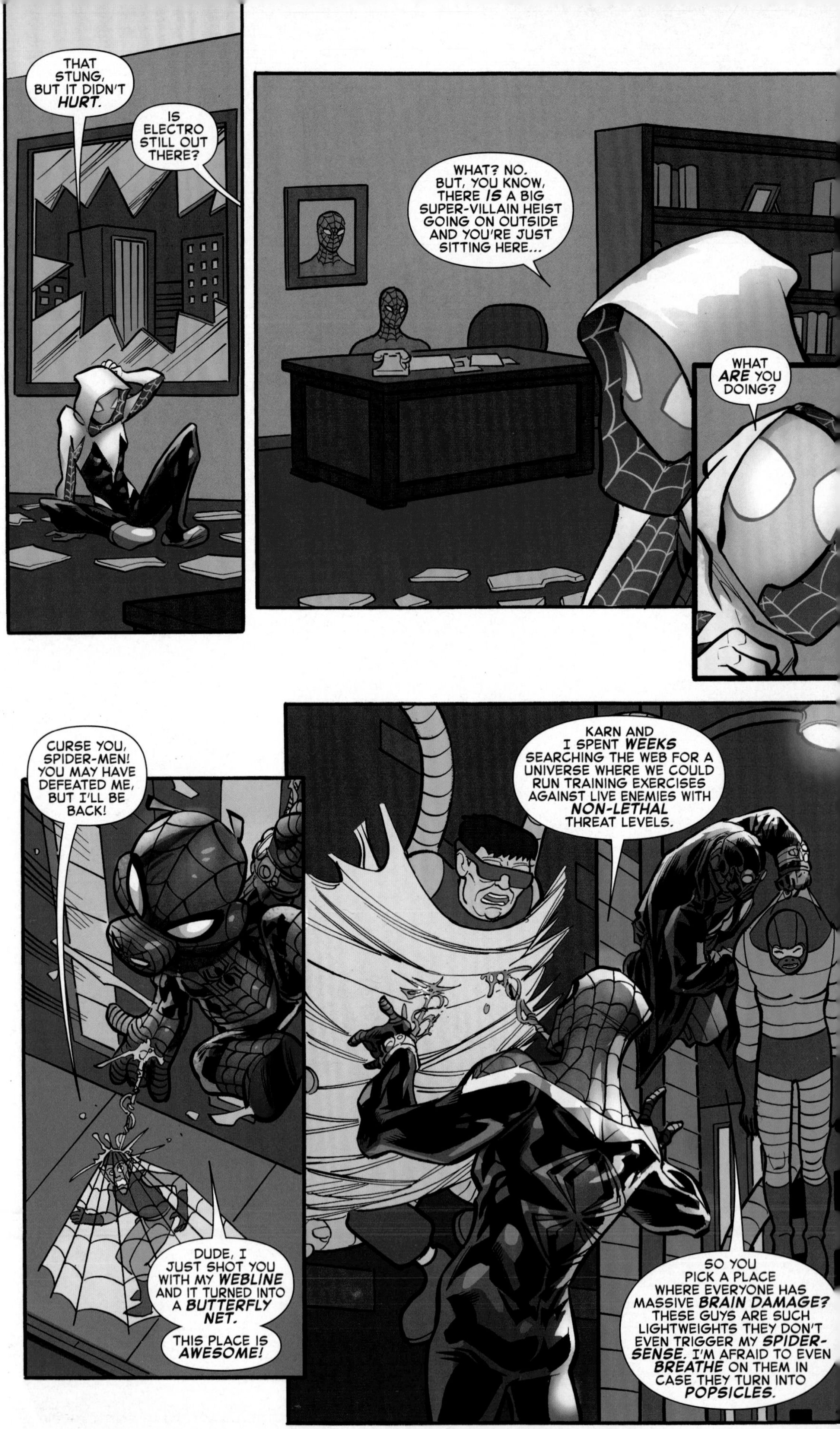
THAT STUNG, BUT IT DIDN'T HURT.
IS ELECTRO STILL OUT THERE?
WHAT? NO. BUT, YOU KNOW, THERE IS A BIG SUPER-VILLAIN HEIST GOING ON OUTSIDE AND YOU'RE JUST SITTING HERE...
WHAT ARE YOU DOING?
CURSE YOU, SPIDER-MEN! YOU MAY HAVE DEFEATED ME, BUT I'LL BE BACK!
DUDE, I JUST SHOT YOU WITH MY WEBLINE AND IT TURNED INTO A BUTTERFLY NET.
THIS PLACE IS AWESOME!
KARN AND I SPENT WEEKS SEARCHING THE WEB FOR A UNIVERSE WHERE WE COULD RUN TRAINING EXERCISES AGAINST LIVE ENEMIES WITH NON-LETHAL THREAT LEVELS.
SO YOU PICK A PLACE WHERE EVERYONE HAS MASSIVE BRAIN DAMAGE? THESE GUYS ARE SUCH LIGHTWEIGHTS THEY DON'T EVEN TRIGGER MY SPIDER-SENSE. I'M AFRAID TO EVEN BREATHE ON THEM IN CASE THEY TURN INTO POPSICLES.

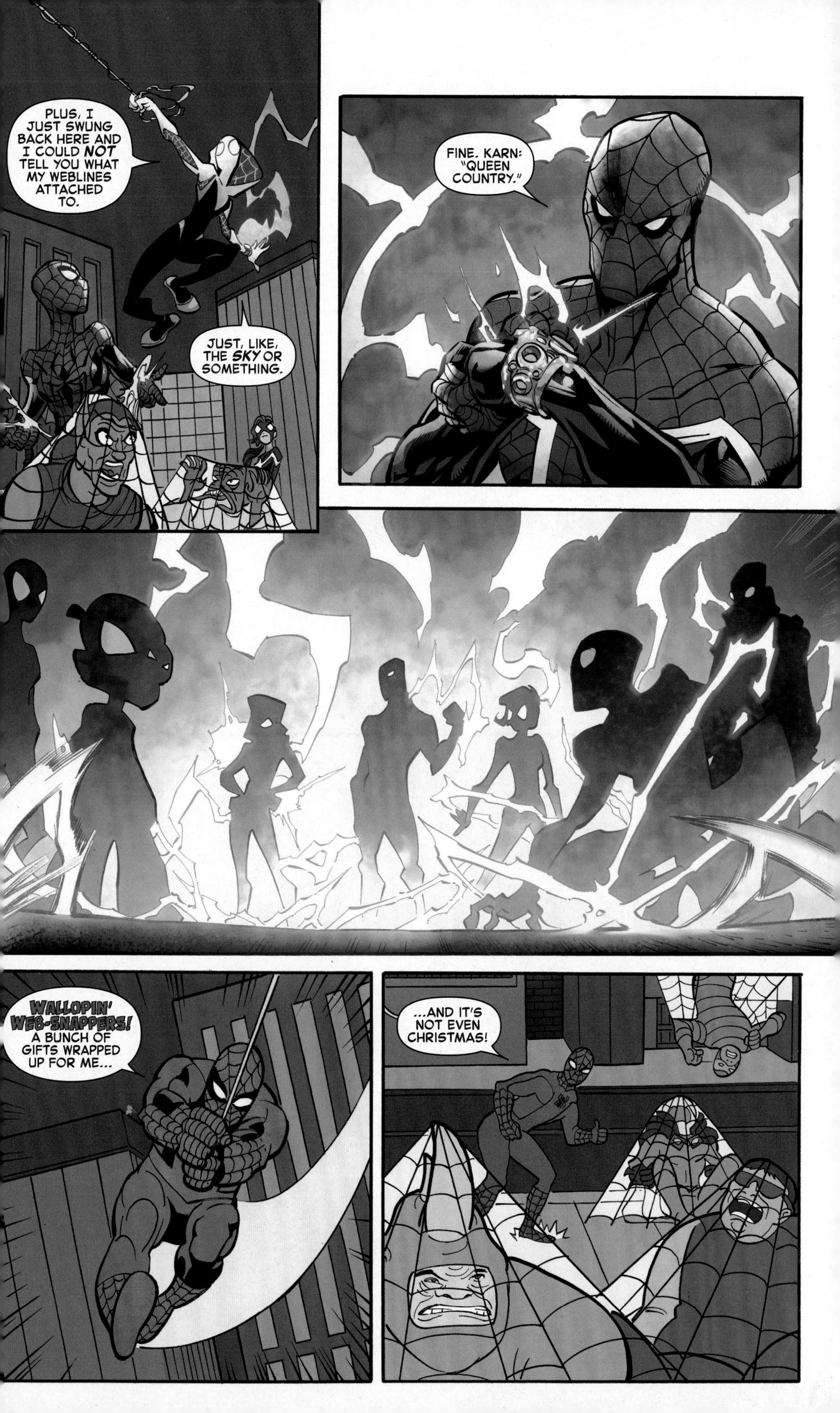
PLUS, I JUST SWUNG BACK HERE AND I COULD NOT TELL YOU WHAT MY WEBLINES ATTACHED TO.
JUST, LIKE, THE SKY OR SOMETHING.
FINE. KARN: "QUEEN COUNTRY."
WALLOPIN' WEB-SNAPPERS! A BUNCH OF GIFTS WRAPPED UP FOR ME...
...AND IT'S NOT EVEN CHRISTMAS!

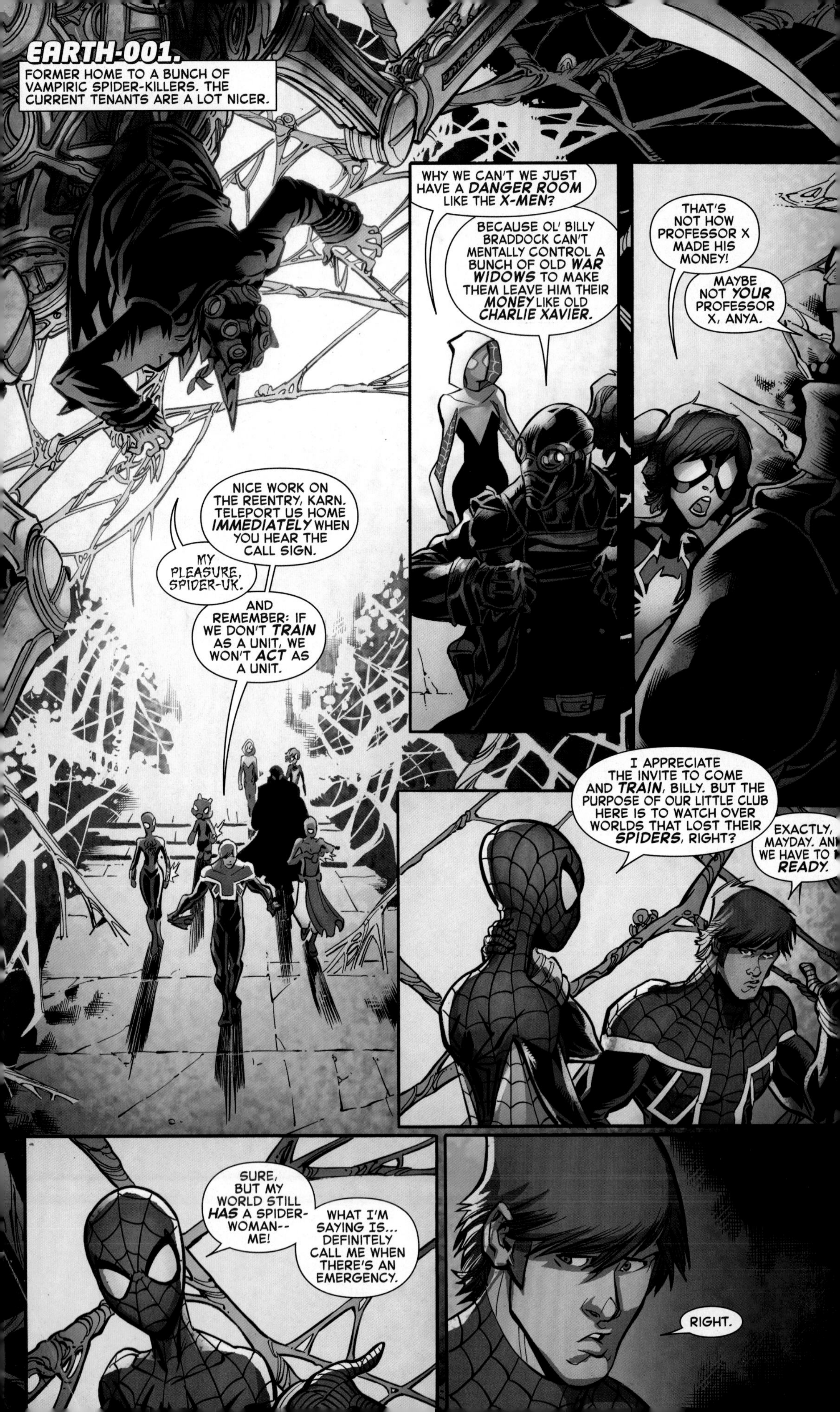
EARTH-001.
FORMER HOME TO A BUNCH OF VAMPIRIC SPIDER-KILLERS. THE CURRENT TENANTS ARE A LOT NICER.
NICE WORK ON THE REENTRY, KARN. TELEPORT US HOME IMMEDIATELY WHEN YOU HEAR THE CALL SIGN.
MY PLEASURE, SPIDER-UK.
AND REMEMBER: IF WE DON'T TRAIN AS A UNIT, WE WON'T ACT AS A UNIT.
WHY WE CAN'T WE JUST HAVE A DANGER ROOM LIKE THE X-MEN?
BECAUSE OL' BILLY BRADDOCK CAN'T MENTALLY CONTROL A BUNCH OF OLD WAR WIDOWS TO MAKE THEM LEAVE HIM THEIR MONEY LIKE OLD CHARLIE XAVIER.
THAT'S NOT HOW PROFESSOR X MADE HIS MONEY!
MAYBE NOT YOUR PROFESSOR X, ANYA.
I APPRECIATE THE INVITE TO COME AND TRAIN, BILLY. BUT THE PURPOSE OF OUR LITTLE CLUB HERE IS TO WATCH OVER WORLDS THAT LOST THEIR SPIDERS, RIGHT?
SURE, BUT MY WORLD STILL HAS A SPIDER-WOMAN-- ME!
WHAT I'M SAYING IS... DEFINITELY CALL ME WHEN THERE'S AN EMERGENCY.
RIGHT.

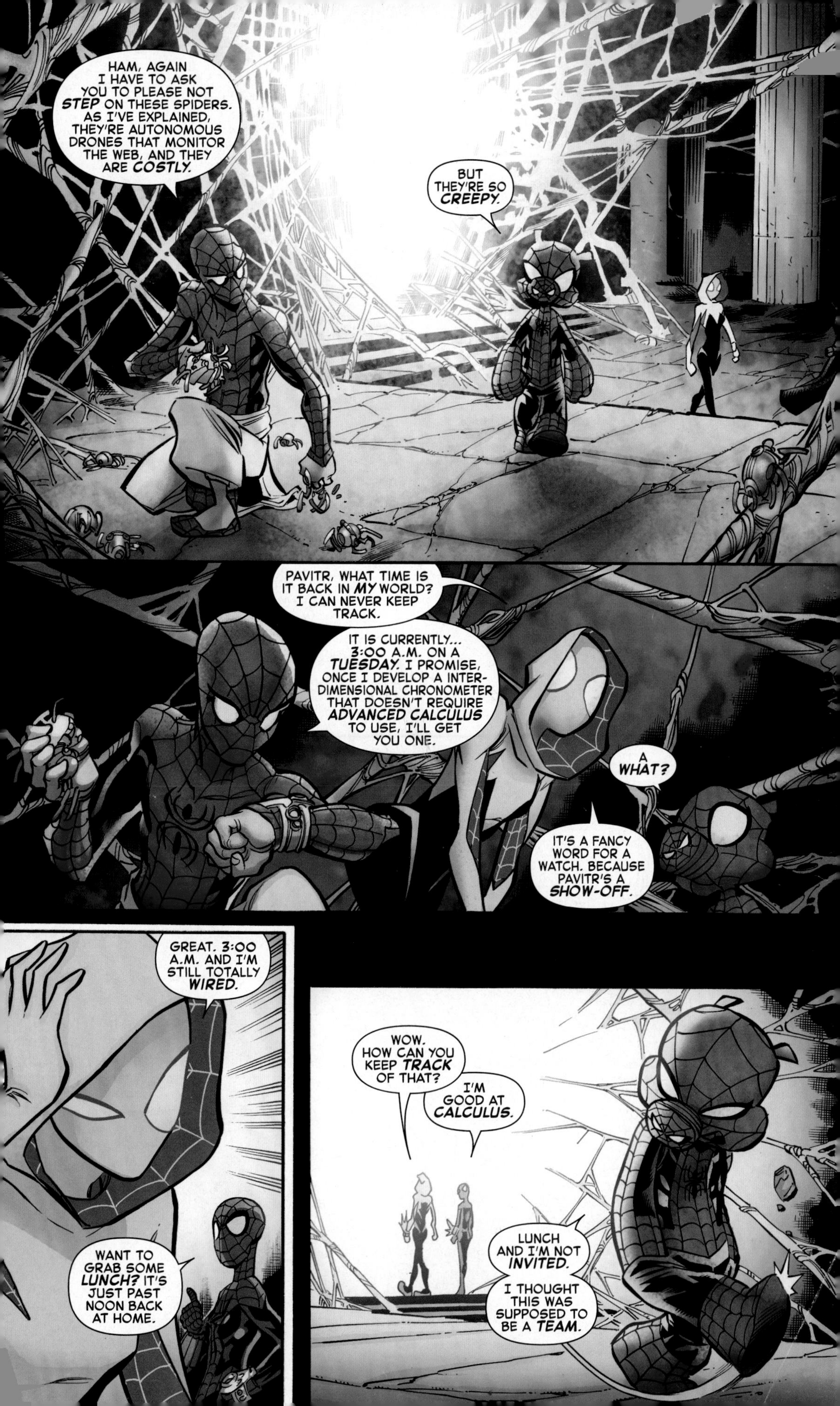
HAM, AGAIN I HAVE TO ASK YOU TO PLEASE NOT STEP ON THESE SPIDERS. AS I'VE EXPLAINED, THEY'RE AUTONOMOUS DRONES THAT MONITOR THE WEB, AND THEY ARE COSTLY.
BUT THEY'RE SO CREEPY.
PAVITR, WHAT TIME IS IT BACK IN MY WORLD? I CAN NEVER KEEP TRACK.
IT IS CURRENTLY... 3:00 A.M. ON A TUESDAY. I PROMISE, ONCE I DEVELOP A INTER-DIMENSIONAL CHRONOMETER THAT DOESN'T REQUIRE ADVANCED CALCULUS TO USE, I'LL GET YOU ONE.
A WHAT?
IT'S A FANCY WORD FOR A WATCH. BECAUSE PAVITR'S A SHOW-OFF.
GREAT. 3:00 A.M. AND I'M STILL TOTALLY WIRED.
WANT TO GRAB SOME LUNCH? IT'S JUST PAST NOON BACK AT HOME.
WOW. HOW CAN YOU KEEP TRACK OF THAT?
I'M GOOD AT CALCULUS.
LUNCH AND I'M NOT INVITED.
I THOUGHT THIS WAS SUPPOSED TO BE A TEAM.

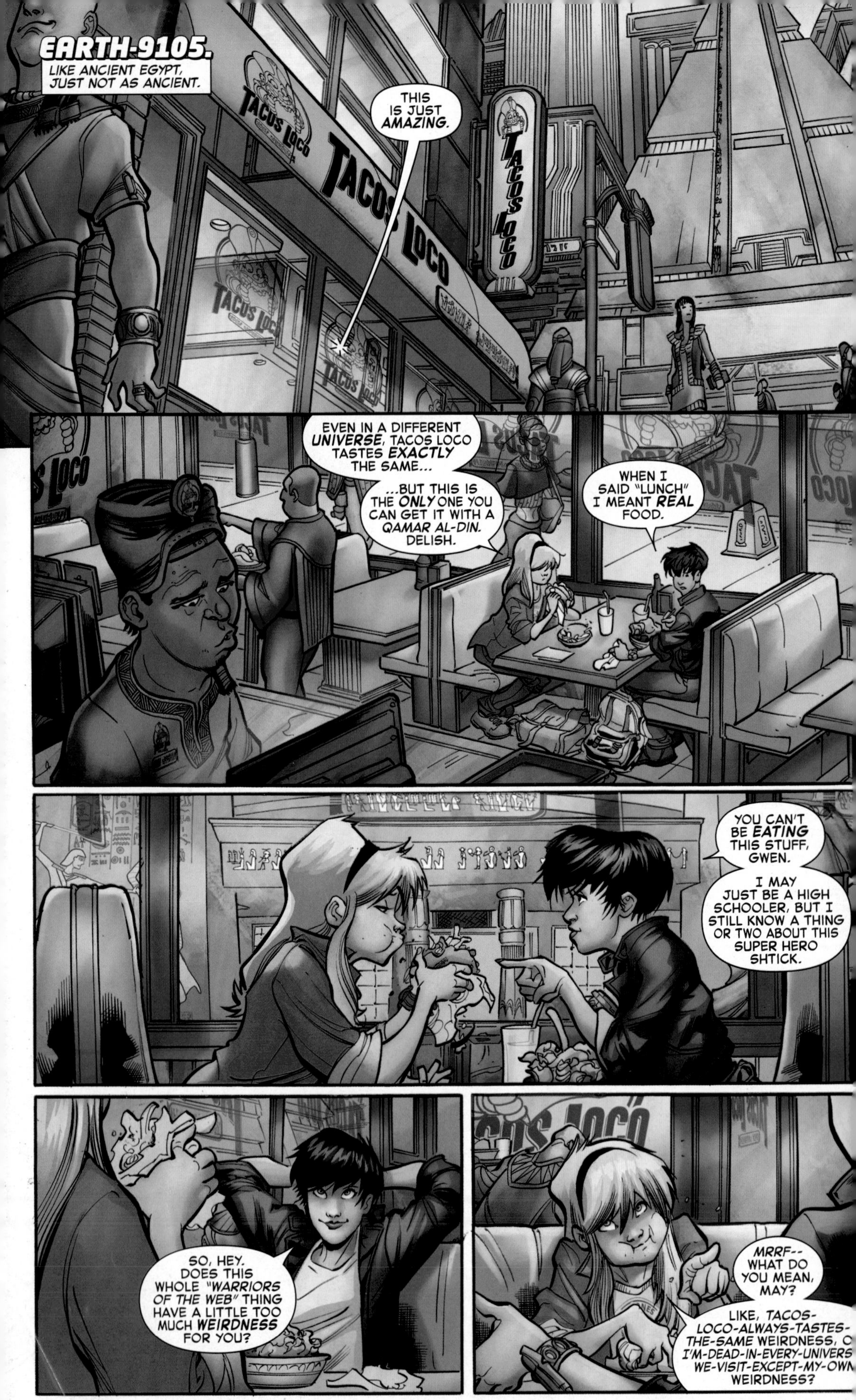
EARTH-9105.
LIKE ANCIENT EGYPT, JUST NOT AS ANCIENT.
THIS IS JUST AMAZING.
TACOS LOCO
EVEN IN A DIFFERENT UNIVERSE, TACOS LOCO TASTES EXACTLY THE SAME...
...BUT THIS IS THE ONLY ONE YOU CAN GET IT WITH A QAMAR AL-DIN. DELISH.
WHEN I SAID "LUNCH" I MEANT REAL FOOD.
YOU CAN'T BE EATING THIS STUFF, GWEN.
I MAY JUST BE A HIGH SCHOOLER, BUT I STILL KNOW A THING OR TWO ABOUT THIS SUPER HERO SHTICK.
SO, HEY. DOES THIS WHOLE "WARRIORS OF THE WEB" THING HAVE A LITTLE TOO MUCH WEIRDNESS FOR YOU?
MRRF-- WHAT DO YOU MEAN, MAY?
LIKE, TACOS-LOCO-ALWAYS-TASTES-THE-SAME WEIRDNESS, O I'M-DEAD-IN-EVERY-UNIVERS WE-VISIT-EXCEPT-MY-OWN WEIRDNESS?

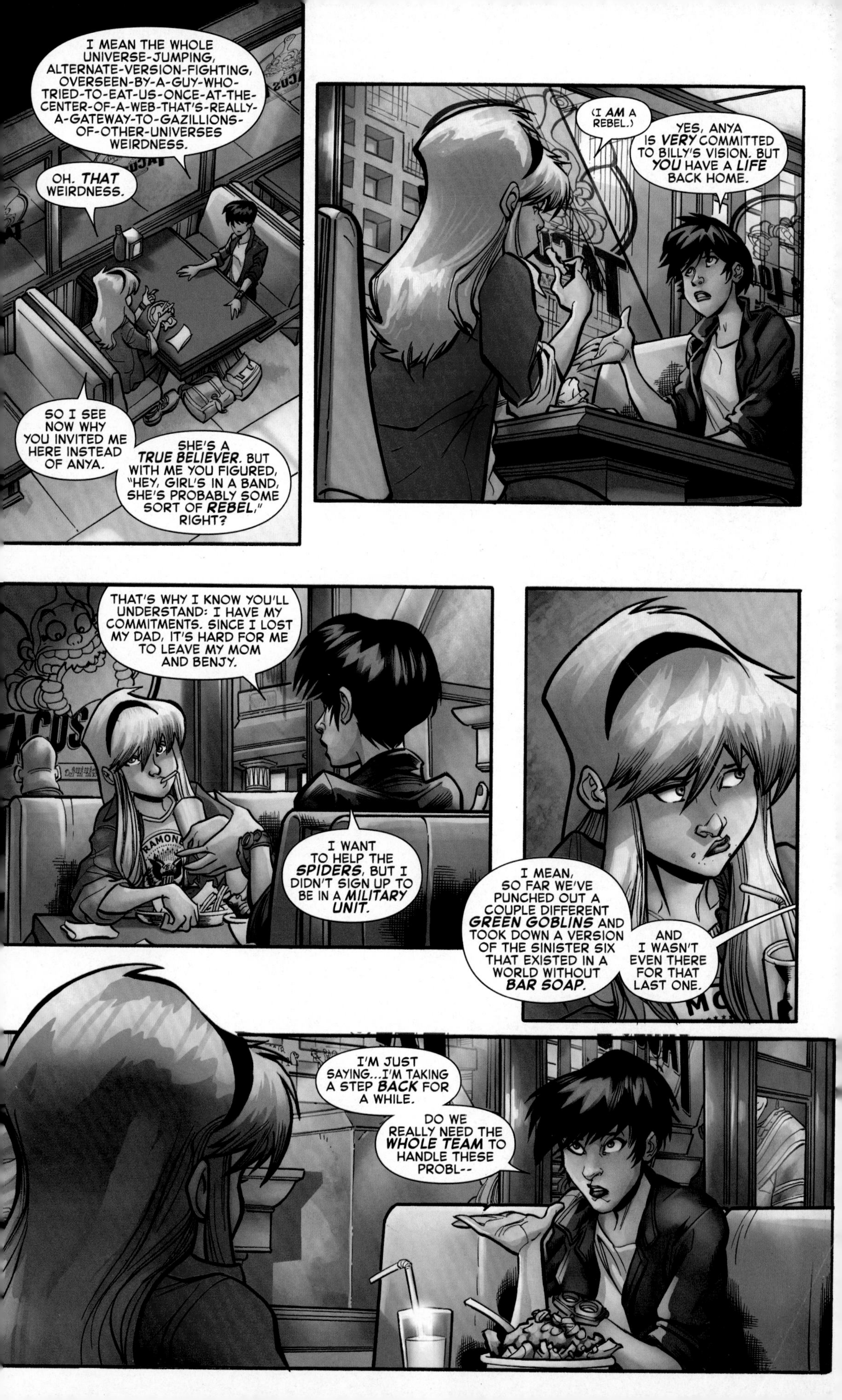

I MEAN THE WHOLE UNIVERSE-JUMPING, ALTERNATE-VERSION-FIGHTING, OVERSEEN-BY-A-GUY-WHO-TRIED-TO-EAT-US-ONCE-AT-THE-CENTER-OF-A-WEB-THAT'S-REALLY-A-GATEWAY-TO-GAZILLIONS-OF-OTHER-UNIVERSES WEIRDNESS.
OH. *THAT* WEIRDNESS.
SO I SEE NOW WHY YOU INVITED ME HERE INSTEAD OF ANYA.
SHE'S A *TRUE BELIEVER*. BUT WITH ME YOU FIGURED, "HEY, GIRL'S IN A BAND, SHE'S PROBABLY SOME SORT OF *REBEL*," RIGHT?
(I *AM* A REBEL.)
YES, ANYA IS *VERY* COMMITTED TO BILLY'S VISION. BUT *YOU* HAVE A *LIFE* BACK HOME.
THAT'S WHY I KNOW YOU'LL UNDERSTAND: I HAVE MY COMMITMENTS. SINCE I LOST MY DAD, IT'S HARD FOR ME TO LEAVE MY MOM AND BENJY.
I WANT TO HELP THE *SPIDERS*, BUT I DIDN'T SIGN UP TO BE IN A *MILITARY UNIT*.
I MEAN, SO FAR WE'VE PUNCHED OUT A COUPLE DIFFERENT *GREEN GOBLINS* AND TOOK DOWN A VERSION OF THE SINISTER SIX THAT EXISTED IN A WORLD WITHOUT *BAR SOAP*.
AND I WASN'T EVEN THERE FOR THAT LAST ONE.
I'M JUST SAYING... I'M TAKING A STEP *BACK* FOR A WHILE.
DO WE REALLY NEED THE *WHOLE TEAM* TO HANDLE THESE PROBL--

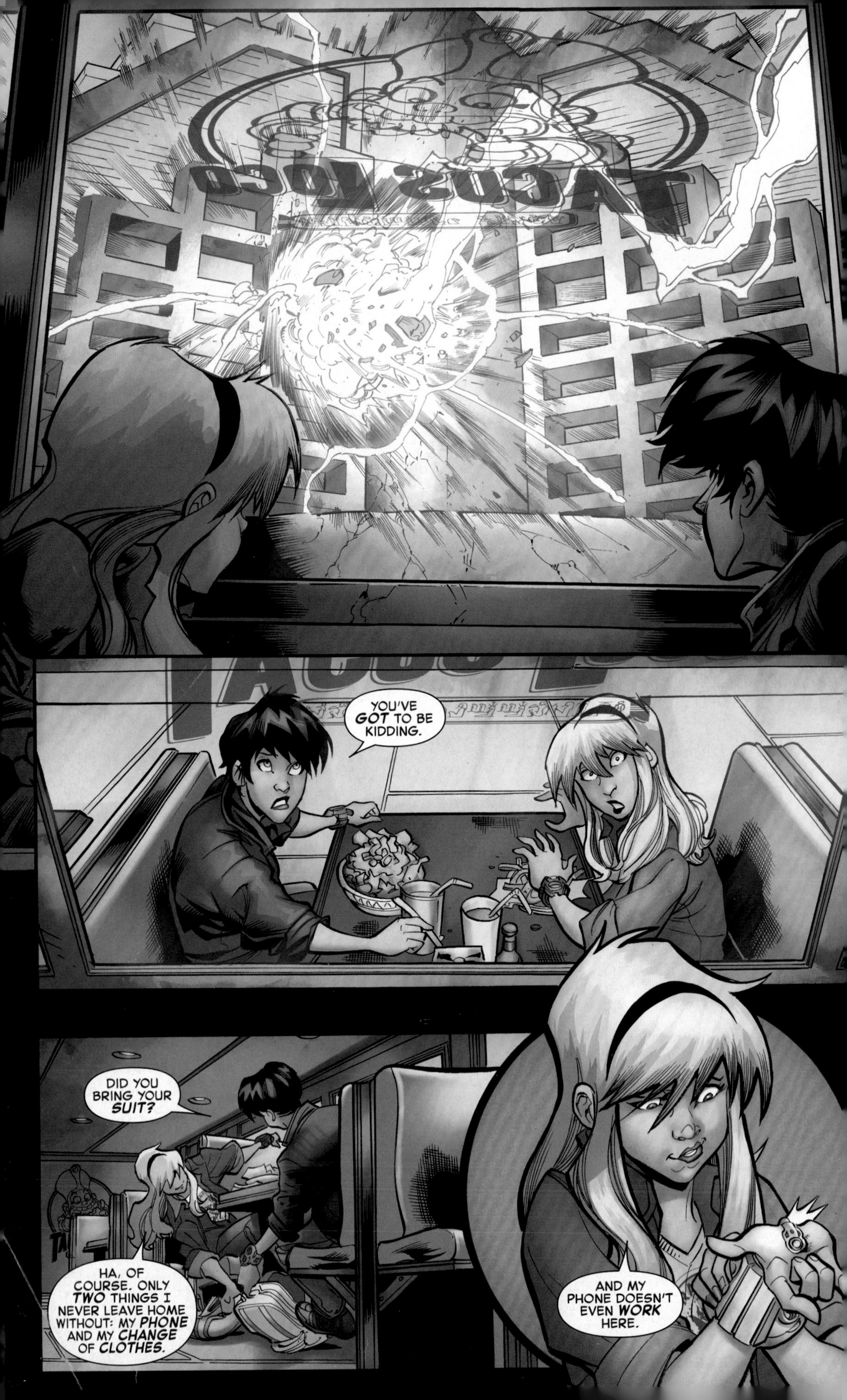
TACOS LOCO
YOU'VE GOT TO BE KIDDING.
DID YOU BRING YOUR SUIT?
HA, OF COURSE. ONLY TWO THINGS I NEVER LEAVE HOME WITHOUT: MY PHONE AND MY CHANGE OF CLOTHES.
AND MY PHONE DOESN'T EVEN WORK HERE.

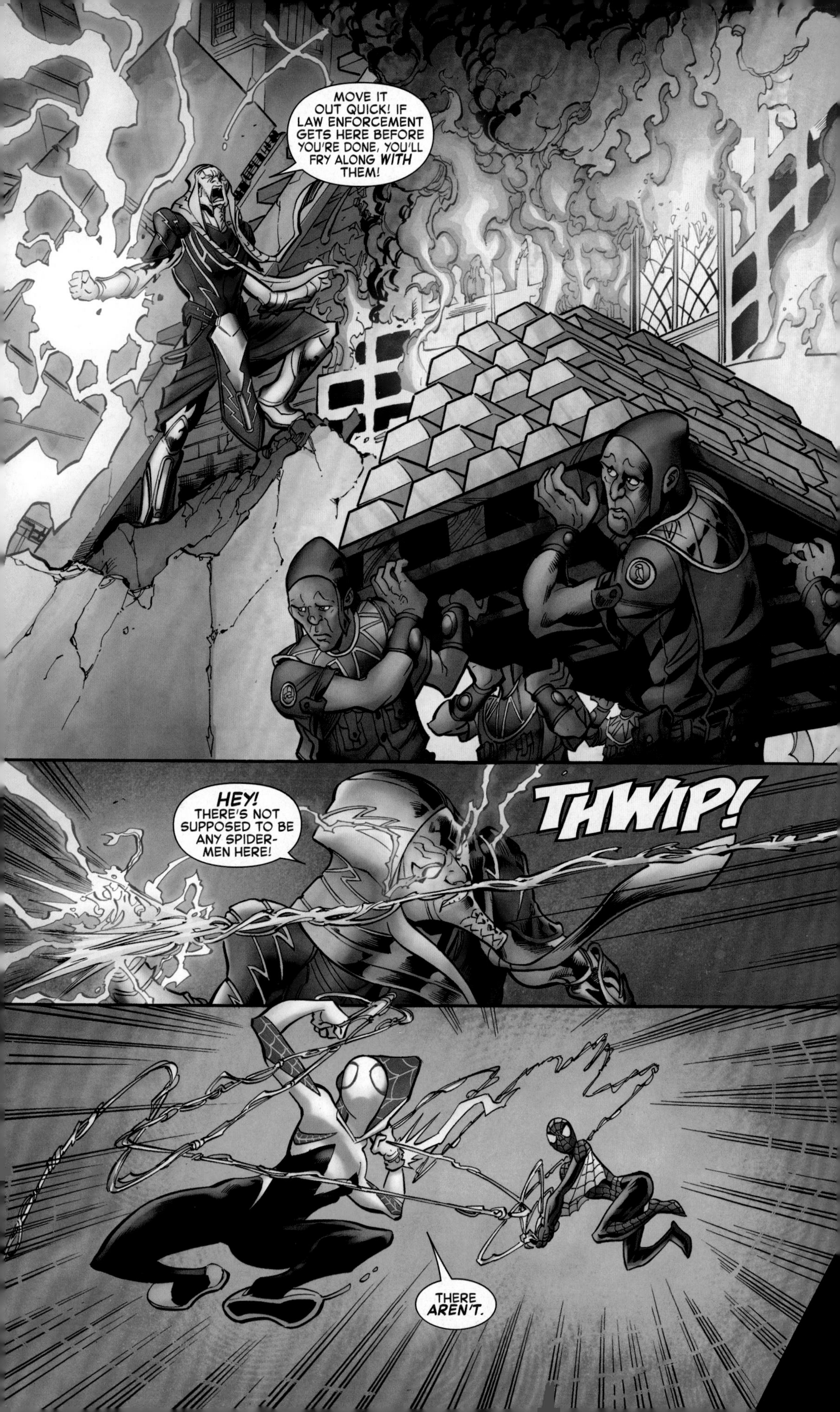
MOVE IT OUT QUICK! IF LAW ENFORCEMENT GETS HERE BEFORE YOU'RE DONE, YOU'LL FRY ALONG WITH THEM!
HEY! THERE'S NOT SUPPOSED TO BE ANY SPIDER-MEN HERE!
THWIP!
THERE AREN'T.

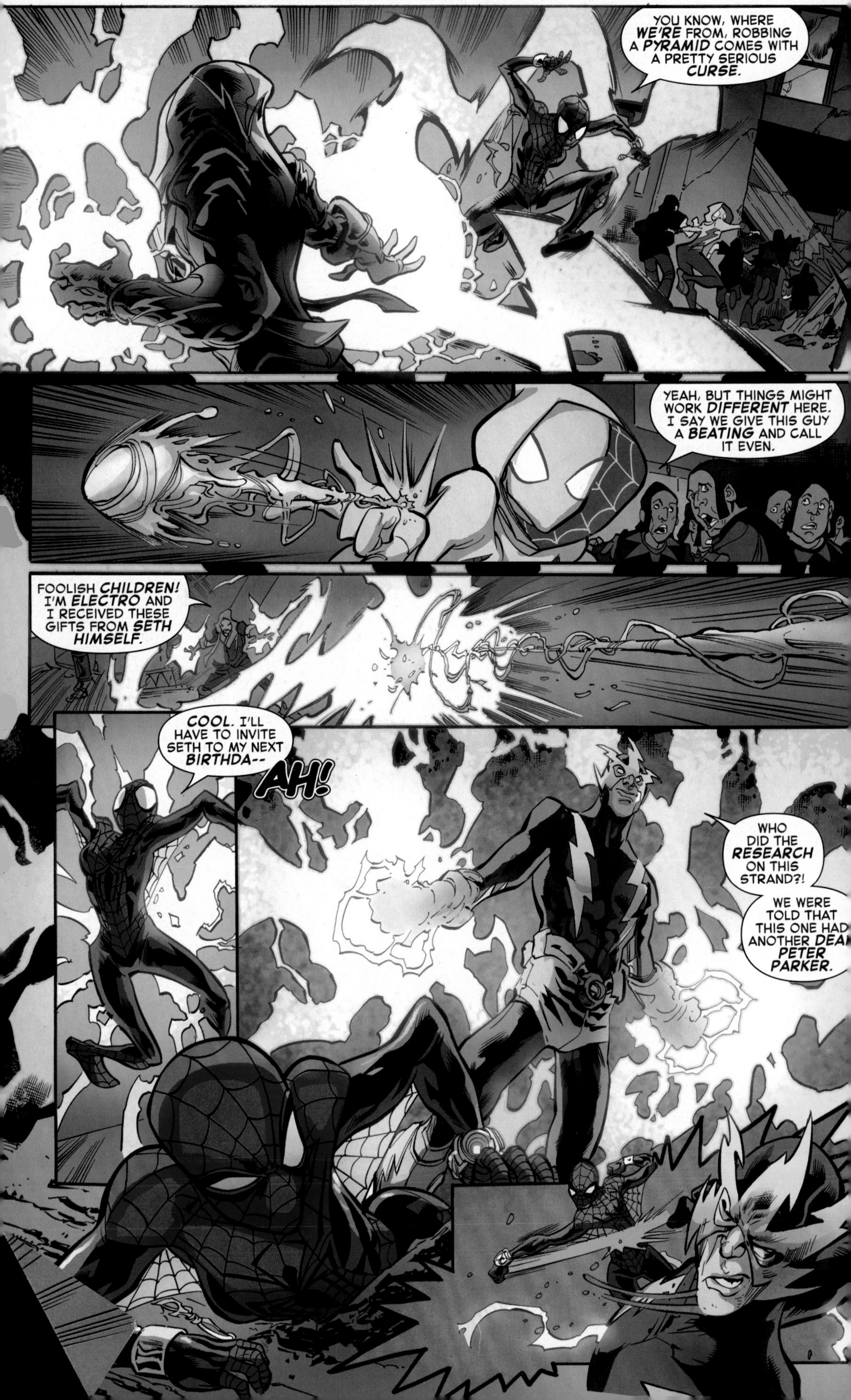

YOU KNOW, WHERE WE'RE FROM, ROBBING A PYRAMID COMES WITH A PRETTY SERIOUS CURSE.
YEAH, BUT THINGS MIGHT WORK DIFFERENT HERE. I SAY WE GIVE THIS GUY A BEATING AND CALL IT EVEN.
FOOLISH CHILDREN! I'M ELECTRO AND I RECEIVED THESE GIFTS FROM SETH HIMSELF.
COOL. I'LL HAVE TO INVITE SETH TO MY NEXT BIRTHDA--
AH!
WHO DID THE RESEARCH ON THIS STRAND?!
WE WERE TOLD THAT THIS ONE HAD ANOTHER DEAD PETER PARKER.

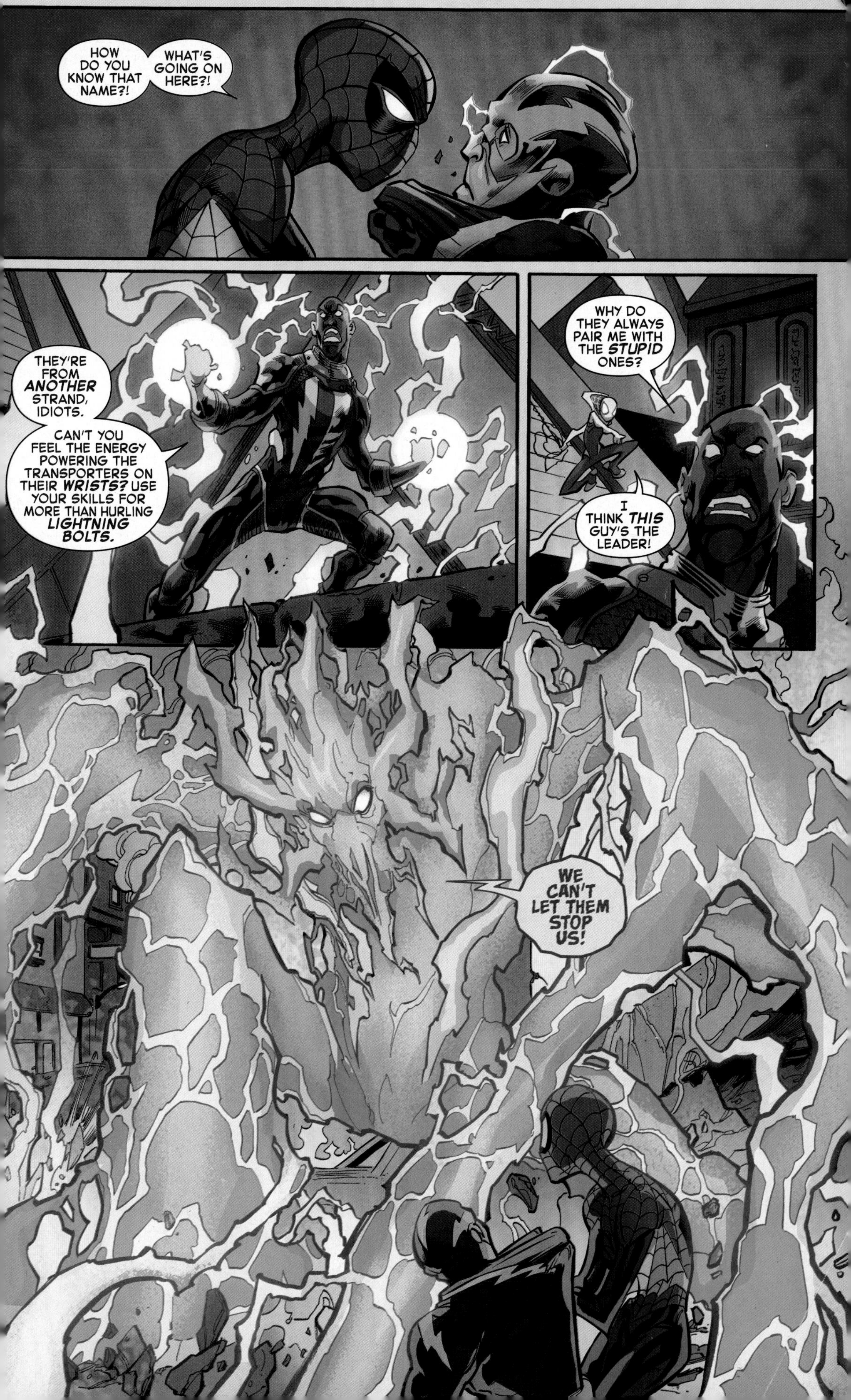
HOW DO YOU KNOW THAT NAME?!
WHAT'S GOING ON HERE?!
THEY'RE FROM ANOTHER STRAND, IDIOTS.
CAN'T YOU FEEL THE ENERGY POWERING THE TRANSPORTERS ON THEIR WRISTS? USE YOUR SKILLS FOR MORE THAN HURLING LIGHTNING BOLTS.
WHY DO THEY ALWAYS PAIR ME WITH THE STUPID ONES?
I THINK THIS GUY'S THE LEADER!
WE CAN'T LET THEM STOP US!

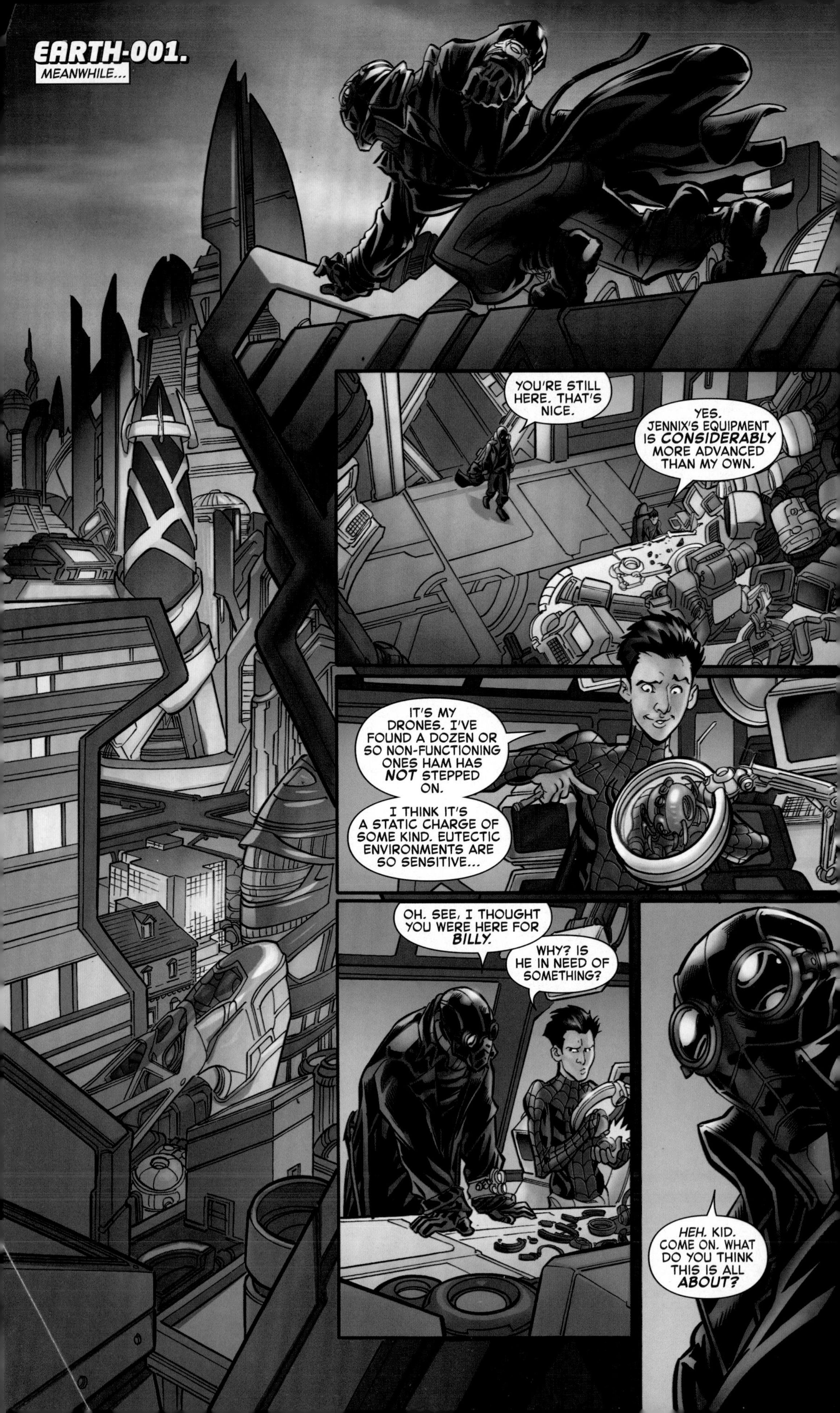
EARTH-001.
MEANWHILE...
YOU'RE STILL HERE. THAT'S NICE.
YES. JENNIX'S EQUIPMENT IS CONSIDERABLY MORE ADVANCED THAN MY OWN.
IT'S MY DRONES. I'VE FOUND A DOZEN OR SO NON-FUNCTIONING ONES HAM HAS NOT STEPPED ON.
I THINK IT'S A STATIC CHARGE OF SOME KIND. EUTECTIC ENVIRONMENTS ARE SO SENSITIVE...
OH. SEE, I THOUGHT YOU WERE HERE FOR BILLY.
WHY? IS HE IN NEED OF SOMETHING?
HEH. KID. COME ON. WHAT DO YOU THINK THIS IS ALL ABOUT?

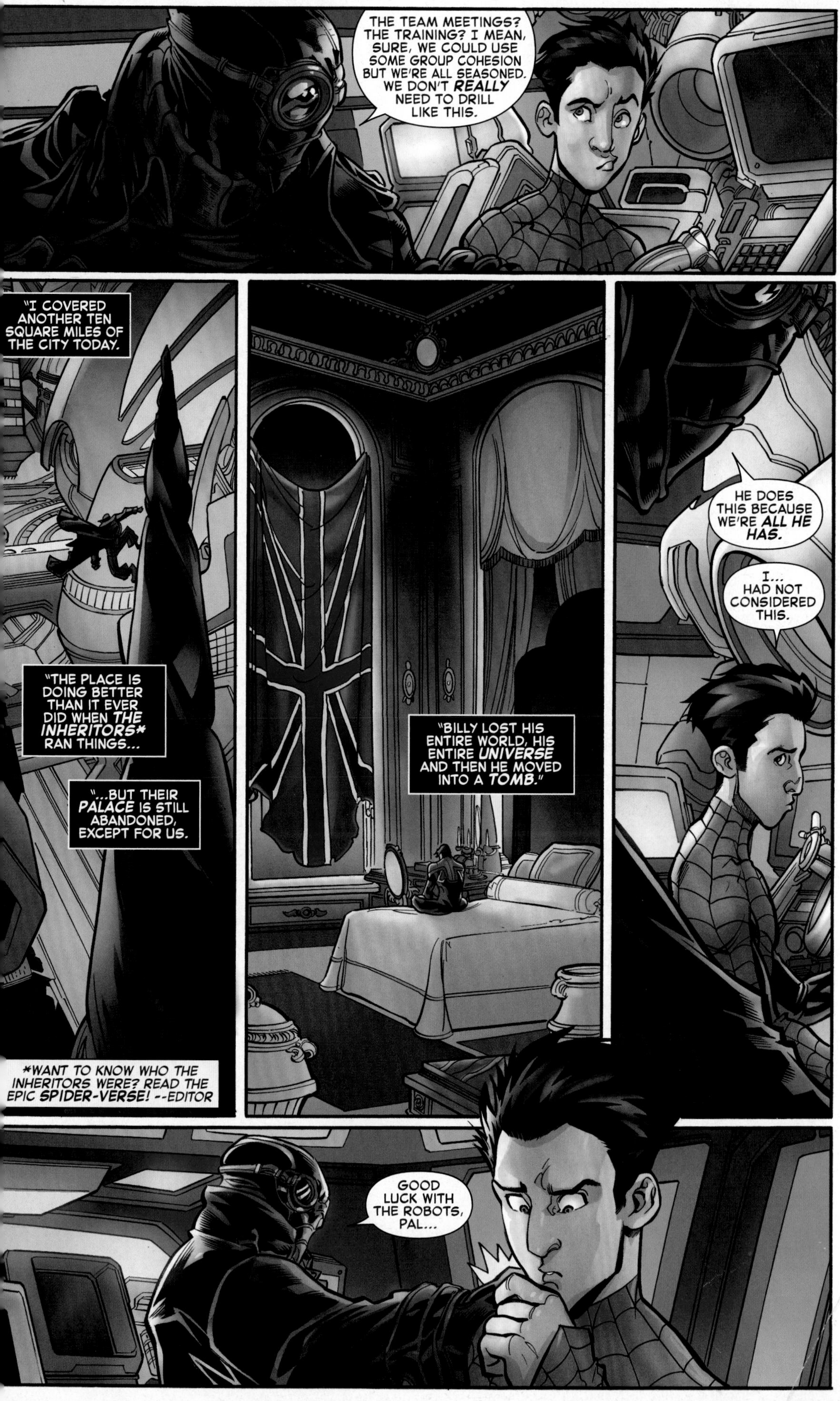
THE TEAM MEETINGS? THE TRAINING? I MEAN, SURE, WE COULD USE SOME GROUP COHESION BUT WE'RE ALL SEASONED. WE DON'T REALLY NEED TO DRILL LIKE THIS.
"I COVERED ANOTHER TEN SQUARE MILES OF THE CITY TODAY.
"THE PLACE IS DOING BETTER THAN IT EVER DID WHEN THE INHERITORS* RAN THINGS...
"...BUT THEIR PALACE IS STILL ABANDONED, EXCEPT FOR US.
*WANT TO KNOW WHO THE INHERITORS WERE? READ THE EPIC SPIDER-VERSE! --EDITOR
"BILLY LOST HIS ENTIRE WORLD, HIS ENTIRE UNIVERSE AND THEN HE MOVED INTO A TOMB."
HE DOES THIS BECAUSE WE'RE ALL HE HAS.
I... HAD NOT CONSIDERED THIS.
GOOD LUCK WITH THE ROBOTS, PAL...

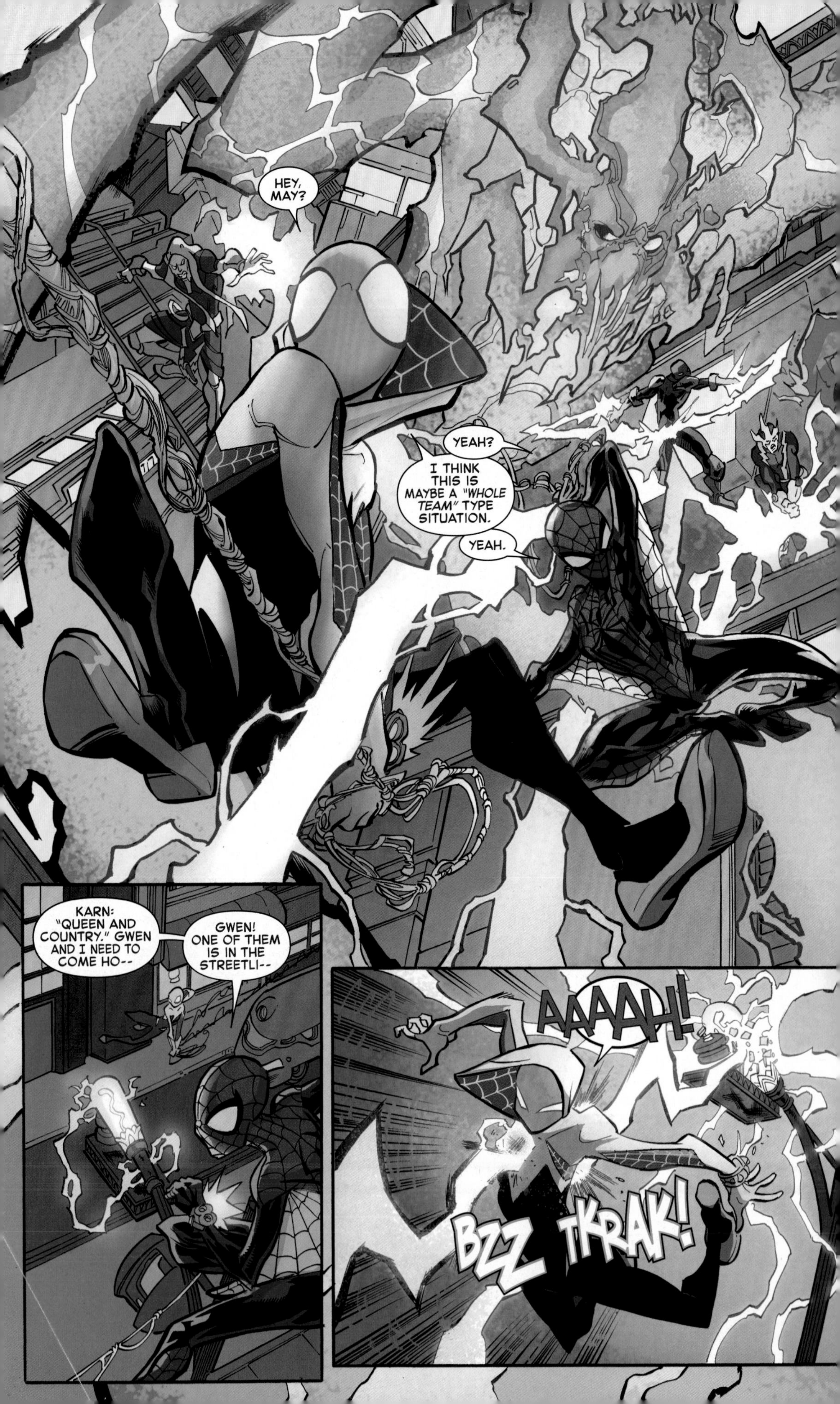

HEY, MAY?
YEAH?
I THINK THIS IS MAYBE A "WHOLE TEAM" TYPE SITUATION.
YEAH.
KARN: "QUEEN AND COUNTRY." GWEN AND I NEED TO COME HO--
GWEN! ONE OF THEM IS IN THE STREETLI--
AAAAH!
BZZ TKRAK!

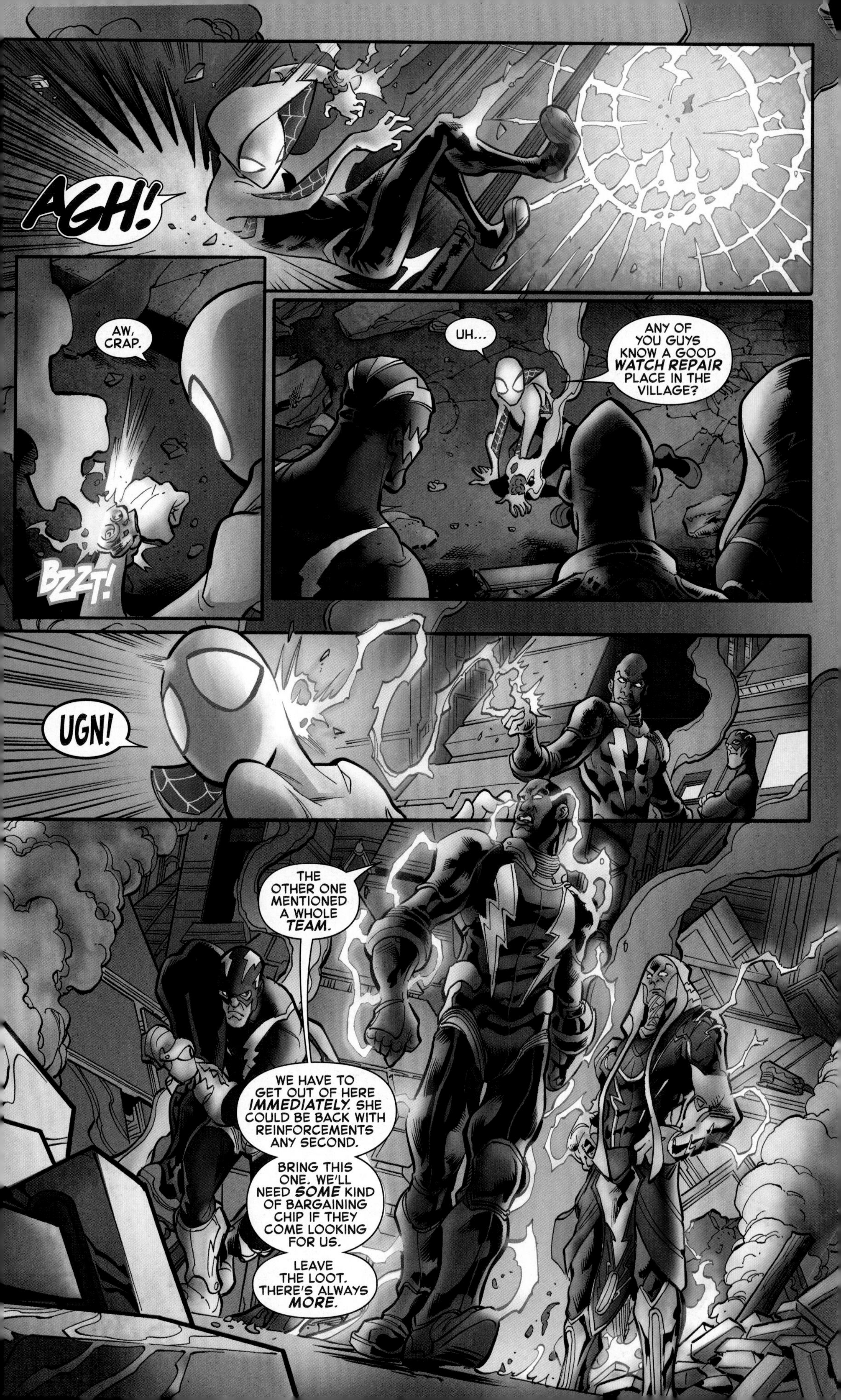
AGH!
AW, CRAP.
BZZT!
UH...
ANY OF YOU GUYS KNOW A GOOD WATCH REPAIR PLACE IN THE VILLAGE?
UGN!
THE OTHER ONE MENTIONED A WHOLE TEAM.
WE HAVE TO GET OUT OF HERE IMMEDIATELY. SHE COULD BE BACK WITH REINFORCEMENTS ANY SECOND.
BRING THIS ONE. WE'LL NEED SOME KIND OF BARGAINING CHIP IF THEY COME LOOKING FOR US.
LEAVE THE LOOT. THERE'S ALWAYS MORE.

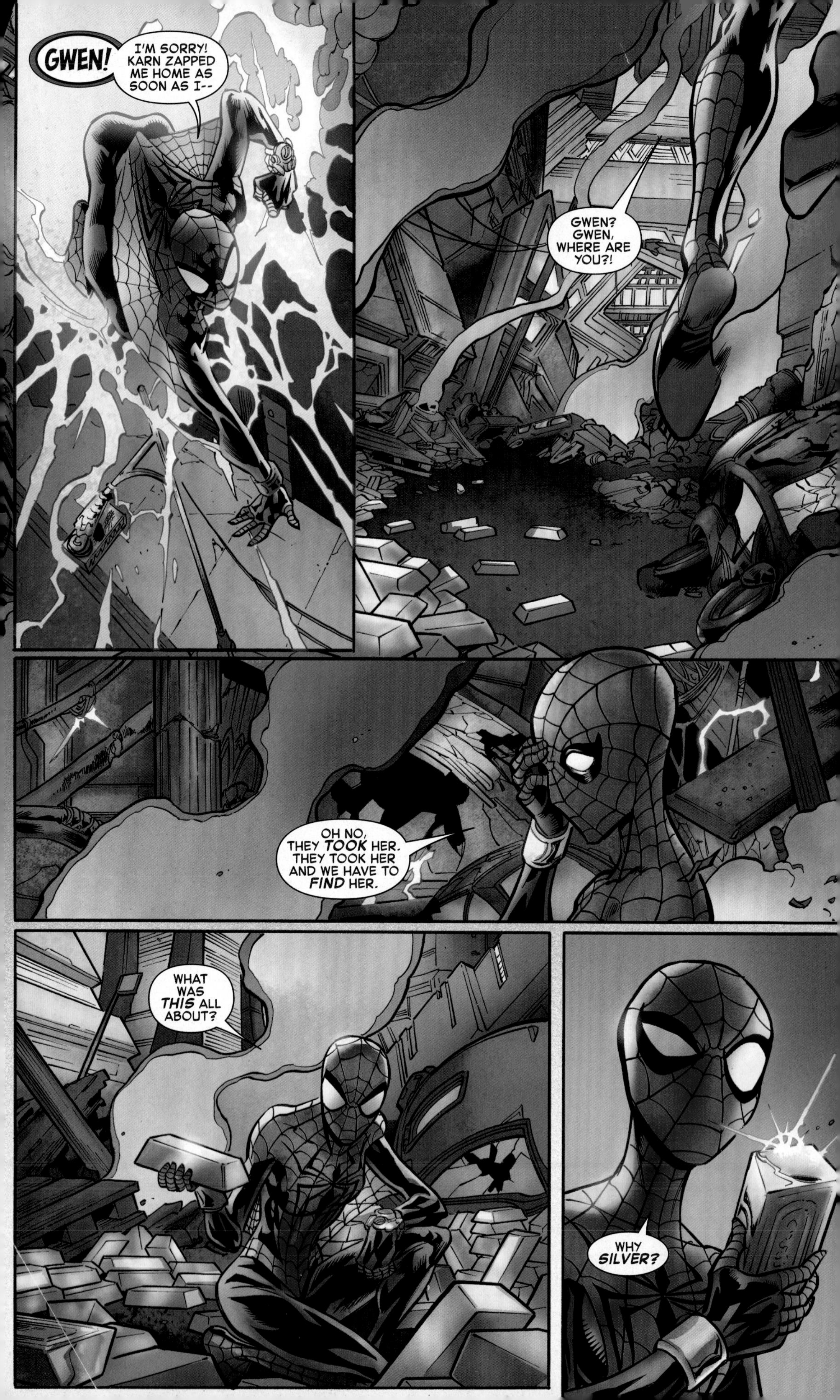
GWEN!
I'M SORRY! KARN ZAPPED ME HOME AS SOON AS I--
GWEN? GWEN, WHERE ARE YOU?!
OH NO, THEY TOOK HER. THEY TOOK HER AND WE HAVE TO FIND HER.
WHAT WAS THIS ALL ABOUT?
WHY SILVER?

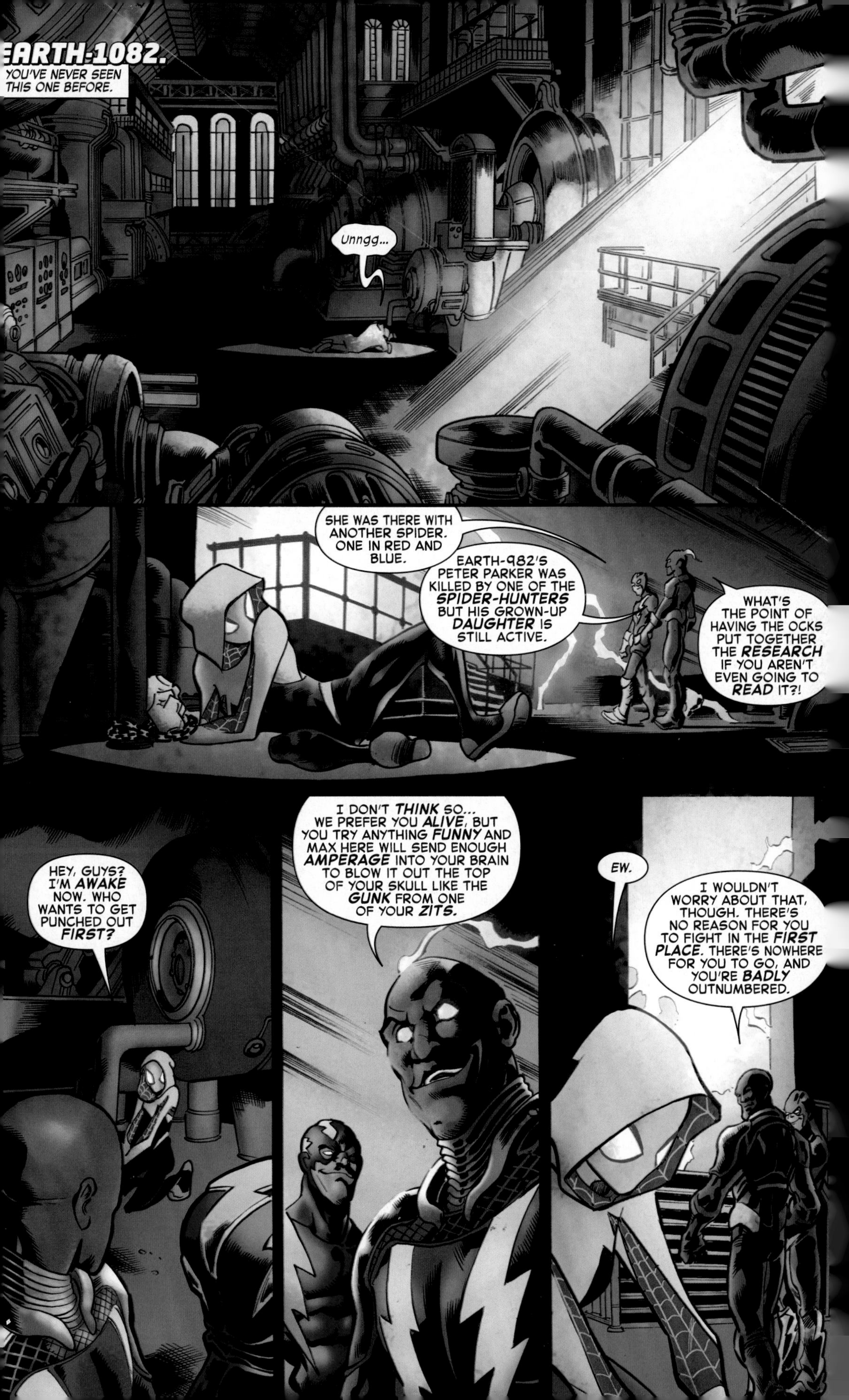
EARTH-1082.
YOU'VE NEVER SEEN THIS ONE BEFORE.
Unngg...
SHE WAS THERE WITH ANOTHER SPIDER. ONE IN RED AND BLUE.
EARTH-982'S PETER PARKER WAS KILLED BY ONE OF THE SPIDER-HUNTERS BUT HIS GROWN-UP DAUGHTER IS STILL ACTIVE.
WHAT'S THE POINT OF HAVING THE OCKS PUT TOGETHER THE RESEARCH IF YOU AREN'T EVEN GOING TO READ IT?!
HEY, GUYS? I'M AWAKE NOW. WHO WANTS TO GET PUNCHED OUT FIRST?
I DON'T THINK SO... WE PREFER YOU ALIVE, BUT YOU TRY ANYTHING FUNNY AND MAX HERE WILL SEND ENOUGH AMPERAGE INTO YOUR BRAIN TO BLOW IT OUT THE TOP OF YOUR SKULL LIKE THE GUNK FROM ONE OF YOUR ZITS.
EW.
I WOULDN'T WORRY ABOUT THAT, THOUGH. THERE'S NO REASON FOR YOU TO FIGHT IN THE FIRST PLACE. THERE'S NOWHERE FOR YOU TO GO, AND YOU'RE BADLY OUTNUMBERED.

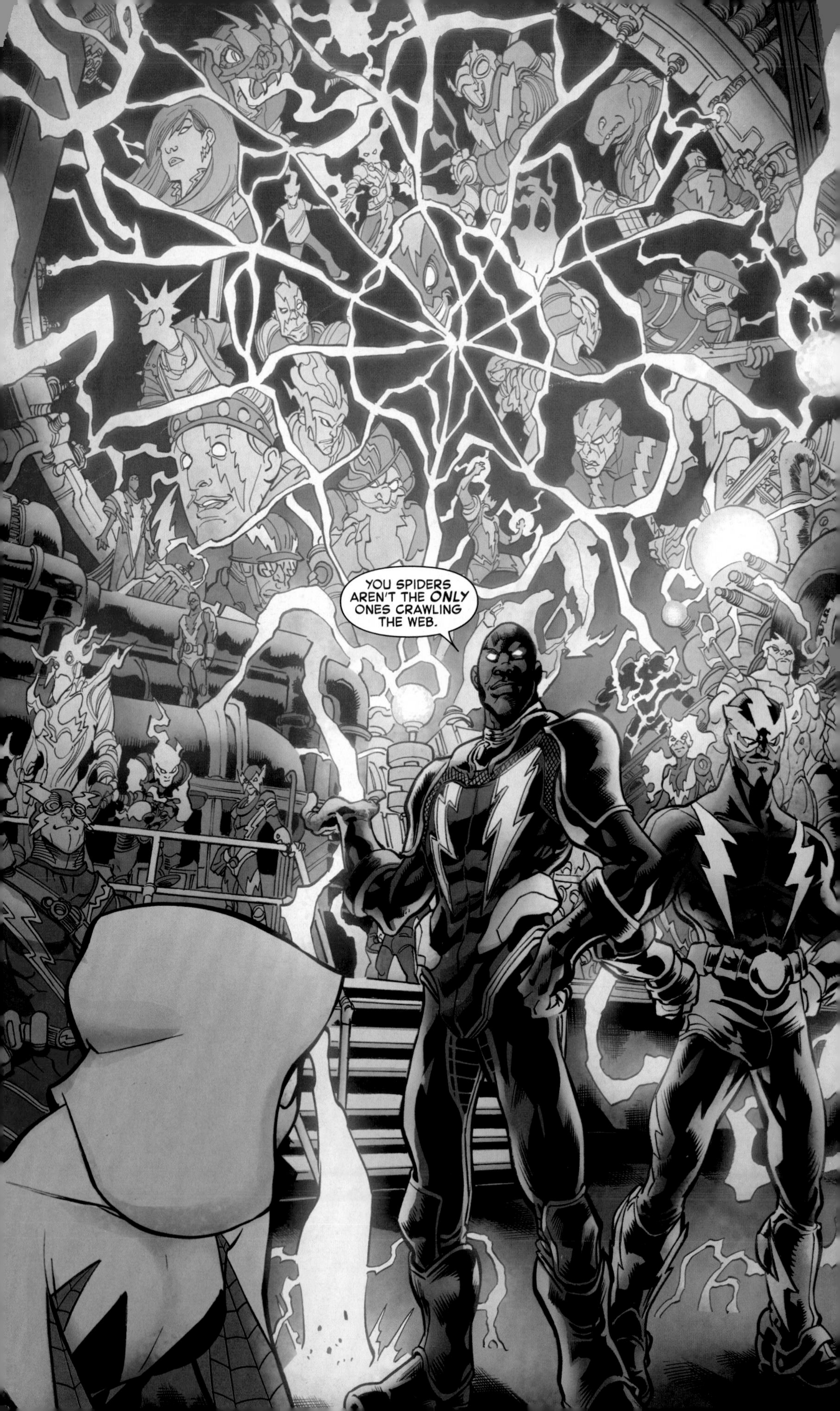
YOU SPIDERS AREN'T THE ONLY ONES CRAWLING THE WEB.

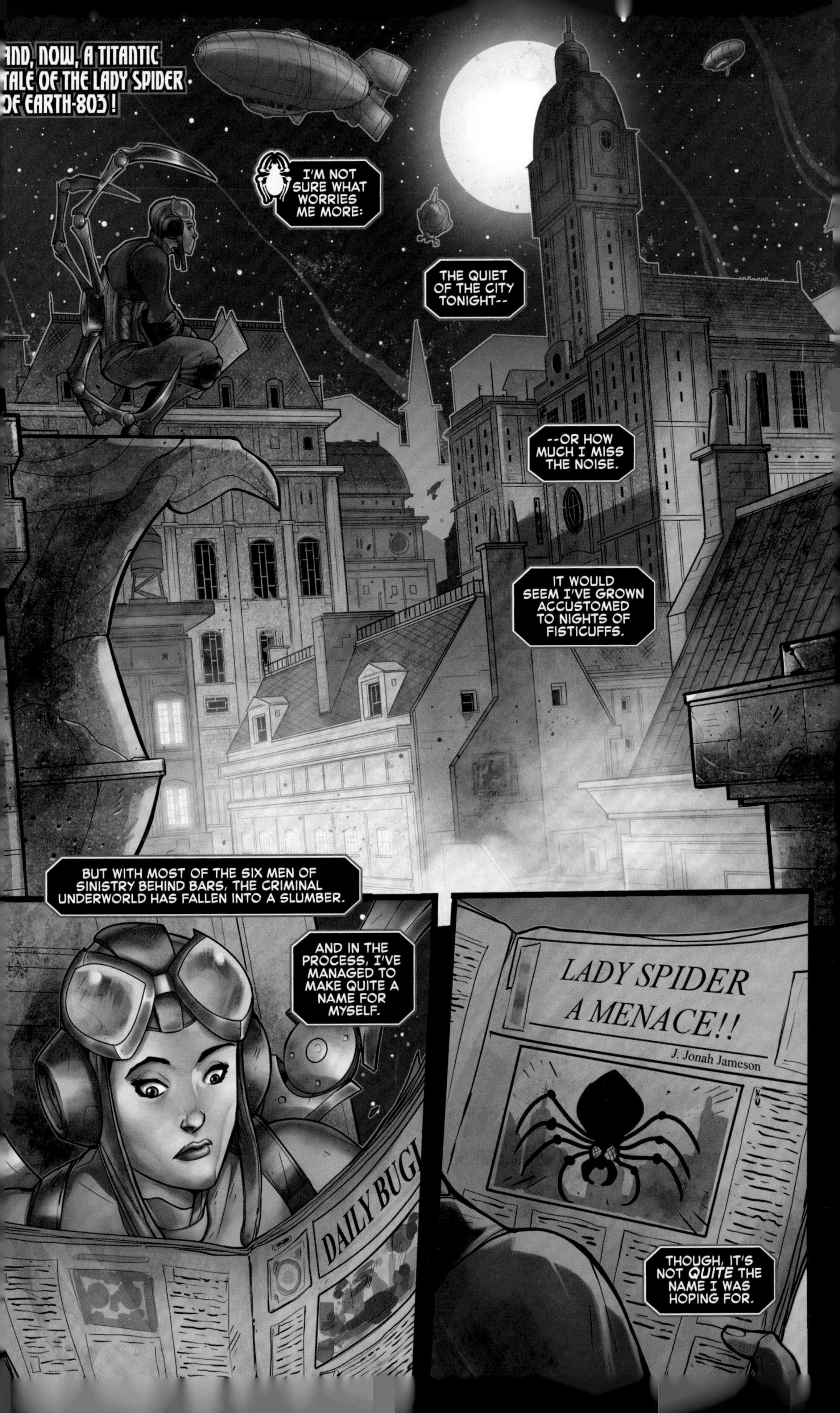

AND, NOW, A TITANTIC TALE OF THE LADY SPIDER OF EARTH-803!
I'M NOT SURE WHAT WORRIES ME MORE:
THE QUIET OF THE CITY TONIGHT--
--OR HOW MUCH I MISS THE NOISE.
IT WOULD SEEM I'VE GROWN ACCUSTOMED TO NIGHTS OF FISTICUFFS.
BUT WITH MOST OF THE SIX MEN OF SINISTRY BEHIND BARS, THE CRIMINAL UNDERWORLD HAS FALLEN INTO A SLUMBER.
AND IN THE PROCESS, I'VE MANAGED TO MAKE QUITE A NAME FOR MYSELF.
LADY SPIDER A MENACE!!
J. Jonah Jameson
THOUGH, IT'S NOT *QUITE* THE NAME I WAS HOPING FOR.

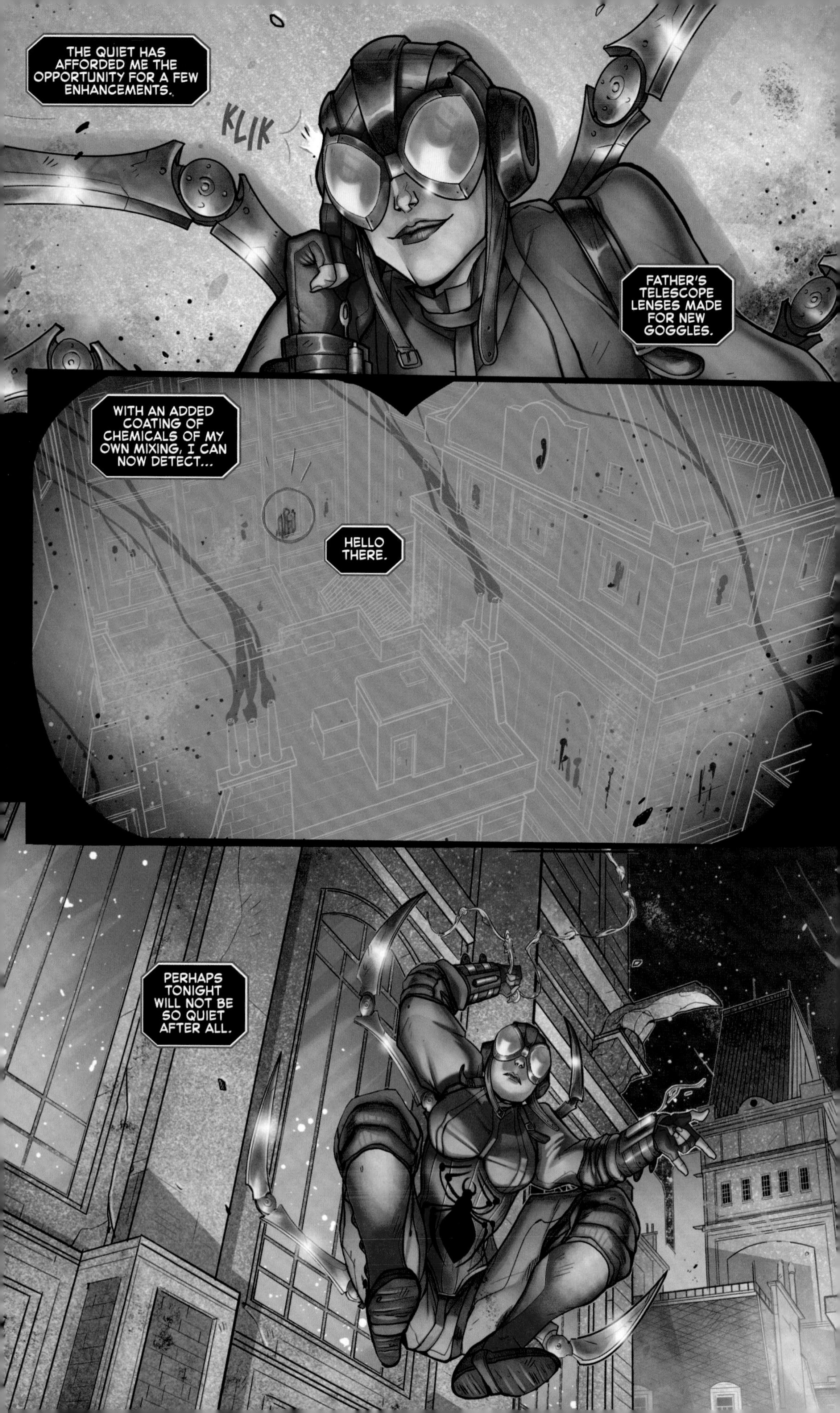
THE QUIET HAS AFFORDED ME THE OPPORTUNITY FOR A FEW ENHANCEMENTS.
KLIK
FATHER'S TELESCOPE LENSES MADE FOR NEW GOGGLES.
WITH AN ADDED COATING OF CHEMICALS OF MY OWN MIXING, I CAN NOW DETECT...
HELLO THERE.
PERHAPS TONIGHT WILL NOT BE SO QUIET AFTER ALL.

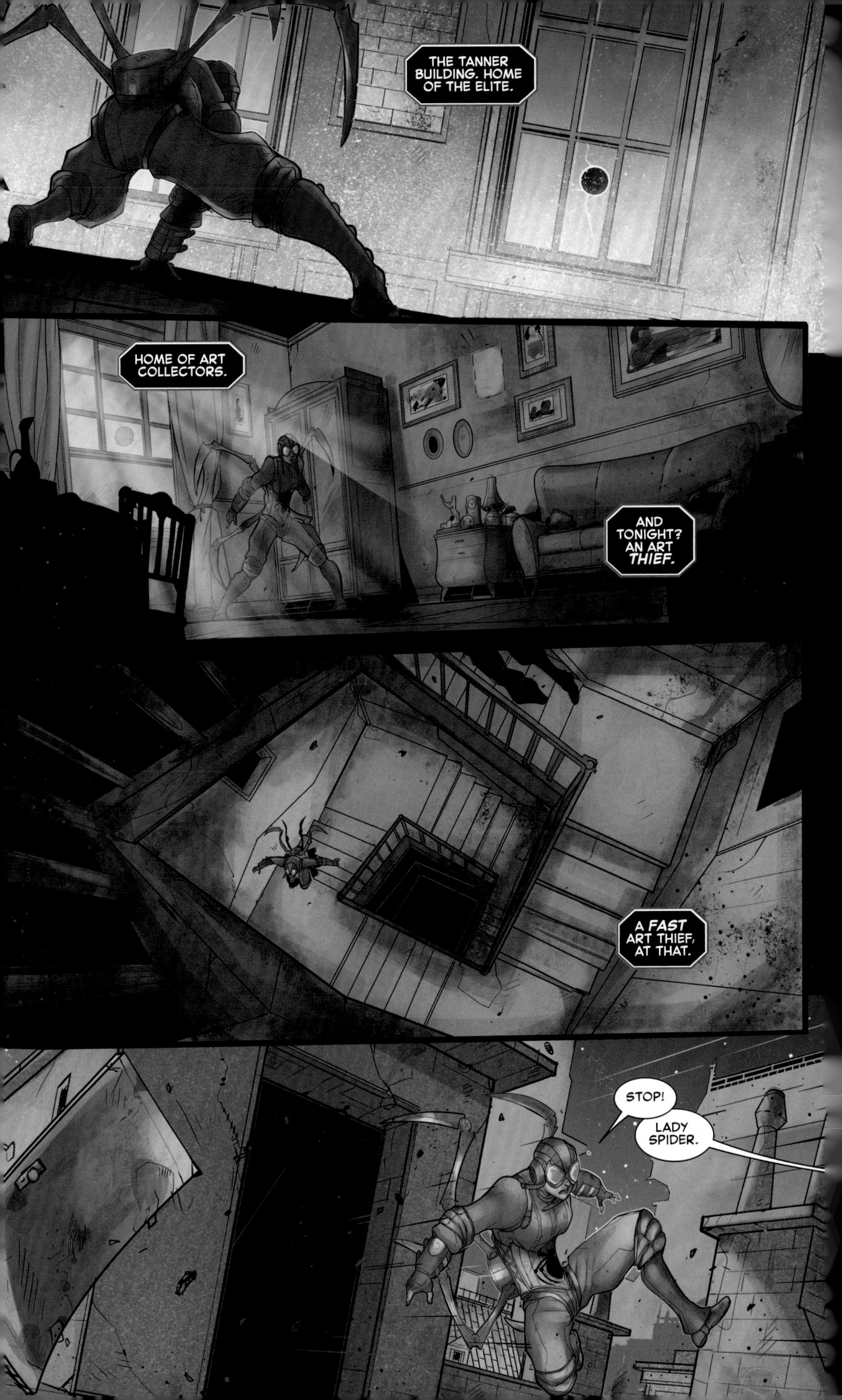
THE TANNER BUILDING. HOME OF THE ELITE.
HOME OF ART COLLECTORS.
AND TONIGHT? AN ART THIEF.
A FAST ART THIEF, AT THAT.
STOP!
LADY SPIDER.

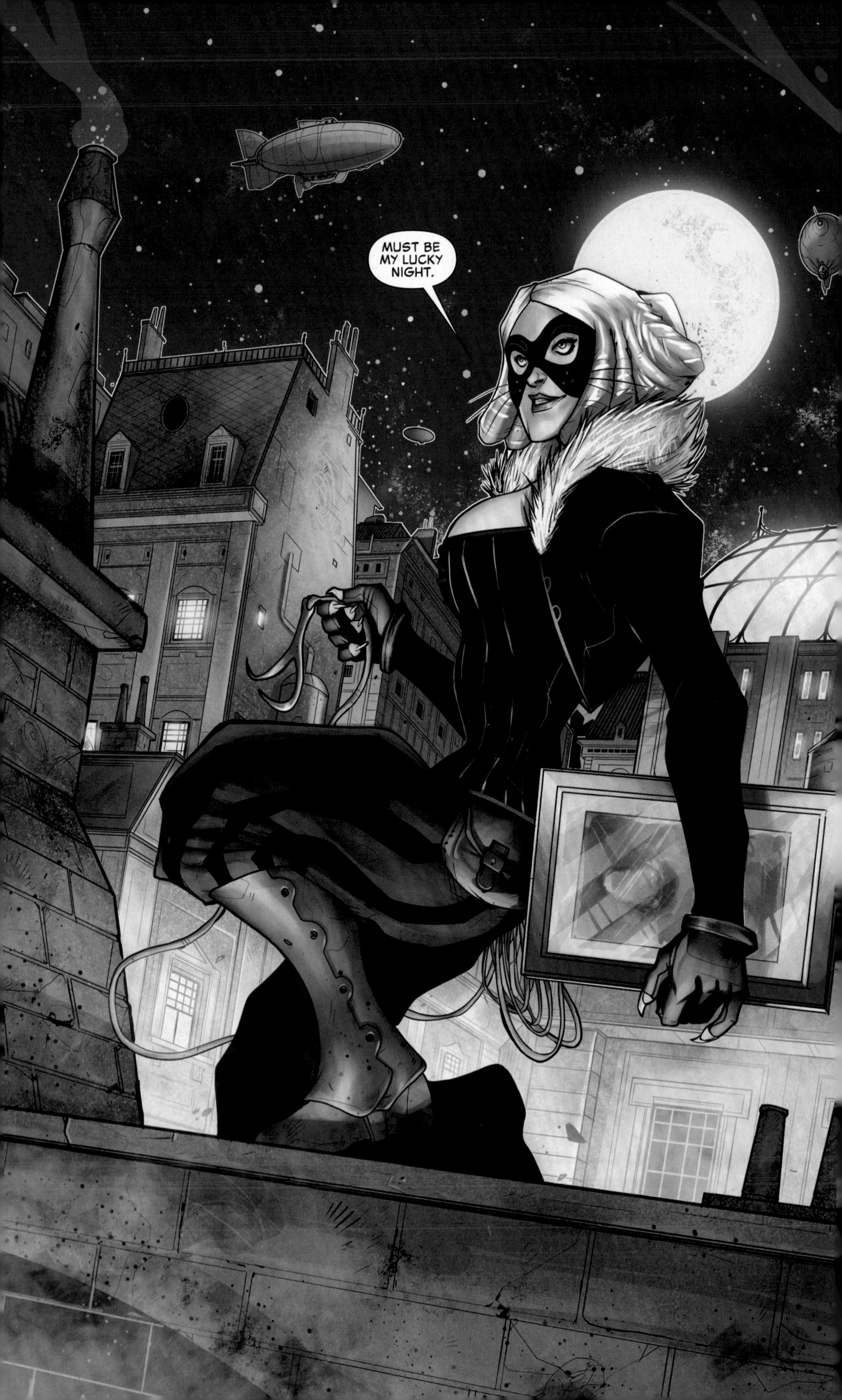
MUST BE MY LUCKY NIGHT.

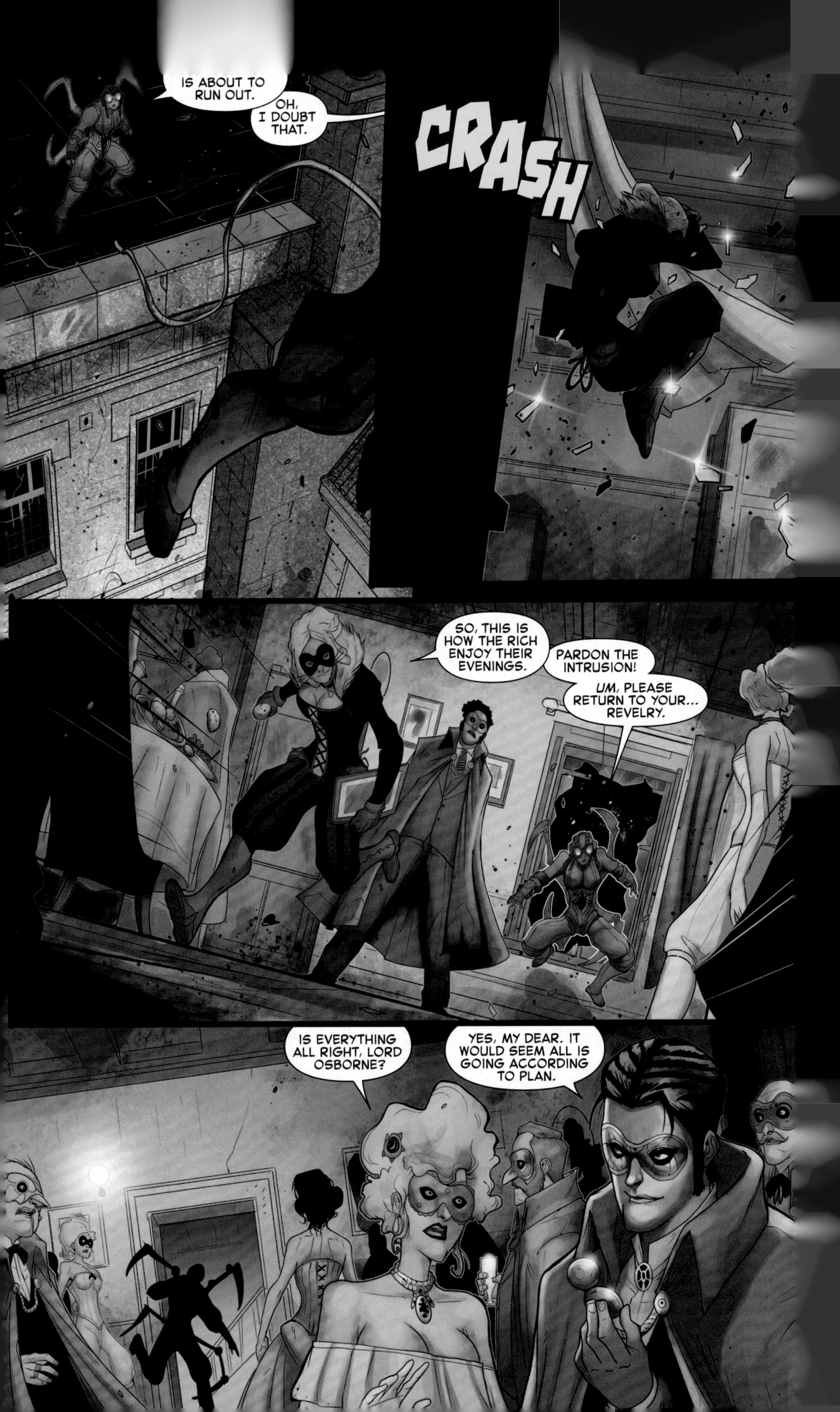
IS ABOUT TO RUN OUT.
OH, I DOUBT THAT.
CRASH
SO, THIS IS HOW THE RICH ENJOY THEIR EVENINGS.
PARDON THE INTRUSION!
UM, PLEASE RETURN TO YOUR... REVELRY.
IS EVERYTHING ALL RIGHT, LORD OSBORNE?
YES, MY DEAR. IT WOULD SEEM ALL IS GOING ACCORDING TO PLAN.

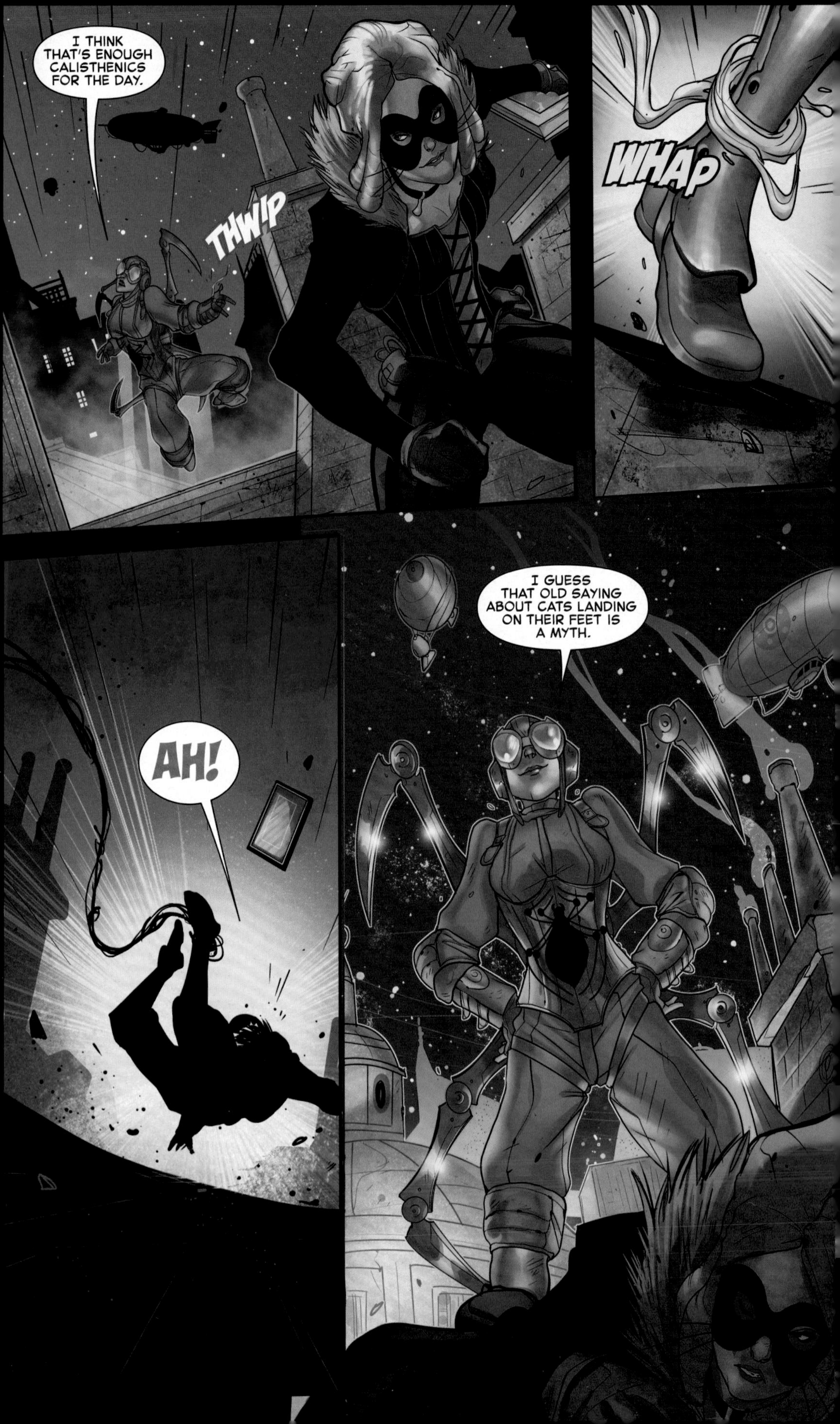
I THINK THAT'S ENOUGH CALISTHENICS FOR THE DAY.
THWIP
WHAP
AH!
I GUESS THAT OLD SAYING ABOUT CATS LANDING ON THEIR FEET IS A MYTH.

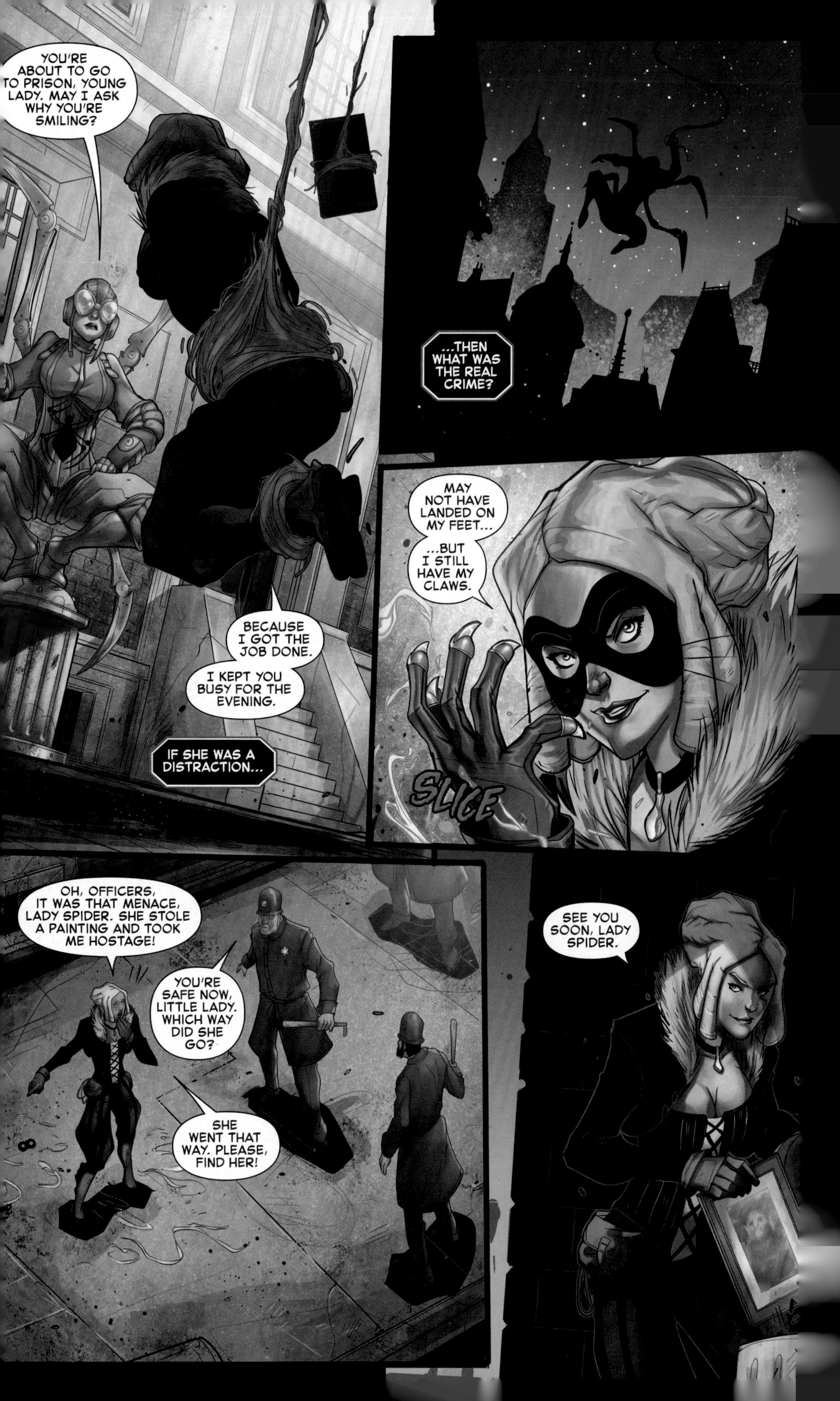
YOU'RE ABOUT TO GO TO PRISON, YOUNG LADY. MAY I ASK WHY YOU'RE SMILING?
BECAUSE I GOT THE JOB DONE.
I KEPT YOU BUSY FOR THE EVENING.
IF SHE WAS A DISTRACTION...
...THEN WHAT WAS THE REAL CRIME?
MAY NOT HAVE LANDED ON MY FEET...
...BUT I STILL HAVE MY CLAWS.
SLICE
OH, OFFICERS, IT WAS THAT MENACE, LADY SPIDER. SHE STOLE A PAINTING AND TOOK ME HOSTAGE!
YOU'RE SAFE NOW, LITTLE LADY. WHICH WAY DID SHE GO?
SHE WENT THAT WAY. PLEASE, FIND HER!
SEE YOU SOON, LADY SPIDER.

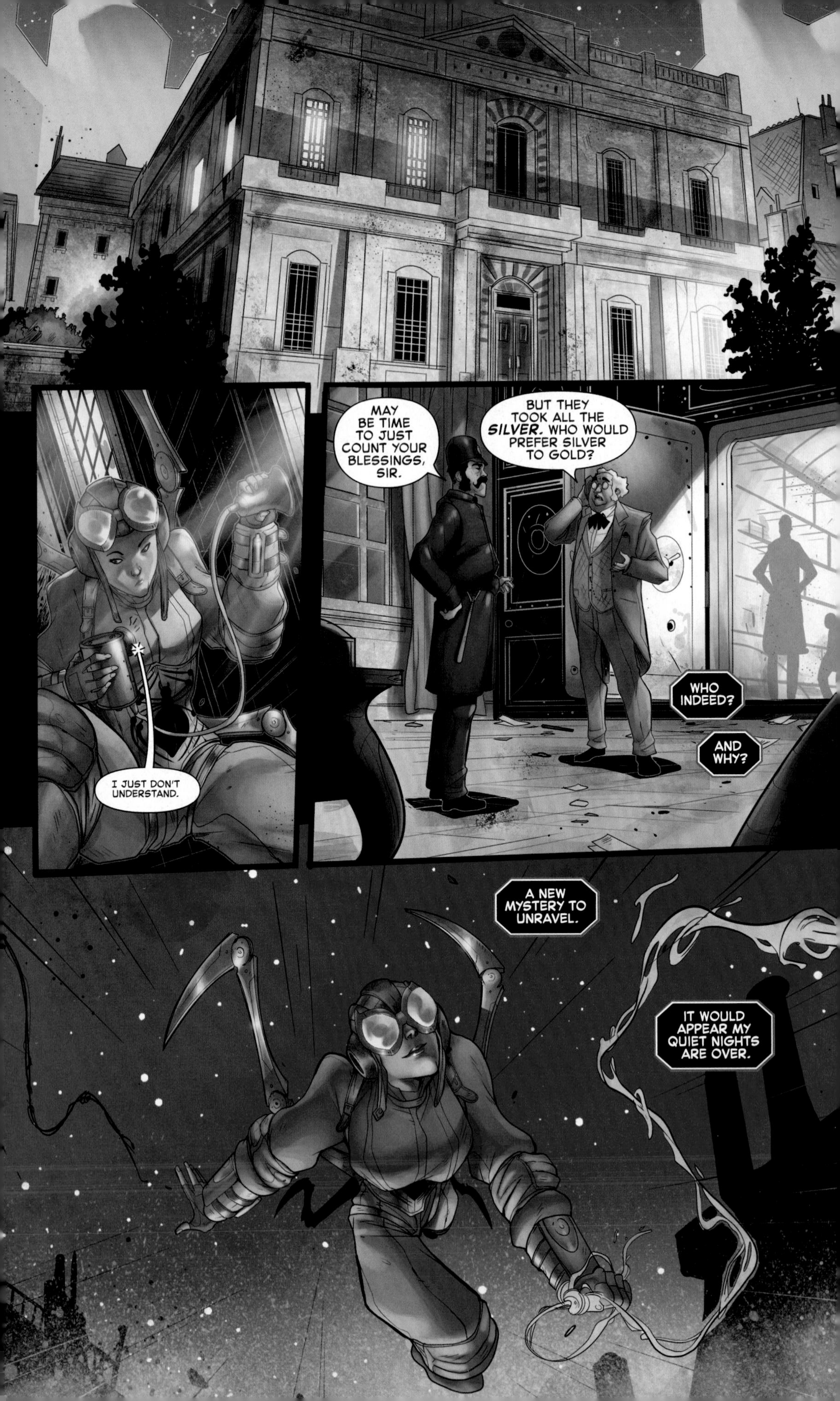
I JUST DON'T UNDERSTAND.
MAY BE TIME TO JUST COUNT YOUR BLESSINGS, SIR.
BUT THEY TOOK ALL THE SILVER. WHO WOULD PREFER SILVER TO GOLD?
WHO INDEED?
AND WHY?
A NEW MYSTERY TO UNRAVEL.
IT WOULD APPEAR MY QUIET NIGHTS ARE OVER.

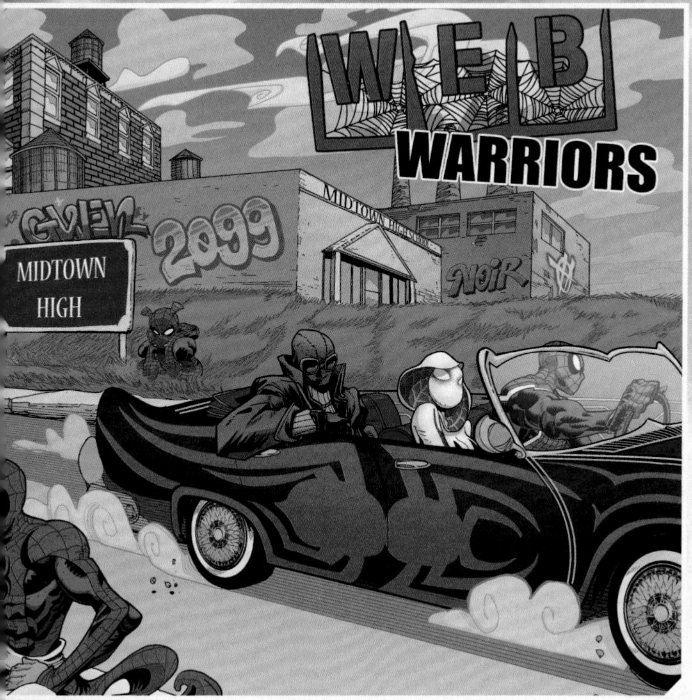
WEB
WARRIORS
GWEN
2099
MIDTOWN
HIGH
MIDTOWN HIGH SCHOOL
NOIR

#1 HIP-HOP VARIANT BY
DAIMON SCOTT

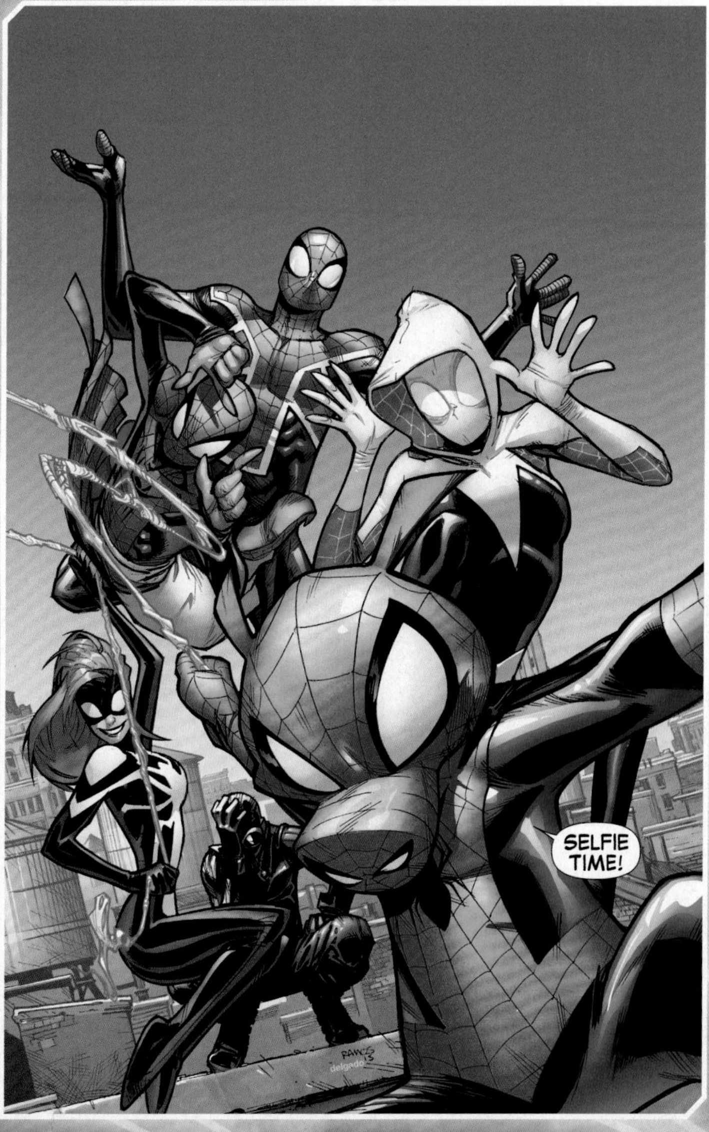
SELFIE
TIME!

#1 VARIANT BY
HUMBERTO RAMOS &
EDGAR DELGADO

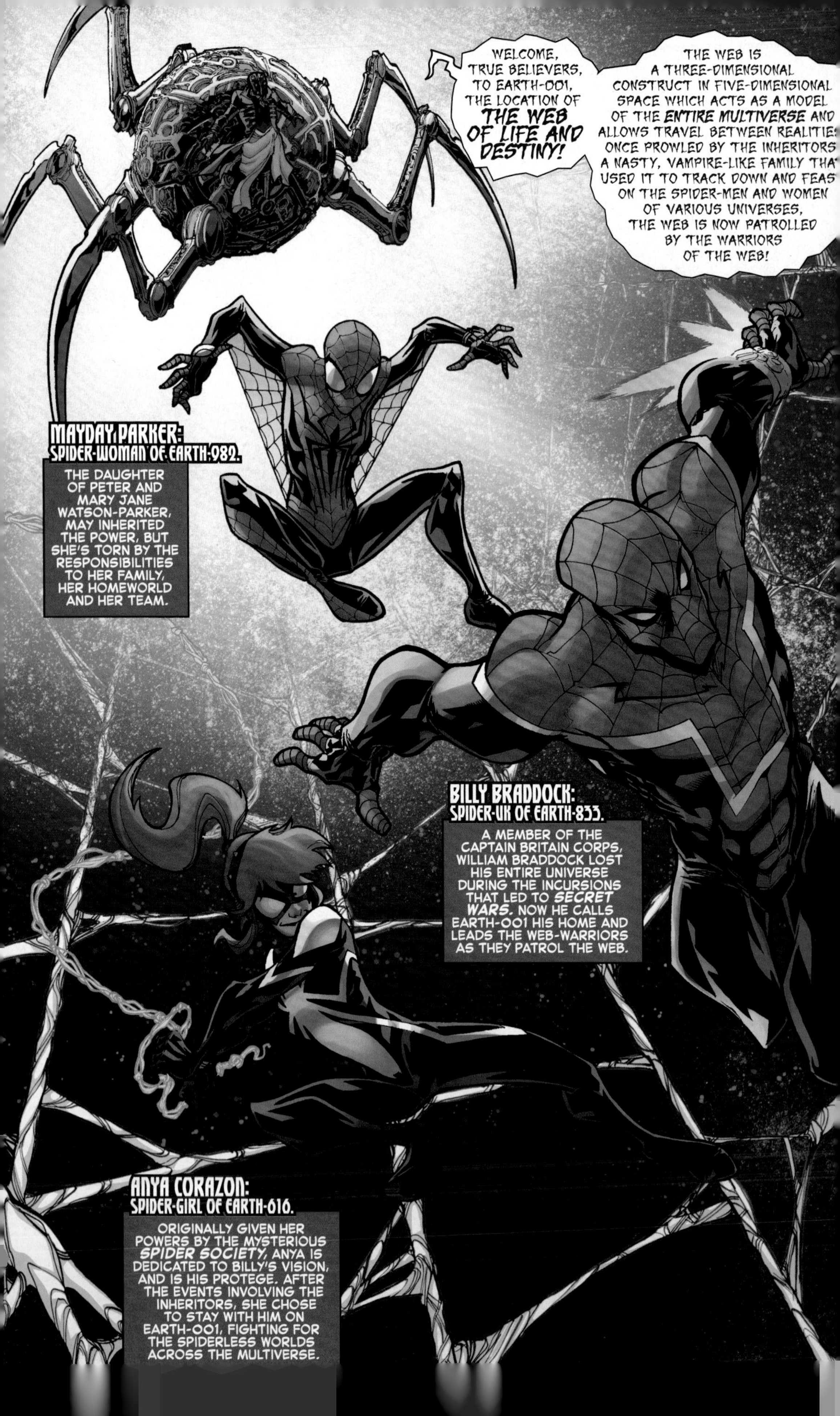
WELCOME, TRUE BELIEVERS, TO EARTH-001, THE LOCATION OF THE WEB OF LIFE AND DESTINY!
THE WEB IS A THREE-DIMENSIONAL CONSTRUCT IN FIVE-DIMENSIONAL SPACE WHICH ACTS AS A MODEL OF THE ENTIRE MULTIVERSE AND ALLOWS TRAVEL BETWEEN REALITIE ONCE PROWLED BY THE INHERITORS A NASTY, VAMPIRE-LIKE FAMILY THA USED IT TO TRACK DOWN AND FEAS ON THE SPIDER-MEN AND WOMEN OF VARIOUS UNIVERSES, THE WEB IS NOW PATROLLED BY THE WARRIORS OF THE WEB!
MAYDAY PARKER: SPIDER-WOMAN OF EARTH-982.
THE DAUGHTER OF PETER AND MARY JANE WATSON-PARKER, MAY INHERITED THE POWER, BUT SHE'S TORN BY THE RESPONSIBILITIES TO HER FAMILY, HER HOMEWORLD AND HER TEAM.
BILLY BRADDOCK: SPIDER-UK OF EARTH-833.
A MEMBER OF THE CAPTAIN BRITAIN CORPS, WILLIAM BRADDOCK LOST HIS ENTIRE UNIVERSE DURING THE INCURSIONS THAT LED TO SECRET WARS. NOW HE CALLS EARTH-001 HIS HOME AND LEADS THE WEB-WARRIORS AS THEY PATROL THE WEB.
ANYA CORAZON: SPIDER-GIRL OF EARTH-616.
ORIGINALLY GIVEN HER POWERS BY THE MYSTERIOUS SPIDER SOCIETY, ANYA IS DEDICATED TO BILLY'S VISION, AND IS HIS PROTEGE. AFTER THE EVENTS INVOLVING THE INHERITORS, SHE CHOSE TO STAY WITH HIM ON EARTH-001, FIGHTING FOR THE SPIDERLESS WORLDS ACROSS THE MULTIVERSE.

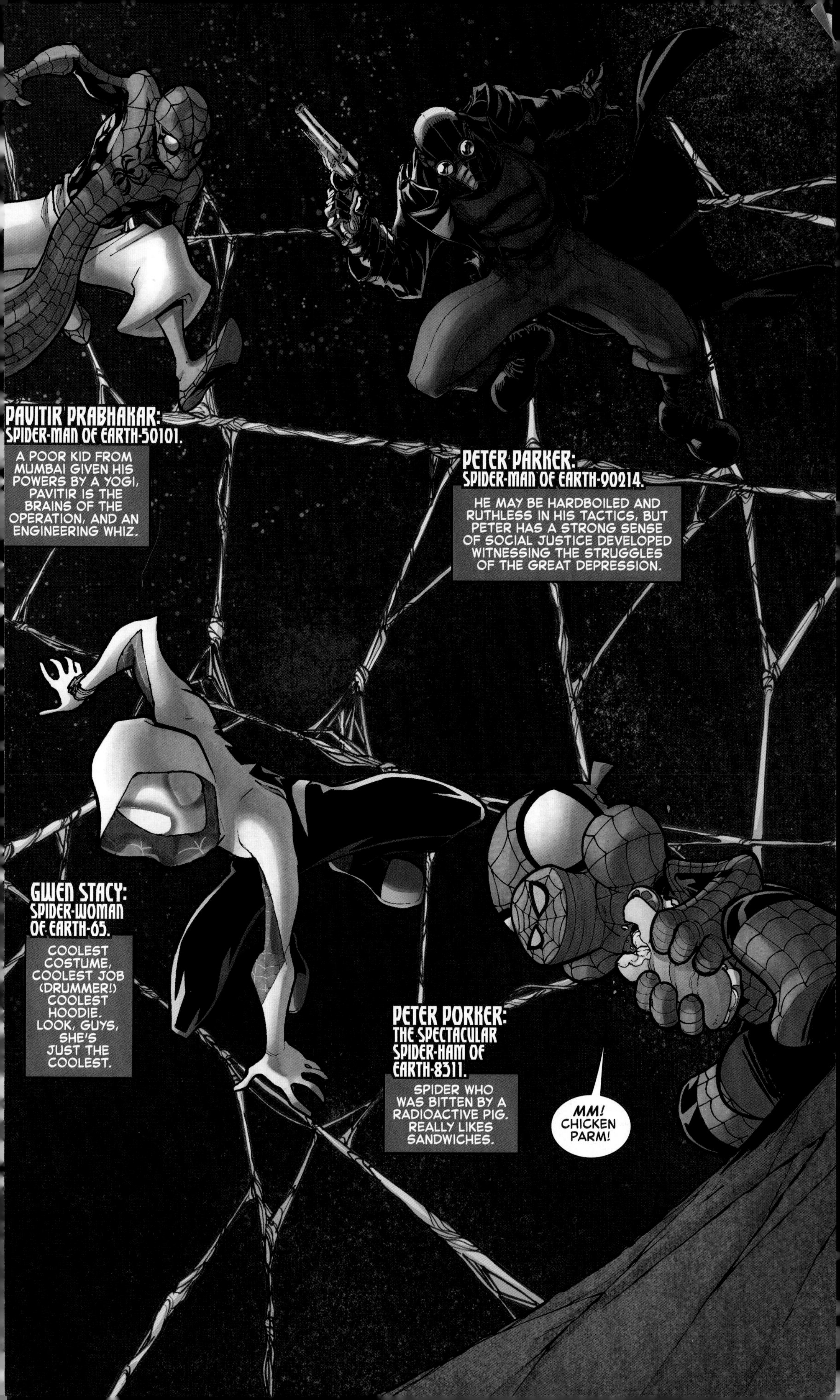
PAVITIR PRABHAKAR:
SPIDER-MAN OF EARTH-50101.
A POOR KID FROM MUMBAI GIVEN HIS POWERS BY A YOGI, PAVITIR IS THE BRAINS OF THE OPERATION, AND AN ENGINEERING WHIZ.
PETER PARKER:
SPIDER-MAN OF EARTH-90214.
HE MAY BE HARDBOILED AND RUTHLESS IN HIS TACTICS, BUT PETER HAS A STRONG SENSE OF SOCIAL JUSTICE DEVELOPED WITNESSING THE STRUGGLES OF THE GREAT DEPRESSION.
GWEN STACY:
SPIDER-WOMAN OF EARTH-65.
COOLEST COSTUME, COOLEST JOB (DRUMMER!) COOLEST HOODIE. LOOK, GUYS, SHE'S JUST THE COOLEST.
PETER PORKER:
THE SPECTACULAR SPIDER-HAM OF EARTH-8311.
SPIDER WHO WAS BITTEN BY A RADIOACTIVE PIG. REALLY LIKES SANDWICHES.
MM! CHICKEN PARM!

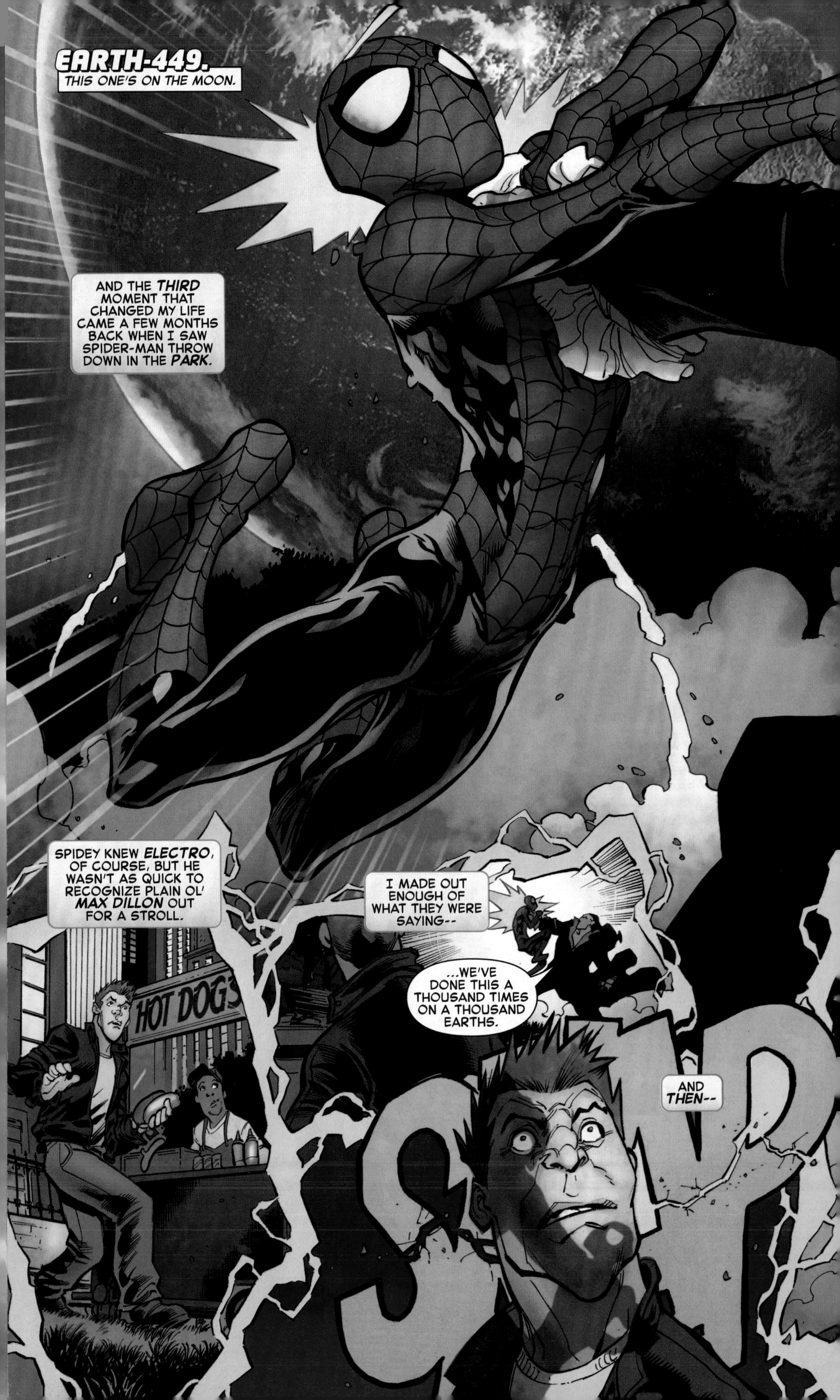
EARTH-449.
THIS ONE'S ON THE MOON.
AND THE THIRD MOMENT THAT CHANGED MY LIFE CAME A FEW MONTHS BACK WHEN I SAW SPIDER-MAN THROW DOWN IN THE PARK.
SPIDEY KNEW ELECTRO, OF COURSE, BUT HE WASN'T AS QUICK TO RECOGNIZE PLAIN OL' MAX DILLON OUT FOR A STROLL.
I MADE OUT ENOUGH OF WHAT THEY WERE SAYING--
...WE'VE DONE THIS A THOUSAND TIMES ON A THOUSAND EARTHS.
HOT DOGS
AND THEN--

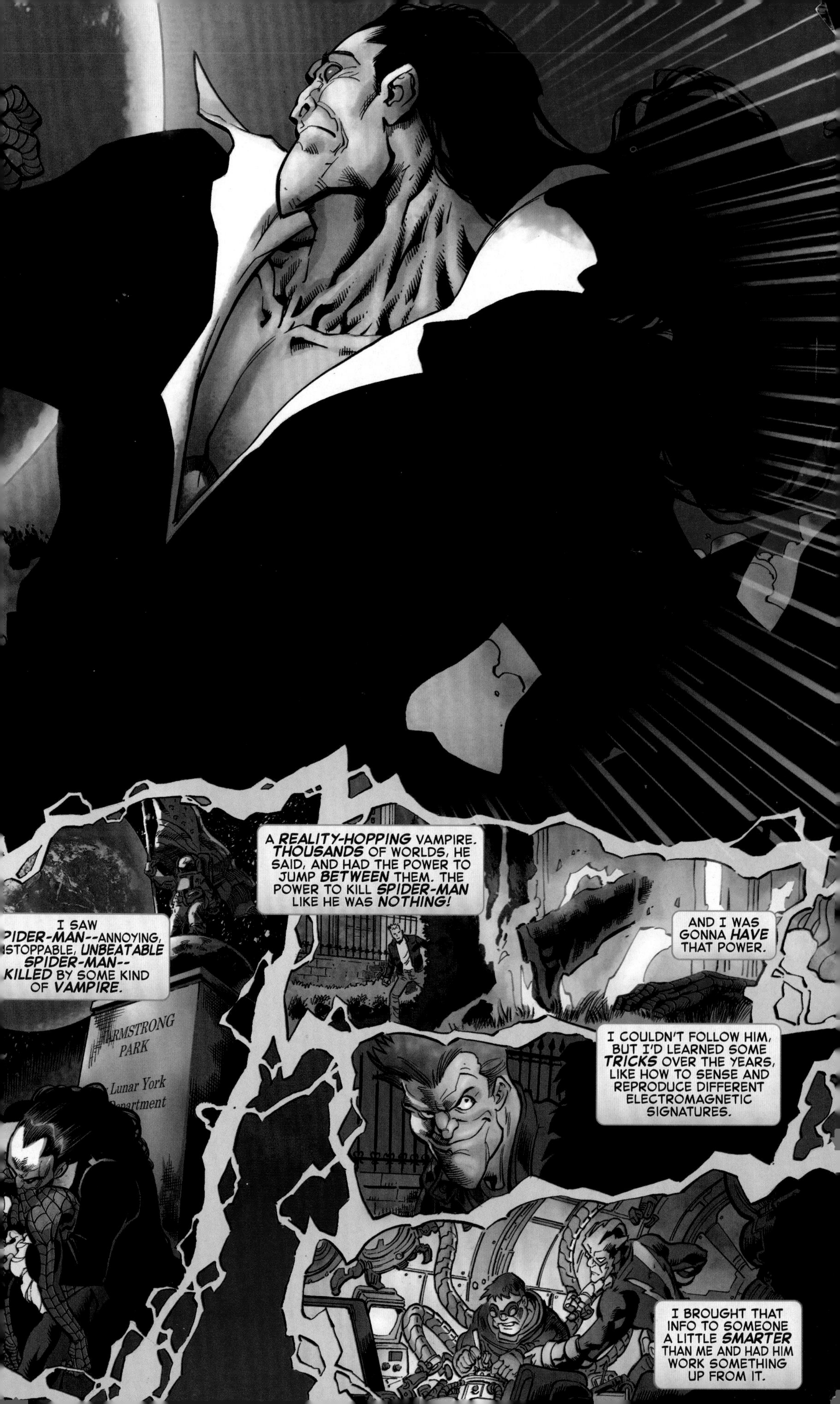

I SAW PIDER-MAN--ANNOYING, STOPPABLE, UNBEATABLE SPIDER-MAN-- KILLED BY SOME KIND OF VAMPIRE.
A REALITY-HOPPING VAMPIRE. THOUSANDS OF WORLDS, HE SAID, AND HAD THE POWER TO JUMP BETWEEN THEM. THE POWER TO KILL SPIDER-MAN LIKE HE WAS NOTHING!
AND I WAS GONNA HAVE THAT POWER.
RMSTRONG PARK
Lunar York
Department
I COULDN'T FOLLOW HIM, BUT I'D LEARNED SOME TRICKS OVER THE YEARS, LIKE HOW TO SENSE AND REPRODUCE DIFFERENT ELECTROMAGNETIC SIGNATURES.
I BROUGHT THAT INFO TO SOMEONE A LITTLE SMARTER THAN ME AND HAD HIM WORK SOMETHING UP FROM IT.

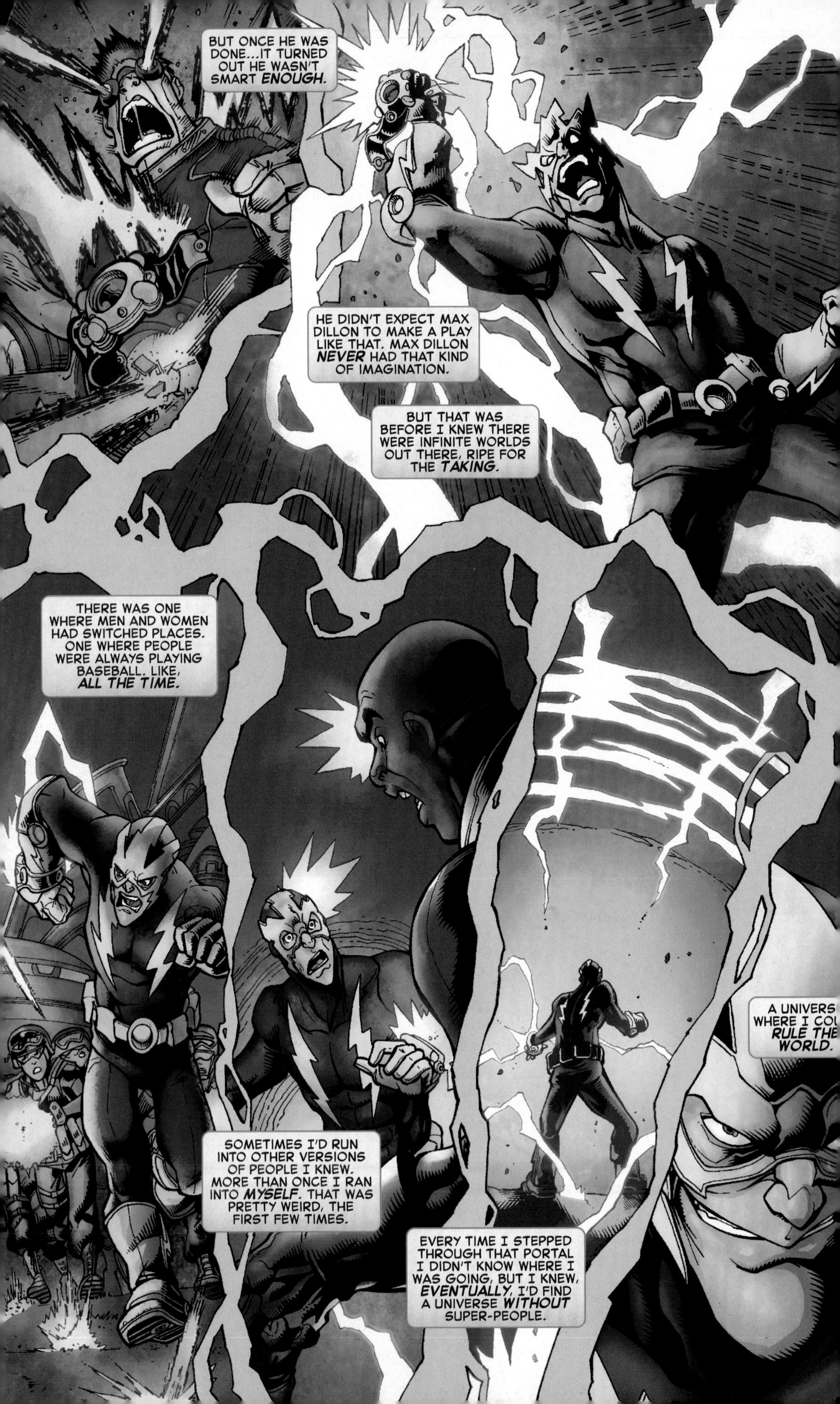

BUT ONCE HE WAS DONE...IT TURNED OUT HE WASN'T SMART ENOUGH.
HE DIDN'T EXPECT MAX DILLON TO MAKE A PLAY LIKE THAT. MAX DILLON NEVER HAD THAT KIND OF IMAGINATION.
BUT THAT WAS BEFORE I KNEW THERE WERE INFINITE WORLDS OUT THERE, RIPE FOR THE TAKING.
THERE WAS ONE WHERE MEN AND WOMEN HAD SWITCHED PLACES. ONE WHERE PEOPLE WERE ALWAYS PLAYING BASEBALL. LIKE, ALL THE TIME.
SOMETIMES I'D RUN INTO OTHER VERSIONS OF PEOPLE I KNEW. MORE THAN ONCE I RAN INTO MYSELF. THAT WAS PRETTY WEIRD, THE FIRST FEW TIMES.
EVERY TIME I STEPPED THROUGH THAT PORTAL I DIDN'T KNOW WHERE I WAS GOING, BUT I KNEW, EVENTUALLY, I'D FIND A UNIVERSE WITHOUT SUPER-PEOPLE.
A UNIVERS WHERE I COU RULE THE WORLD.

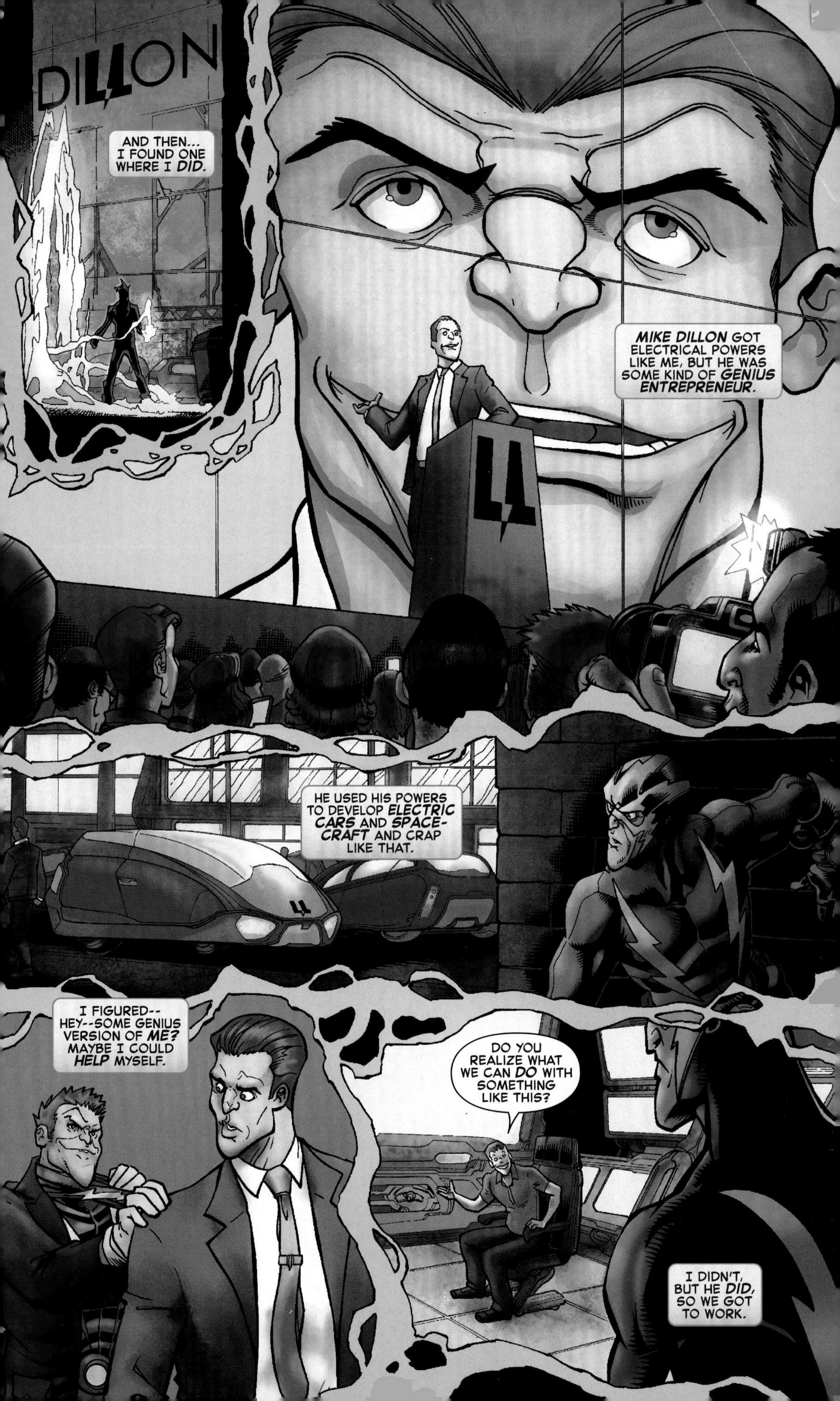
DILLON
AND THEN... I FOUND ONE WHERE I DID.
MIKE DILLON GOT ELECTRICAL POWERS LIKE ME, BUT HE WAS SOME KIND OF GENIUS ENTREPRENEUR.
HE USED HIS POWERS TO DEVELOP ELECTRIC CARS AND SPACE-CRAFT AND CRAP LIKE THAT.
I FIGURED-- HEY--SOME GENIUS VERSION OF ME? MAYBE I COULD HELP MYSELF.
DO YOU REALIZE WHAT WE CAN DO WITH SOMETHING LIKE THIS?
I DIDN'T, BUT HE DID, SO WE GOT TO WORK.

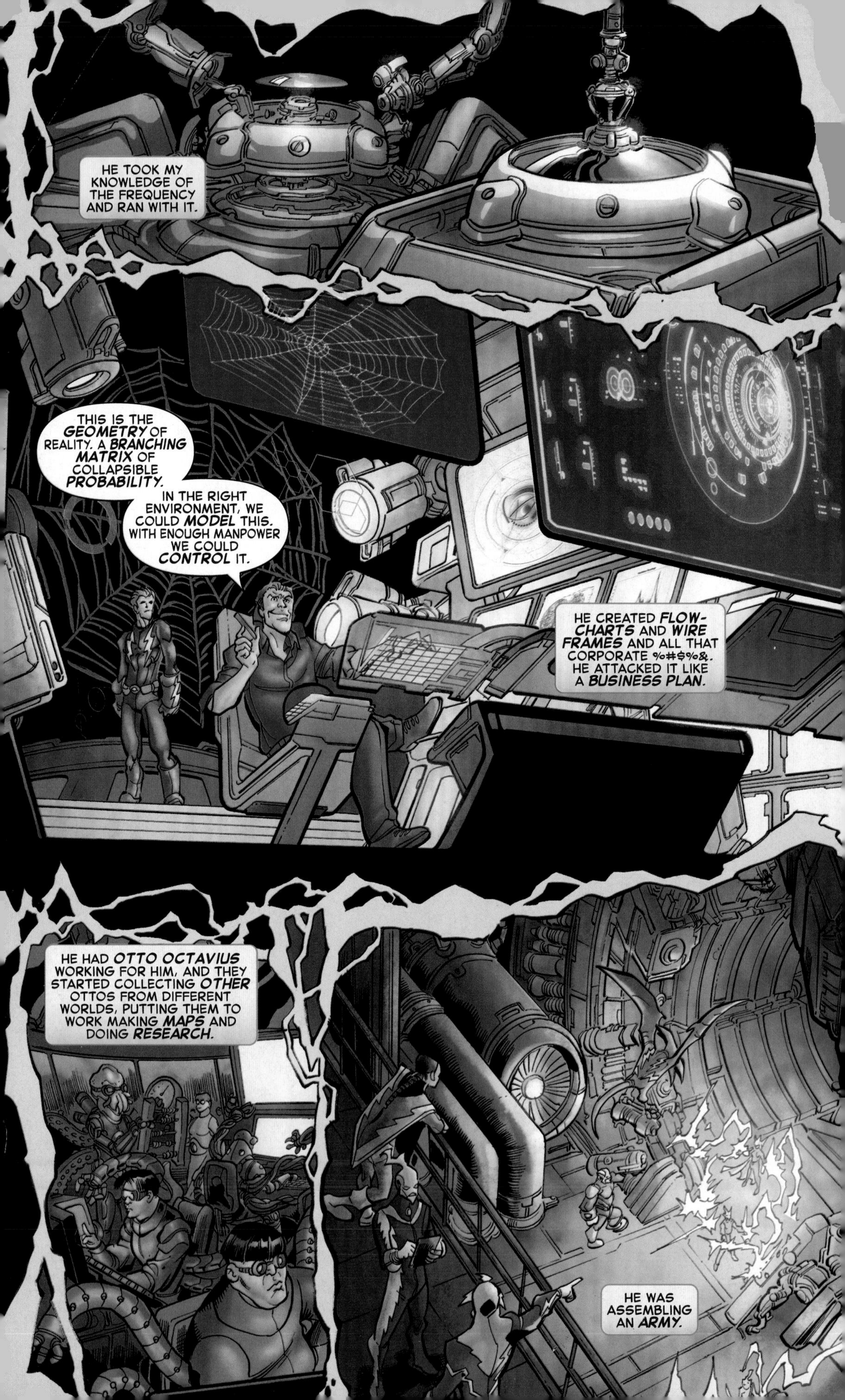

HE TOOK MY KNOWLEDGE OF THE FREQUENCY AND RAN WITH IT.
THIS IS THE GEOMETRY OF REALITY. A BRANCHING MATRIX OF COLLAPSIBLE PROBABILITY.
IN THE RIGHT ENVIRONMENT, WE COULD MODEL THIS. WITH ENOUGH MANPOWER WE COULD CONTROL IT.
HE CREATED FLOW-CHARTS AND WIRE FRAMES AND ALL THAT CORPORATE %#$%&. HE ATTACKED IT LIKE A BUSINESS PLAN.
HE HAD OTTO OCTAVIUS WORKING FOR HIM, AND THEY STARTED COLLECTING OTHER OTTOS FROM DIFFERENT WORLDS, PUTTING THEM TO WORK MAKING MAPS AND DOING RESEARCH.
HE WAS ASSEMBLING AN ARMY.

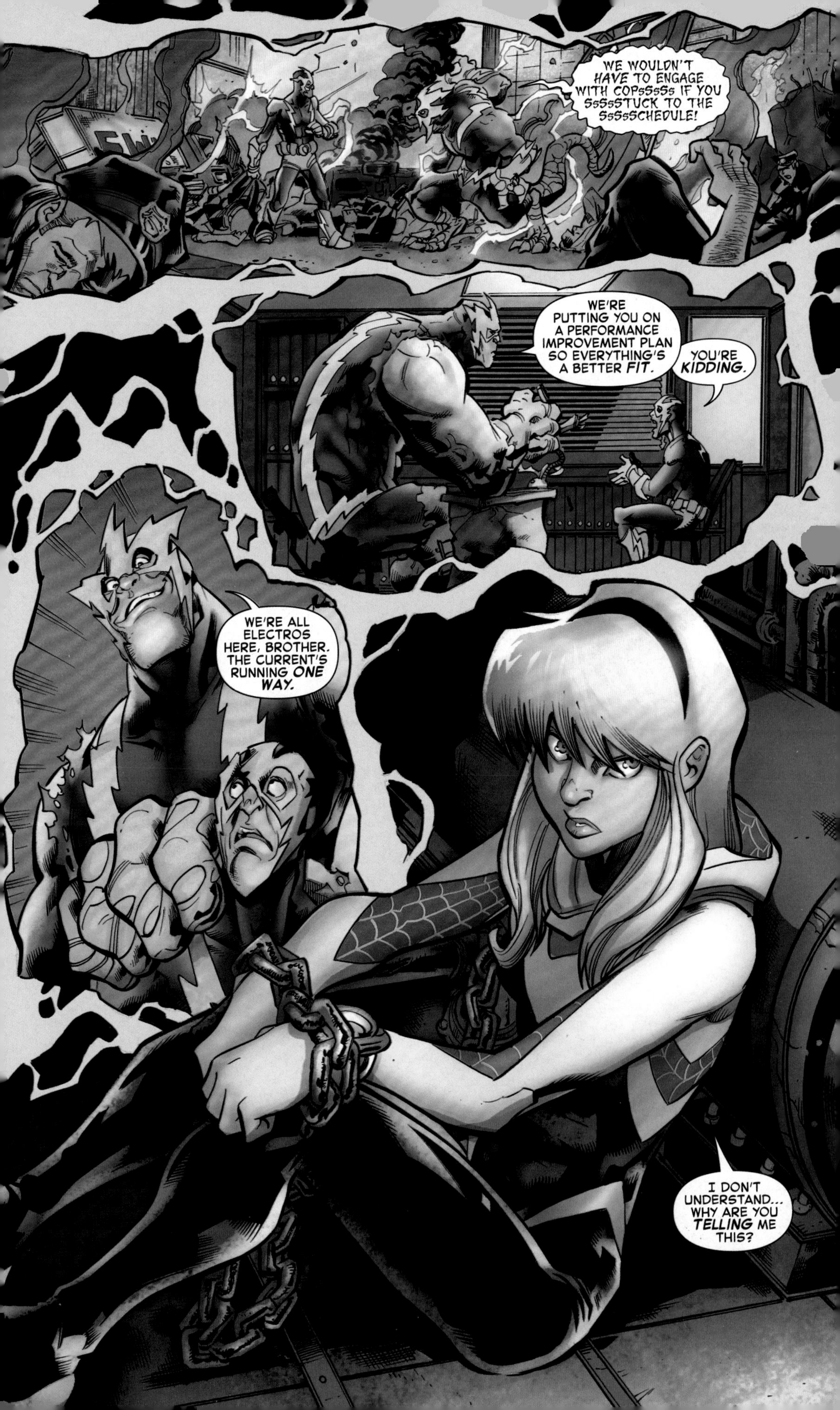
WE WOULDN'T HAVE TO ENGAGE WITH COPsSsSs IF YOU SsSsSTUCK TO THE SsSsSCHEDULE!
WE'RE PUTTING YOU ON A PERFORMANCE IMPROVEMENT PLAN SO EVERYTHING'S A BETTER FIT.
YOU'RE KIDDING.
WE'RE ALL ELECTROS HERE, BROTHER. THE CURRENT'S RUNNING ONE WAY.
I DON'T UNDERSTAND... WHY ARE YOU TELLING ME THIS?

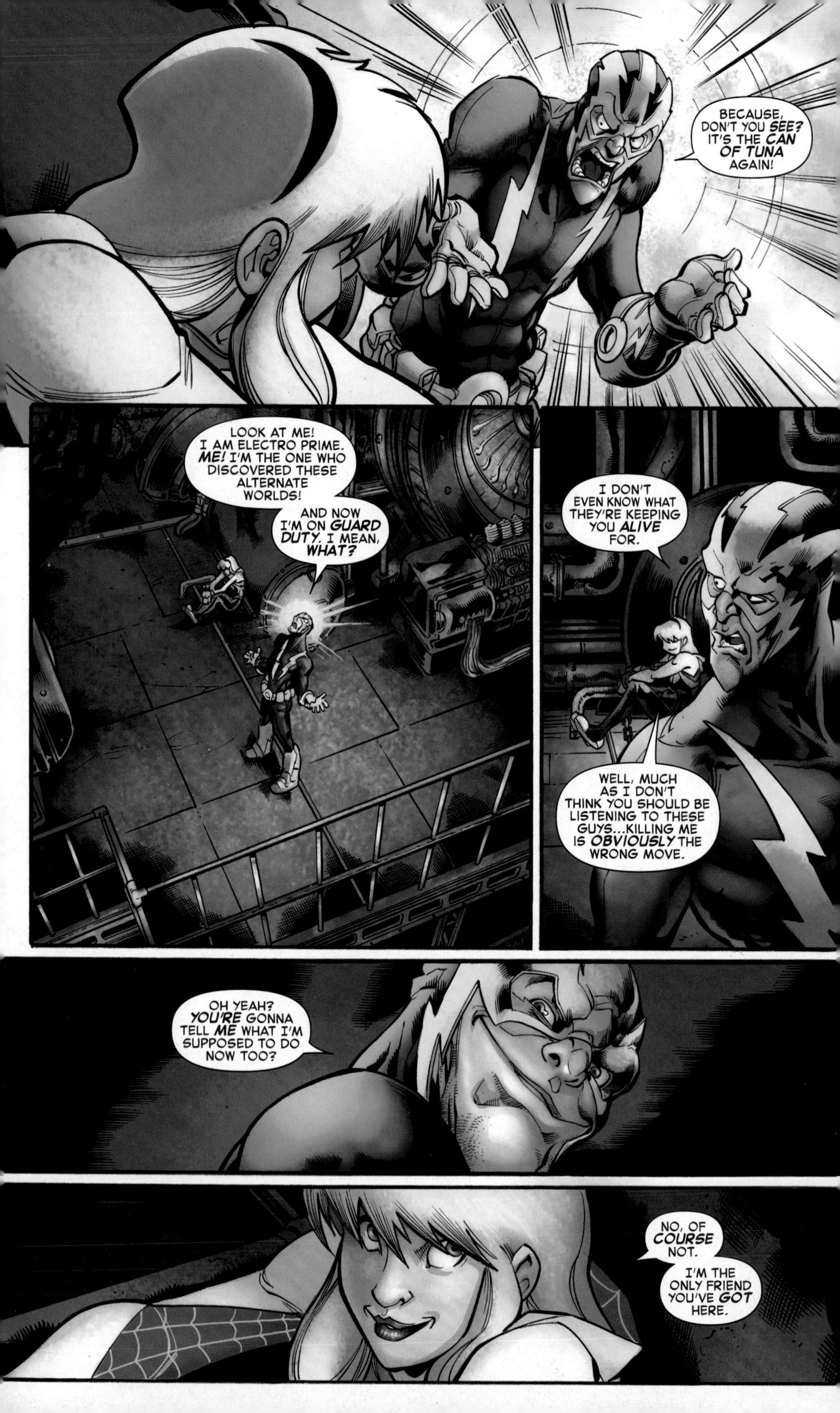
BECAUSE, DON'T YOU SEE? IT'S THE CAN OF TUNA AGAIN!
LOOK AT ME! I AM ELECTRO PRIME. ME! I'M THE ONE WHO DISCOVERED THESE ALTERNATE WORLDS!
AND NOW I'M ON GUARD DUTY. I MEAN, WHAT?
I DON'T EVEN KNOW WHAT THEY'RE KEEPING YOU ALIVE FOR.
WELL, MUCH AS I DON'T THINK YOU SHOULD BE LISTENING TO THESE GUYS...KILLING ME IS OBVIOUSLY THE WRONG MOVE.
OH YEAH? YOU'RE GONNA TELL ME WHAT I'M SUPPOSED TO DO NOW TOO?
NO, OF COURSE NOT.
I'M THE ONLY FRIEND YOU'VE GOT HERE.

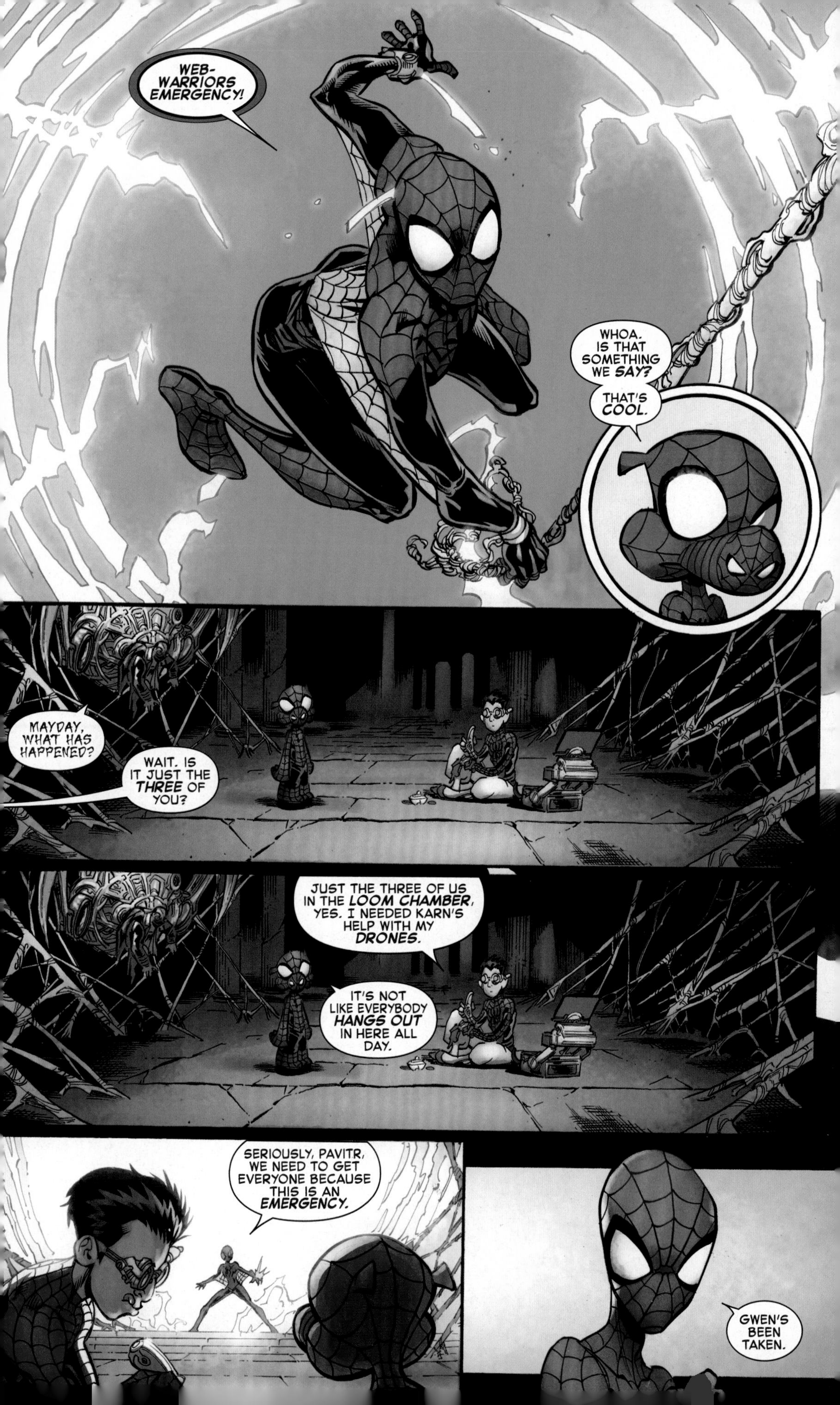
WEB-WARRIORS EMERGENCY!
WHOA. IS THAT SOMETHING WE SAY?
THAT'S COOL.
MAYDAY, WHAT HAS HAPPENED?
WAIT. IS IT JUST THE THREE OF YOU?
JUST THE THREE OF US IN THE LOOM CHAMBER, YES. I NEEDED KARN'S HELP WITH MY DRONES.
IT'S NOT LIKE EVERYBODY HANGS OUT IN HERE ALL DAY.
SERIOUSLY, PAVITR, WE NEED TO GET EVERYONE BECAUSE THIS IS AN EMERGENCY.
GWEN'S BEEN TAKEN.

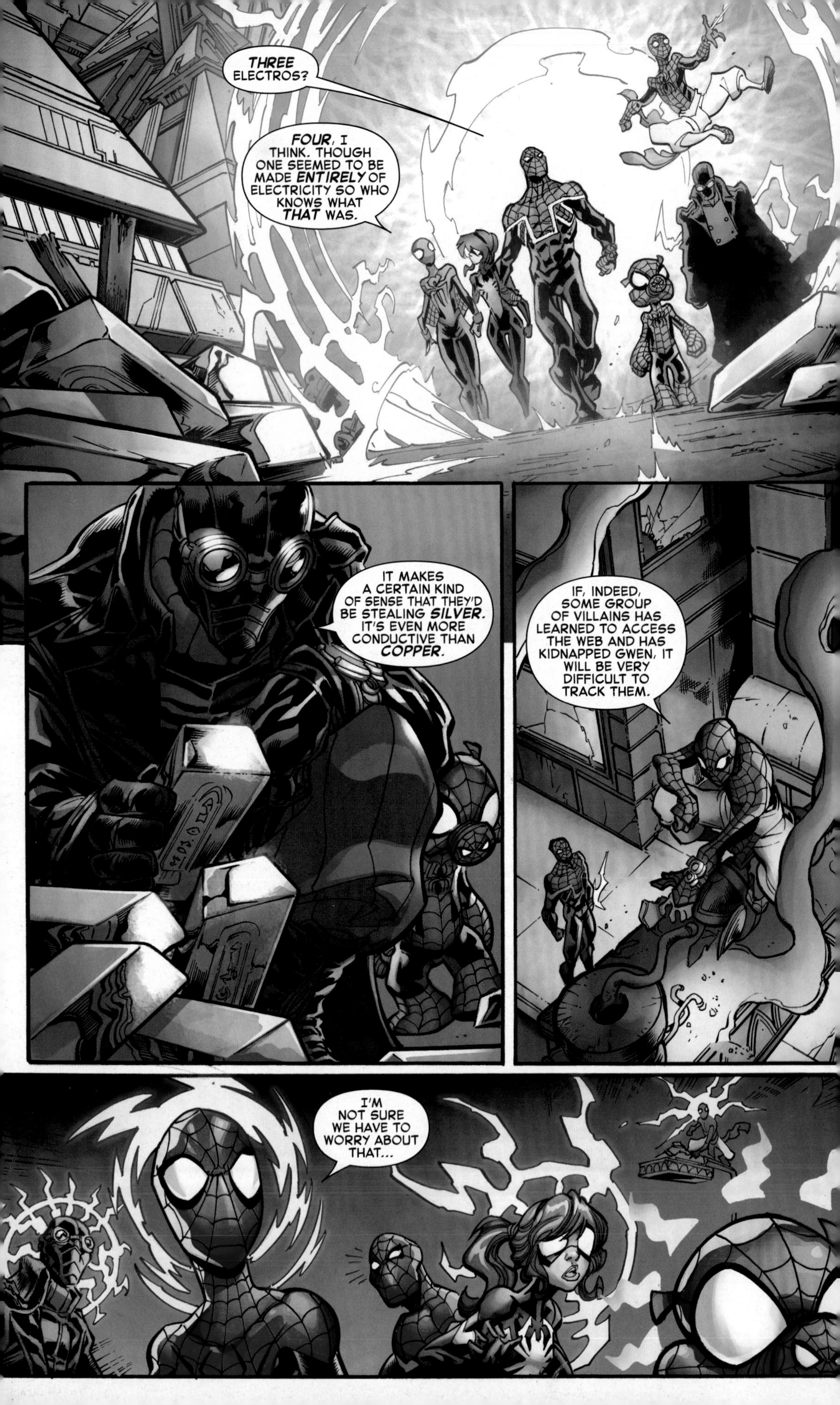
THREE ELECTROS?
FOUR, I THINK. THOUGH ONE SEEMED TO BE MADE ENTIRELY OF ELECTRICITY SO WHO KNOWS WHAT THAT WAS.
IT MAKES A CERTAIN KIND OF SENSE THAT THEY'D BE STEALING SILVER. IT'S EVEN MORE CONDUCTIVE THAN COPPER.
IF, INDEED, SOME GROUP OF VILLAINS HAS LEARNED TO ACCESS THE WEB AND HAS KIDNAPPED GWEN, IT WILL BE VERY DIFFICULT TO TRACK THEM.
I'M NOT SURE WE HAVE TO WORRY ABOUT THAT...

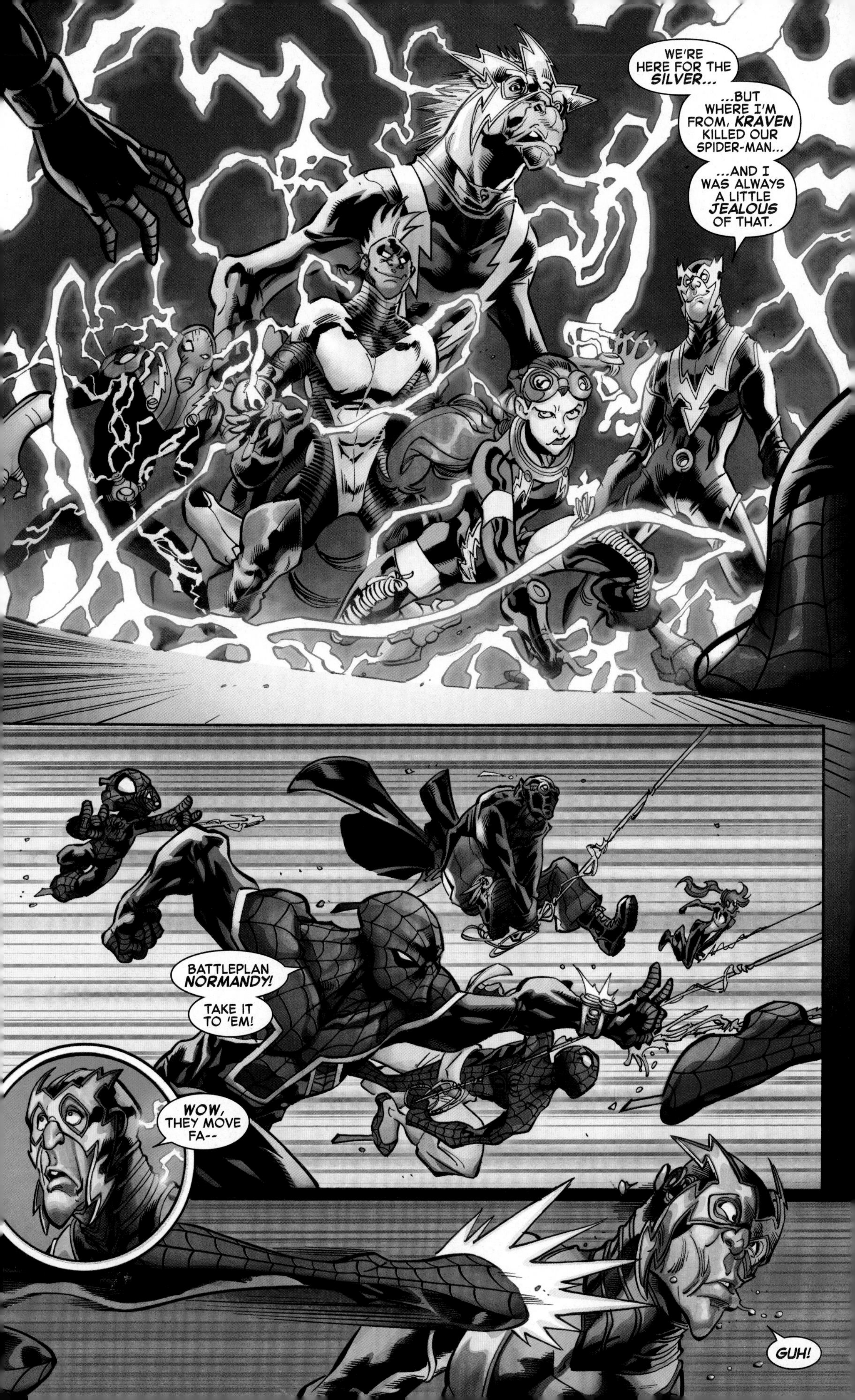
WE'RE HERE FOR THE SILVER...
...BUT WHERE I'M FROM, KRAVEN KILLED OUR SPIDER-MAN...
...AND I WAS ALWAYS A LITTLE JEALOUS OF THAT.
BATTLEPLAN NORMANDY!
TAKE IT TO 'EM!
WOW, THEY MOVE FA--
GUH!

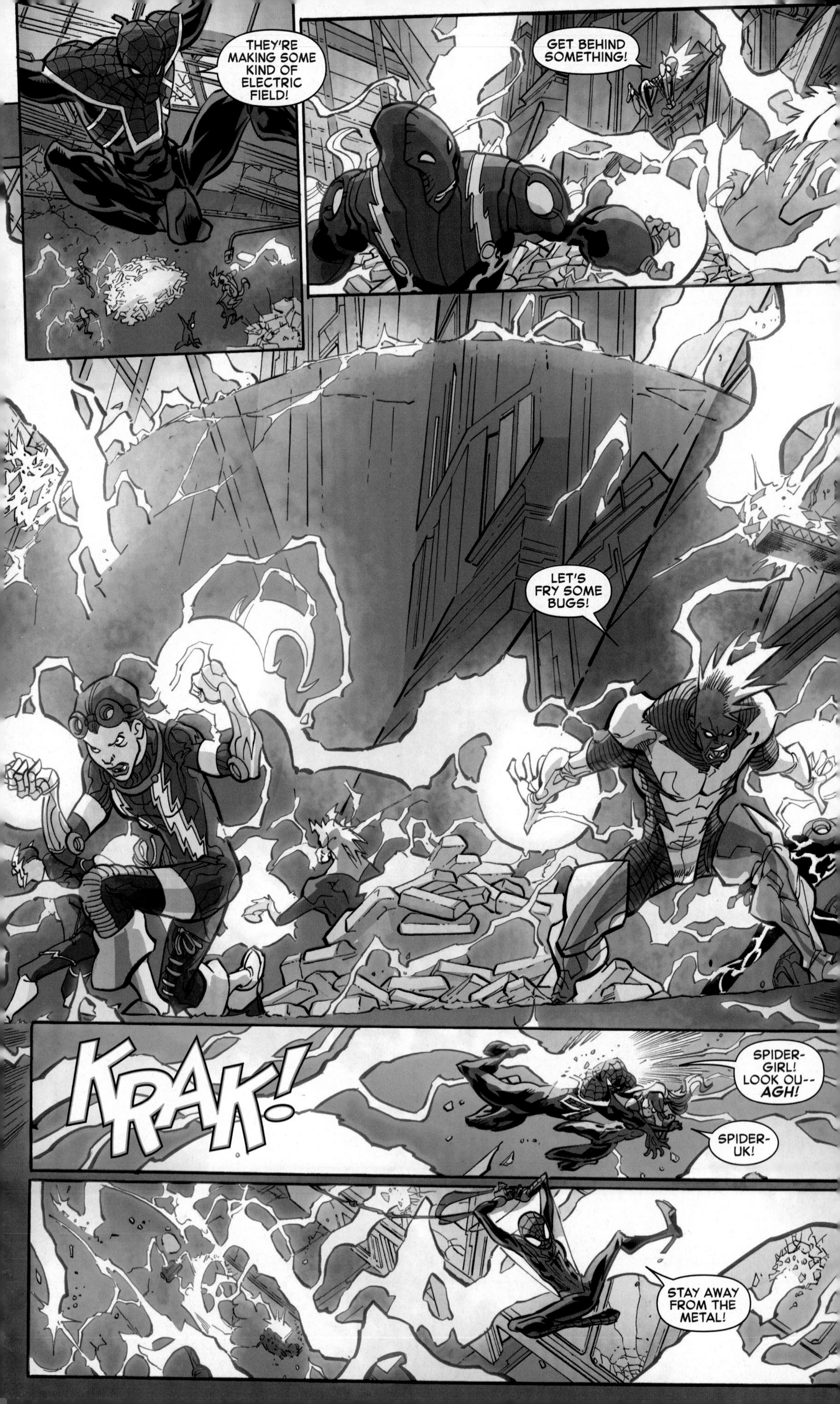
THEY'RE MAKING SOME KIND OF ELECTRIC FIELD!
GET BEHIND SOMETHING!
LET'S FRY SOME BUGS!
KRAK!
SPIDER-GIRL! LOOK OU-- AGH!
SPIDER-UK!
STAY AWAY FROM THE METAL!

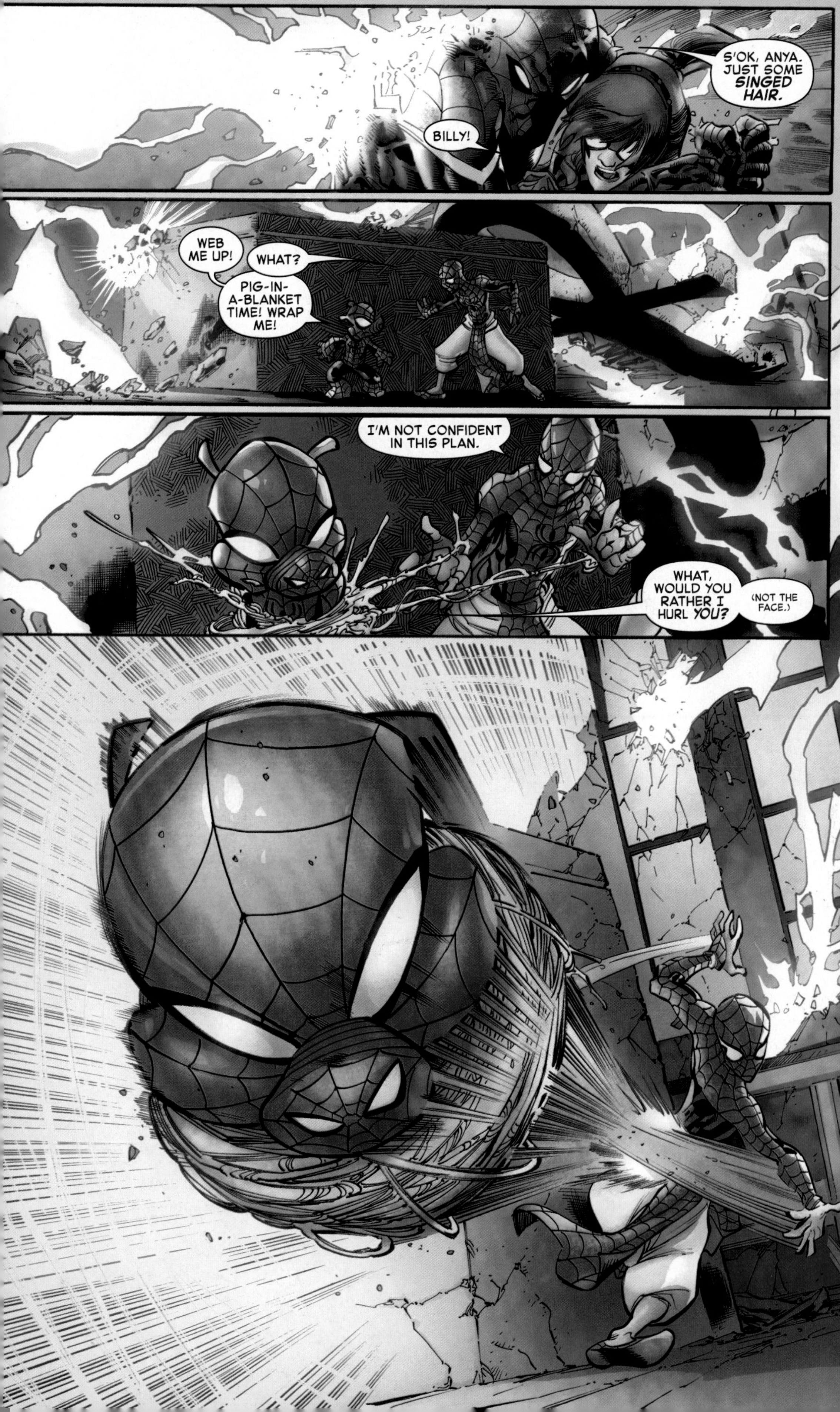
BILLY!
S'OK, ANYA. JUST SOME SINGED HAIR.
WEB ME UP!
WHAT?
PIG-IN-A-BLANKET TIME! WRAP ME!
I'M NOT CONFIDENT IN THIS PLAN.
WHAT, WOULD YOU RATHER I HURL YOU?
(NOT THE FACE.)

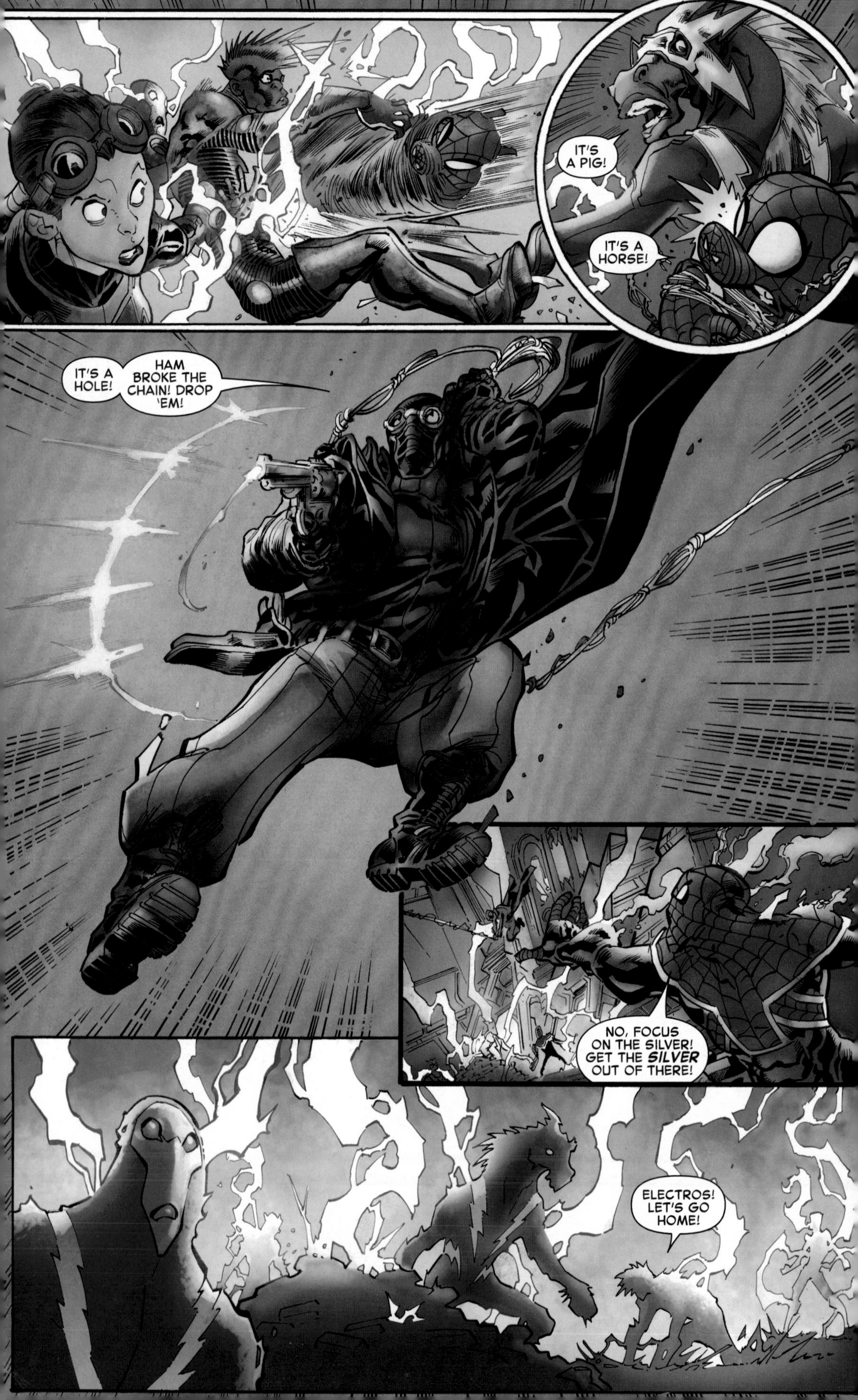
IT'S A PIG!
IT'S A HORSE!
IT'S A HOLE!
HAM BROKE THE CHAIN! DROP 'EM!
NO, FOCUS ON THE SILVER! GET THE *SILVER* OUT OF THERE!
ELECTROS! LET'S GO HOME!

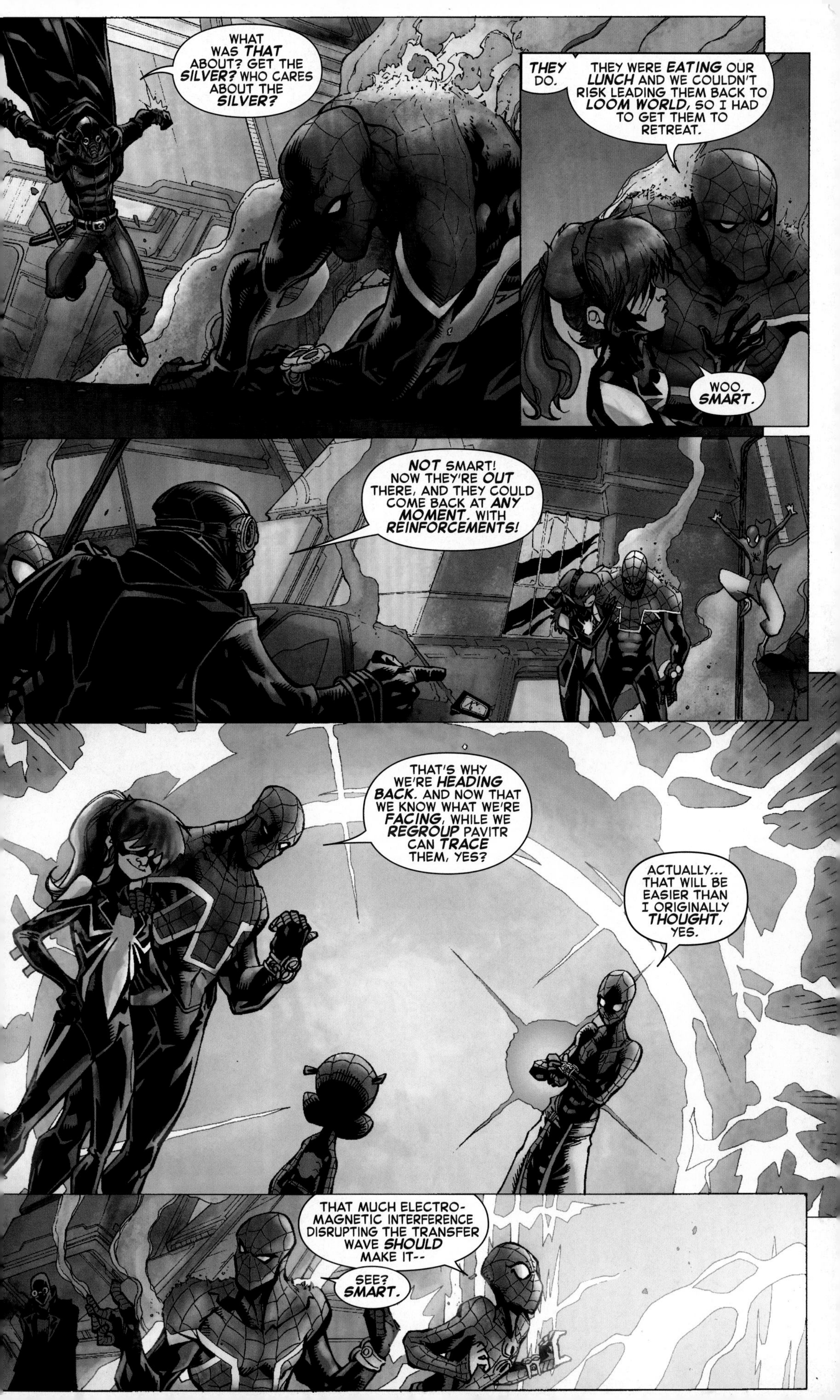

WHAT WAS **THAT** ABOUT? GET THE **SILVER?** WHO CARES ABOUT THE **SILVER?**
THEY DO.
THEY WERE **EATING** OUR **LUNCH** AND WE COULDN'T RISK LEADING THEM BACK TO **LOOM WORLD,** SO I HAD TO GET THEM TO RETREAT.
WOO. **SMART.**
NOT SMART! NOW THEY'RE **OUT** THERE, AND THEY COULD COME BACK AT **ANY MOMENT.** WITH **REINFORCEMENTS!**
THAT'S WHY WE'RE **HEADING BACK.** AND NOW THAT WE KNOW WHAT WE'RE **FACING,** WHILE WE **REGROUP** PAVITR CAN **TRACE** THEM, YES?
ACTUALLY... THAT WILL BE EASIER THAN I ORIGINALLY **THOUGHT,** YES.
THAT MUCH ELECTRO-MAGNETIC INTERFERENCE DISRUPTING THE TRANSFER WAVE **SHOULD** MAKE IT--
SEE? **SMART.**

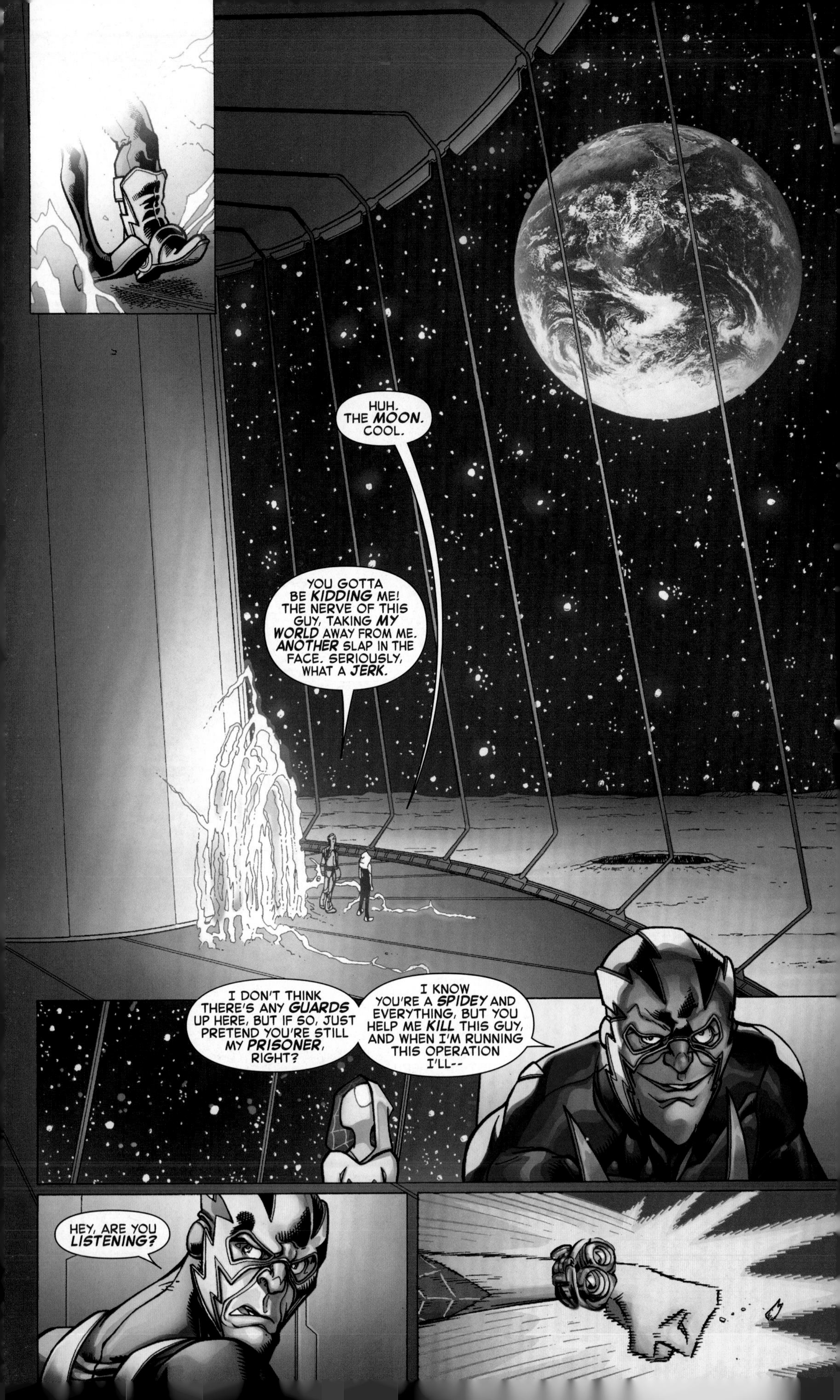

HUH. THE MOON. COOL.
YOU GOTTA BE KIDDING ME! THE NERVE OF THIS GUY, TAKING MY WORLD AWAY FROM ME. ANOTHER SLAP IN THE FACE. SERIOUSLY, WHAT A JERK.
I DON'T THINK THERE'S ANY GUARDS UP HERE, BUT IF SO, JUST PRETEND YOU'RE STILL MY PRISONER, RIGHT?
I KNOW YOU'RE A SPIDEY AND EVERYTHING, BUT YOU HELP ME KILL THIS GUY, AND WHEN I'M RUNNING THIS OPERATION I'LL--
HEY, ARE YOU LISTENING?

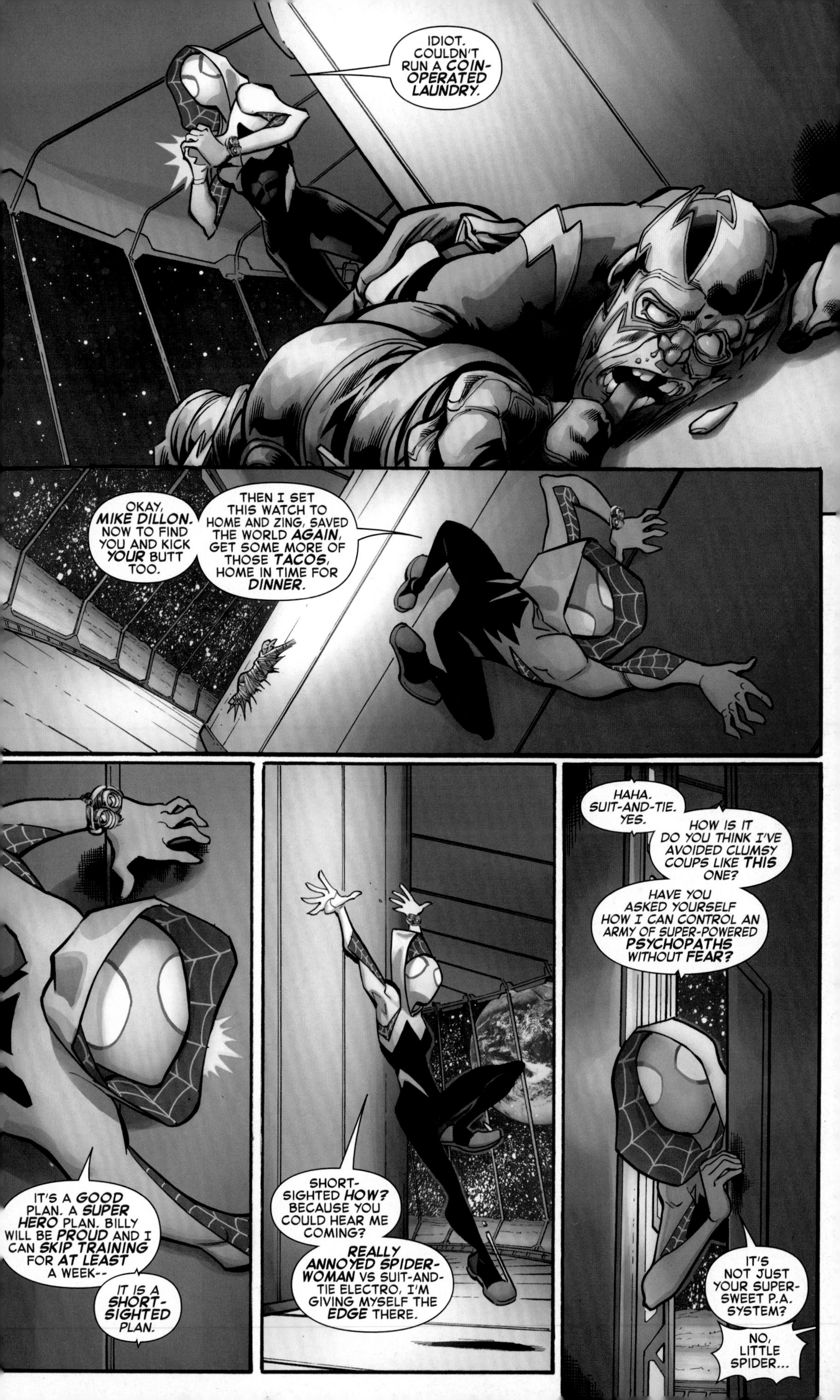
IDIOT. COULDN'T RUN A COIN-OPERATED LAUNDRY.
OKAY, MIKE DILLON. NOW TO FIND YOU AND KICK YOUR BUTT TOO.
THEN I SET THIS WATCH TO HOME AND ZING, SAVED THE WORLD AGAIN, GET SOME MORE OF THOSE TACOS, HOME IN TIME FOR DINNER.
IT'S A GOOD PLAN. A SUPER HERO PLAN. BILLY WILL BE PROUD AND I CAN SKIP TRAINING FOR AT LEAST A WEEK--
IT IS A SHORT-SIGHTED PLAN.
SHORT-SIGHTED HOW? BECAUSE YOU COULD HEAR ME COMING?
REALLY ANNOYED SPIDER-WOMAN VS SUIT-AND-TIE ELECTRO, I'M GIVING MYSELF THE EDGE THERE.
HAHA. SUIT-AND-TIE. YES.
HOW IS IT DO YOU THINK I'VE AVOIDED CLUMSY COUPS LIKE THIS ONE?
HAVE YOU ASKED YOURSELF HOW I CAN CONTROL AN ARMY OF SUPER-POWERED PSYCHOPATHS WITHOUT FEAR?
IT'S NOT JUST YOUR SUPER-SWEET P.A. SYSTEM?
NO, LITTLE SPIDER...

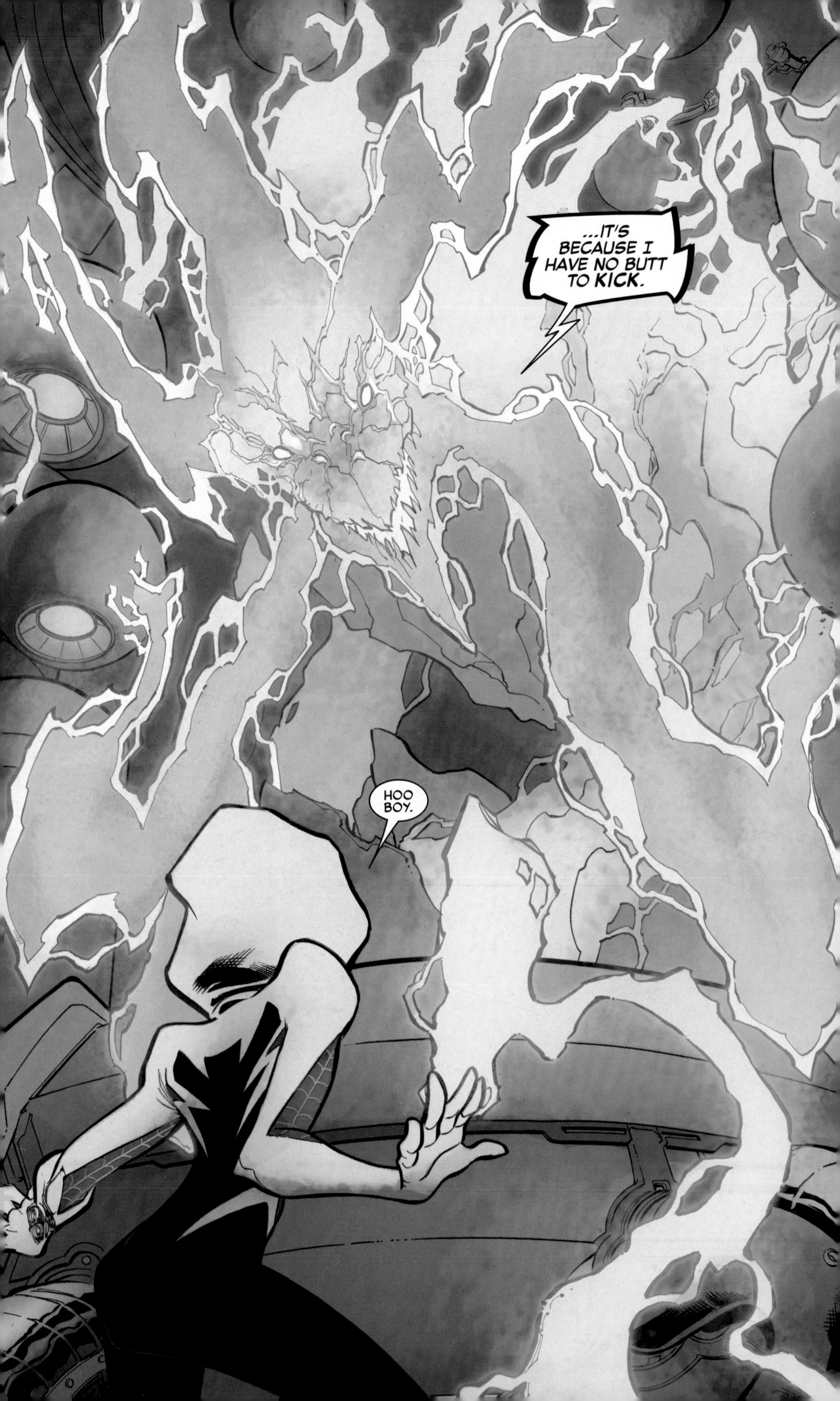
...IT'S BECAUSE I HAVE NO BUTT TO KICK.
HOO BOY.

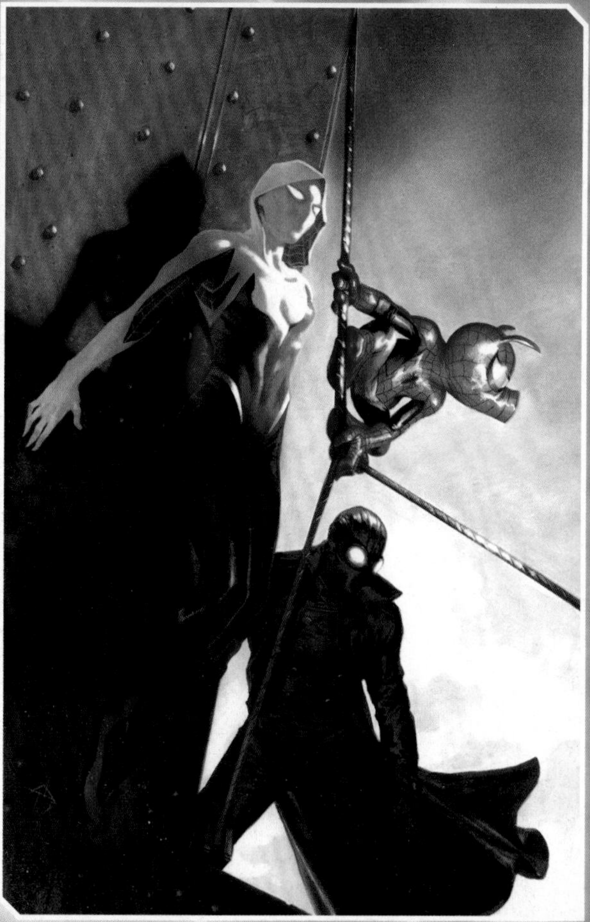

#2 VARIANT BY
GABRIELE DELL'OTTO

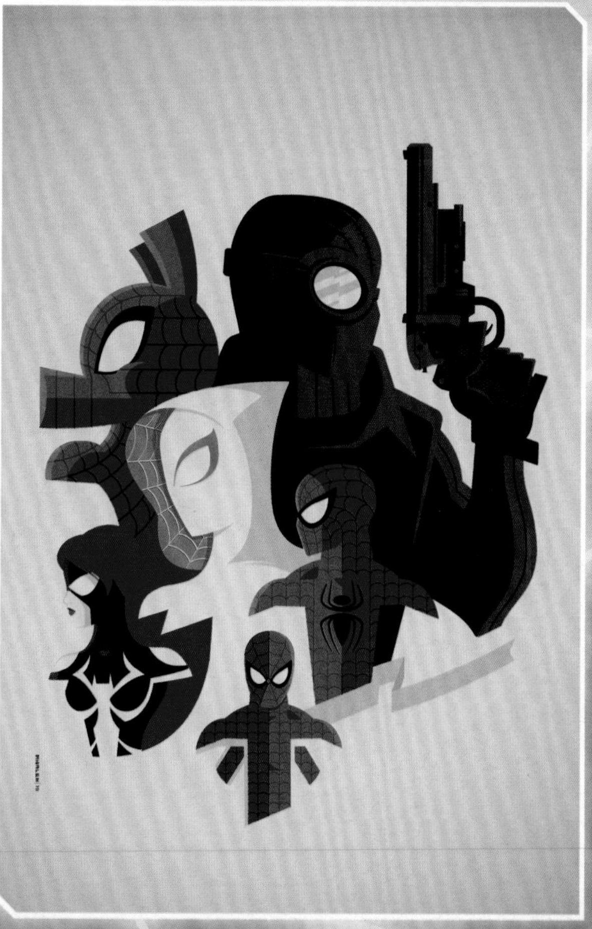

#3 VARIANT BY
TOM WHALEN

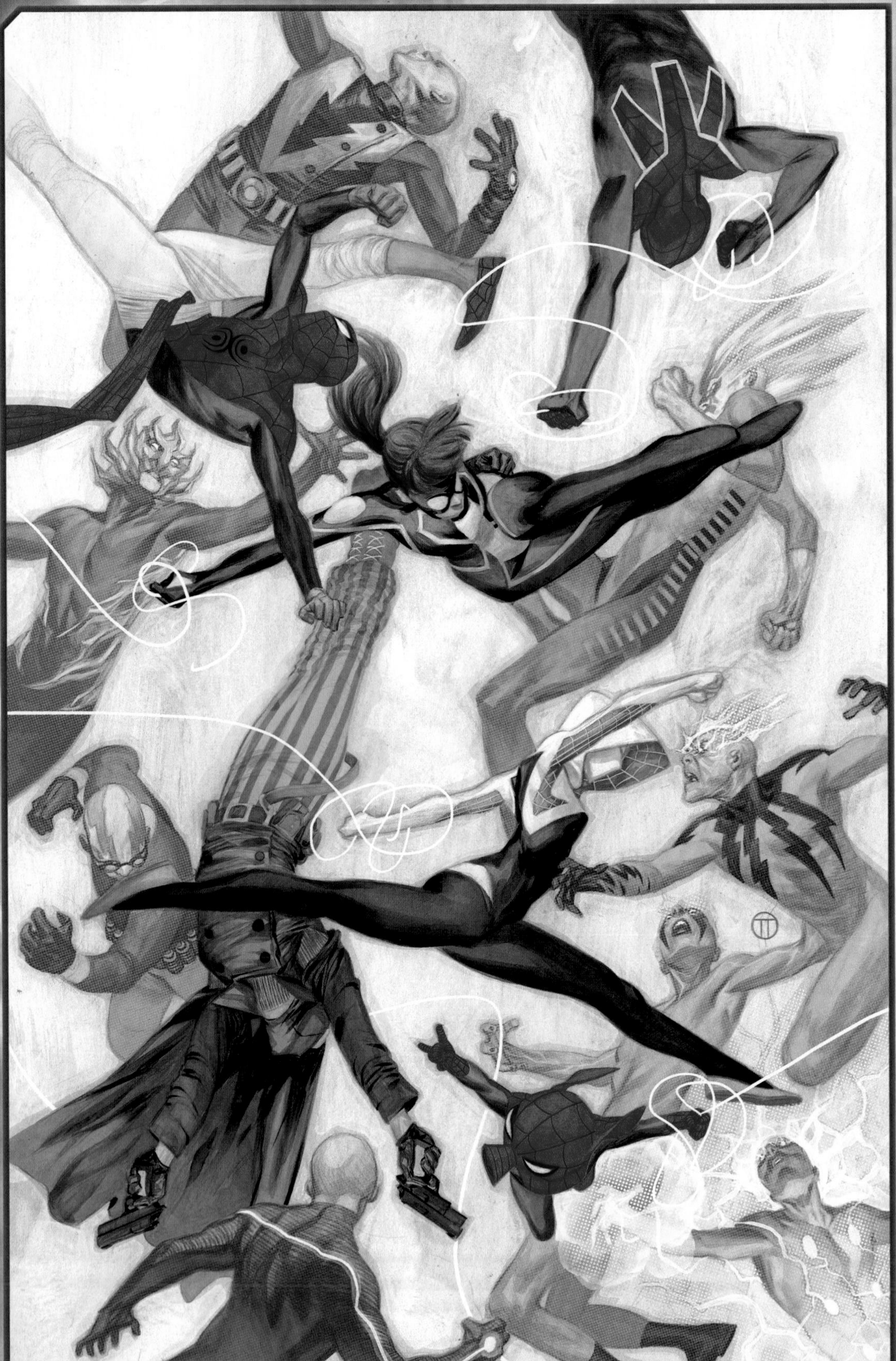

PART THREE : CAPACITY

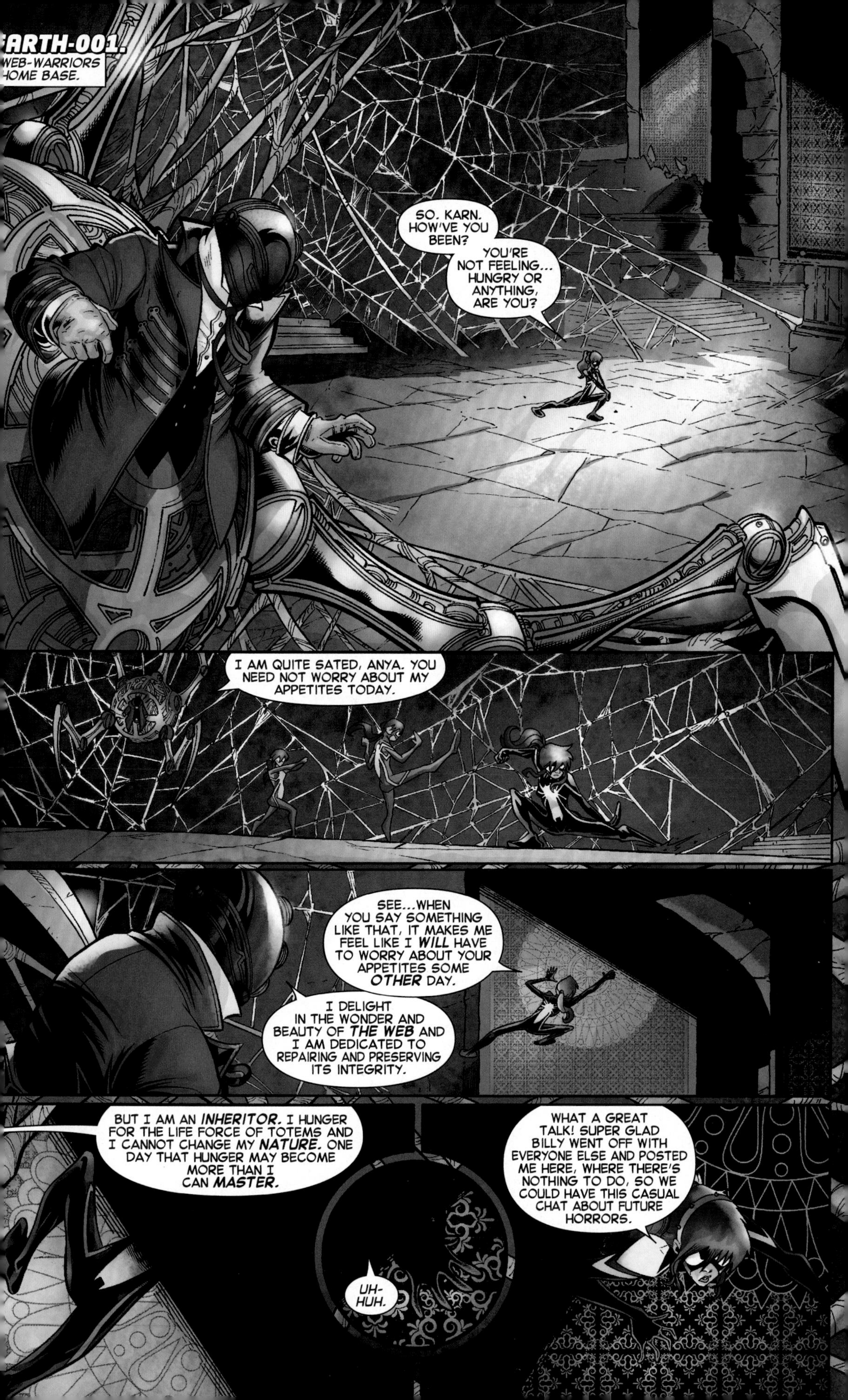
EARTH-001.
WEB-WARRIORS HOME BASE.
SO. KARN. HOW'VE YOU BEEN?
YOU'RE NOT FEELING... HUNGRY OR ANYTHING, ARE YOU?
I AM QUITE SATED, ANYA. YOU NEED NOT WORRY ABOUT MY APPETITES TODAY.
SEE...WHEN YOU SAY SOMETHING LIKE THAT, IT MAKES ME FEEL LIKE I WILL HAVE TO WORRY ABOUT YOUR APPETITES SOME OTHER DAY.
I DELIGHT IN THE WONDER AND BEAUTY OF THE WEB AND I AM DEDICATED TO REPAIRING AND PRESERVING ITS INTEGRITY.
BUT I AM AN INHERITOR. I HUNGER FOR THE LIFE FORCE OF TOTEMS AND I CANNOT CHANGE MY NATURE. ONE DAY THAT HUNGER MAY BECOME MORE THAN I CAN MASTER.
UH-HUH.
WHAT A GREAT TALK! SUPER GLAD BILLY WENT OFF WITH EVERYONE ELSE AND POSTED ME HERE, WHERE THERE'S NOTHING TO DO, SO WE COULD HAVE THIS CASUAL CHAT ABOUT FUTURE HORRORS.

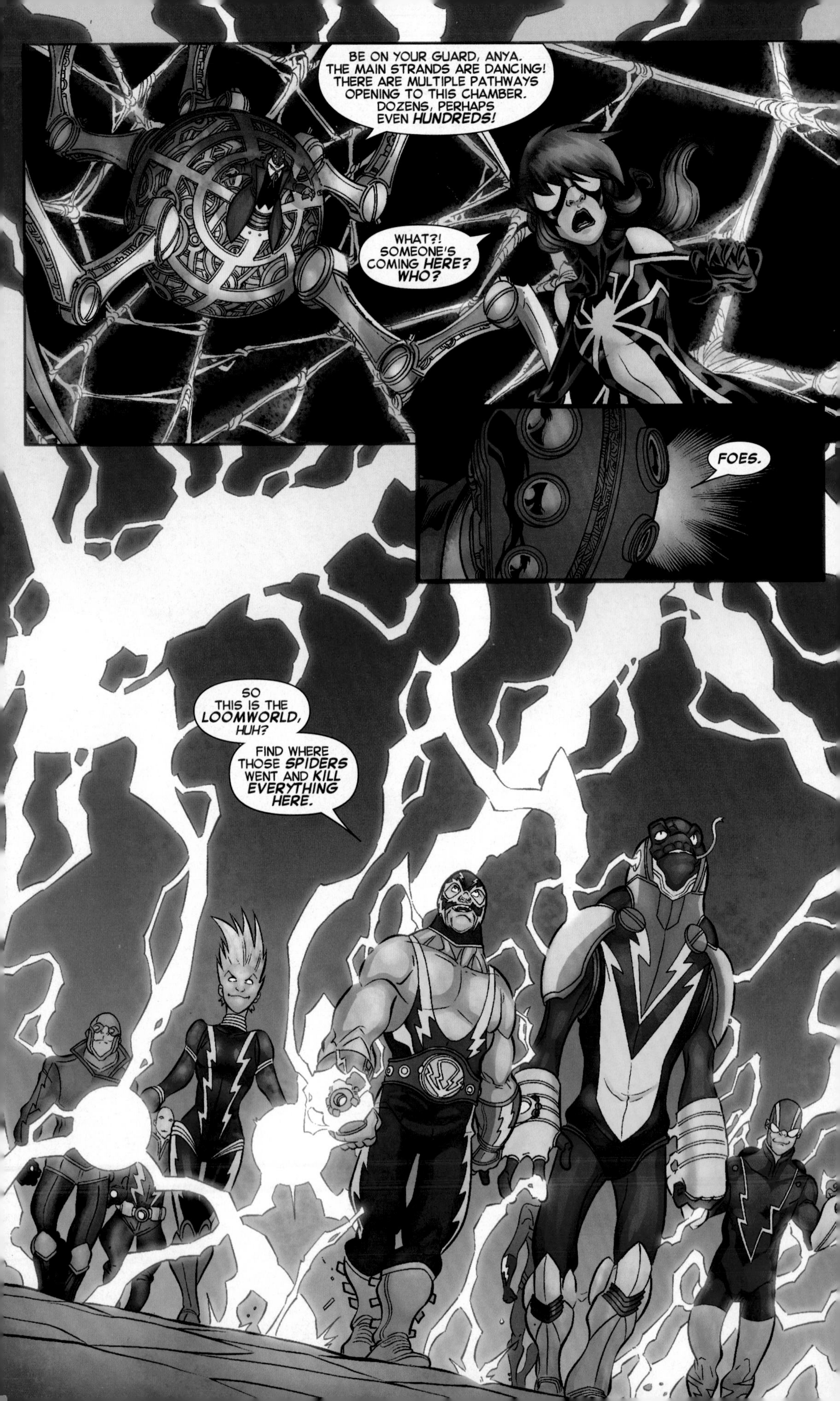
BE ON YOUR GUARD, ANYA. THE MAIN STRANDS ARE DANCING! THERE ARE MULTIPLE PATHWAYS OPENING TO THIS CHAMBER. DOZENS, PERHAPS EVEN HUNDREDS!
WHAT?! SOMEONE'S COMING HERE? WHO?
FOES.
SO THIS IS THE LOOMWORLD, HUH?
FIND WHERE THOSE SPIDERS WENT AND KILL EVERYTHING HERE.

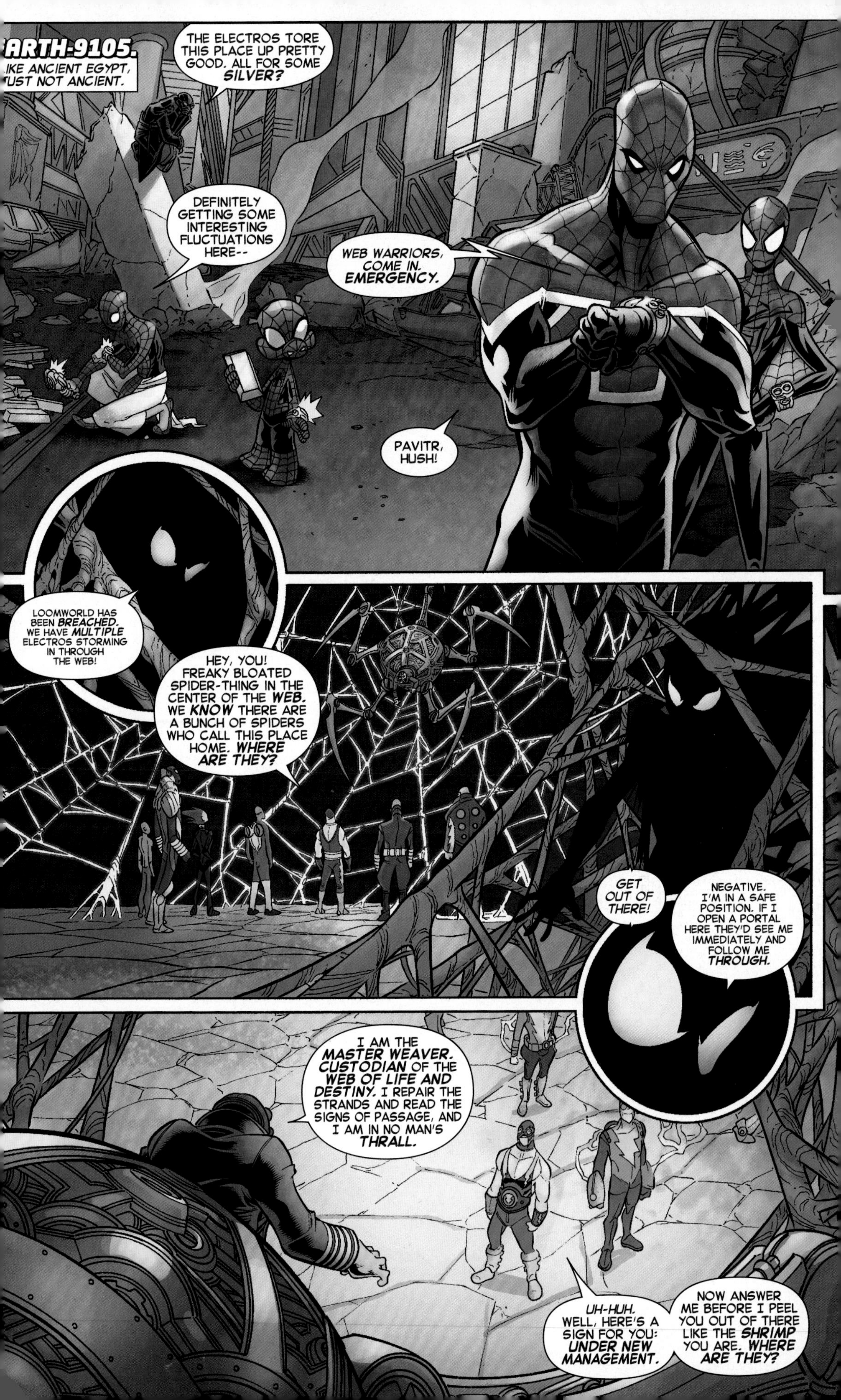

ARTH-9105.
IKE ANCIENT EGYPT, UST NOT ANCIENT.
THE ELECTROS TORE THIS PLACE UP PRETTY GOOD. ALL FOR SOME SILVER?
DEFINITELY GETTING SOME INTERESTING FLUCTUATIONS HERE--
WEB WARRIORS, COME IN. EMERGENCY.
PAVITR, HUSH!
LOOMWORLD HAS BEEN BREACHED. WE HAVE MULTIPLE ELECTROS STORMING IN THROUGH THE WEB!
HEY, YOU! FREAKY BLOATED SPIDER-THING IN THE CENTER OF THE WEB. WE KNOW THERE ARE A BUNCH OF SPIDERS WHO CALL THIS PLACE HOME. WHERE ARE THEY?
GET OUT OF THERE!
NEGATIVE. I'M IN A SAFE POSITION. IF I OPEN A PORTAL HERE THEY'D SEE ME IMMEDIATELY AND FOLLOW ME THROUGH.
I AM THE MASTER WEAVER. CUSTODIAN OF THE WEB OF LIFE AND DESTINY. I REPAIR THE STRANDS AND READ THE SIGNS OF PASSAGE, AND I AM IN NO MAN'S THRALL.
UH-HUH. WELL, HERE'S A SIGN FOR YOU: UNDER NEW MANAGEMENT.
NOW ANSWER ME BEFORE I PEEL YOU OUT OF THERE LIKE THE SHRIMP YOU ARE. WHERE ARE THEY?

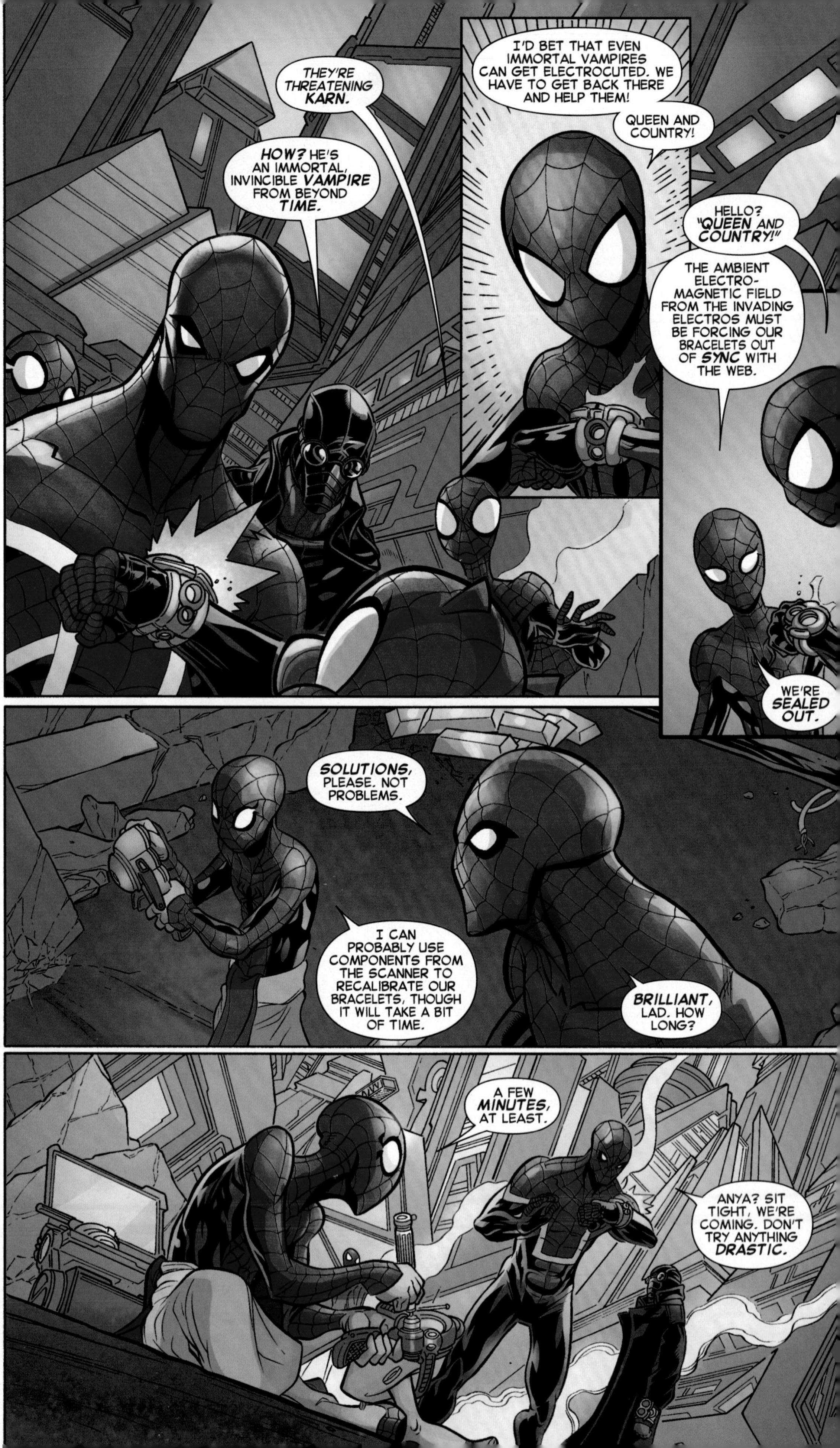
THEY'RE THREATENING KARN.
HOW? HE'S AN IMMORTAL, INVINCIBLE VAMPIRE FROM BEYOND TIME.
I'D BET THAT EVEN IMMORTAL VAMPIRES CAN GET ELECTROCUTED. WE HAVE TO GET BACK THERE AND HELP THEM!
QUEEN AND COUNTRY!
HELLO? "QUEEN AND COUNTRY!"
THE AMBIENT ELECTRO-MAGNETIC FIELD FROM THE INVADING ELECTROS MUST BE FORCING OUR BRACELETS OUT OF SYNC WITH THE WEB.
WE'RE SEALED OUT.
SOLUTIONS, PLEASE. NOT PROBLEMS.
I CAN PROBABLY USE COMPONENTS FROM THE SCANNER TO RECALIBRATE OUR BRACELETS, THOUGH IT WILL TAKE A BIT OF TIME.
BRILLIANT, LAD. HOW LONG?
A FEW MINUTES, AT LEAST.
ANYA? SIT TIGHT, WE'RE COMING. DON'T TRY ANYTHING DRASTIC.

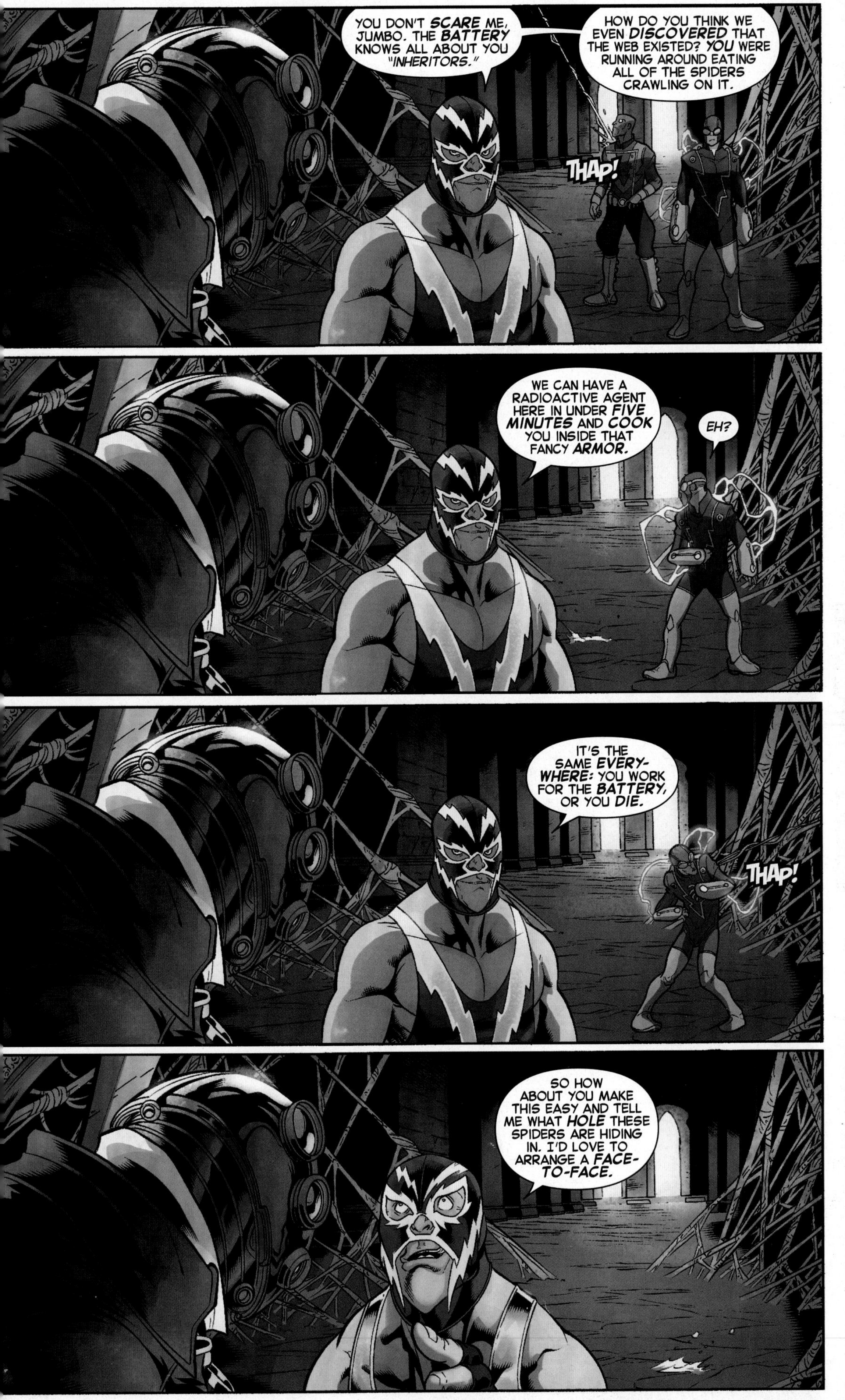

YOU DON'T SCARE ME, JUMBO. THE BATTERY KNOWS ALL ABOUT YOU "INHERITORS."
HOW DO YOU THINK WE EVEN DISCOVERED THAT THE WEB EXISTED? YOU WERE RUNNING AROUND EATING ALL OF THE SPIDERS CRAWLING ON IT.
THAP!
WE CAN HAVE A RADIOACTIVE AGENT HERE IN UNDER FIVE MINUTES AND COOK YOU INSIDE THAT FANCY ARMOR.
EH?
IT'S THE SAME EVERY-WHERE: YOU WORK FOR THE BATTERY, OR YOU DIE.
THAP!
SO HOW ABOUT YOU MAKE THIS EASY AND TELL ME WHAT HOLE THESE SPIDERS ARE HIDING IN. I'D LOVE TO ARRANGE A FACE-TO-FACE.

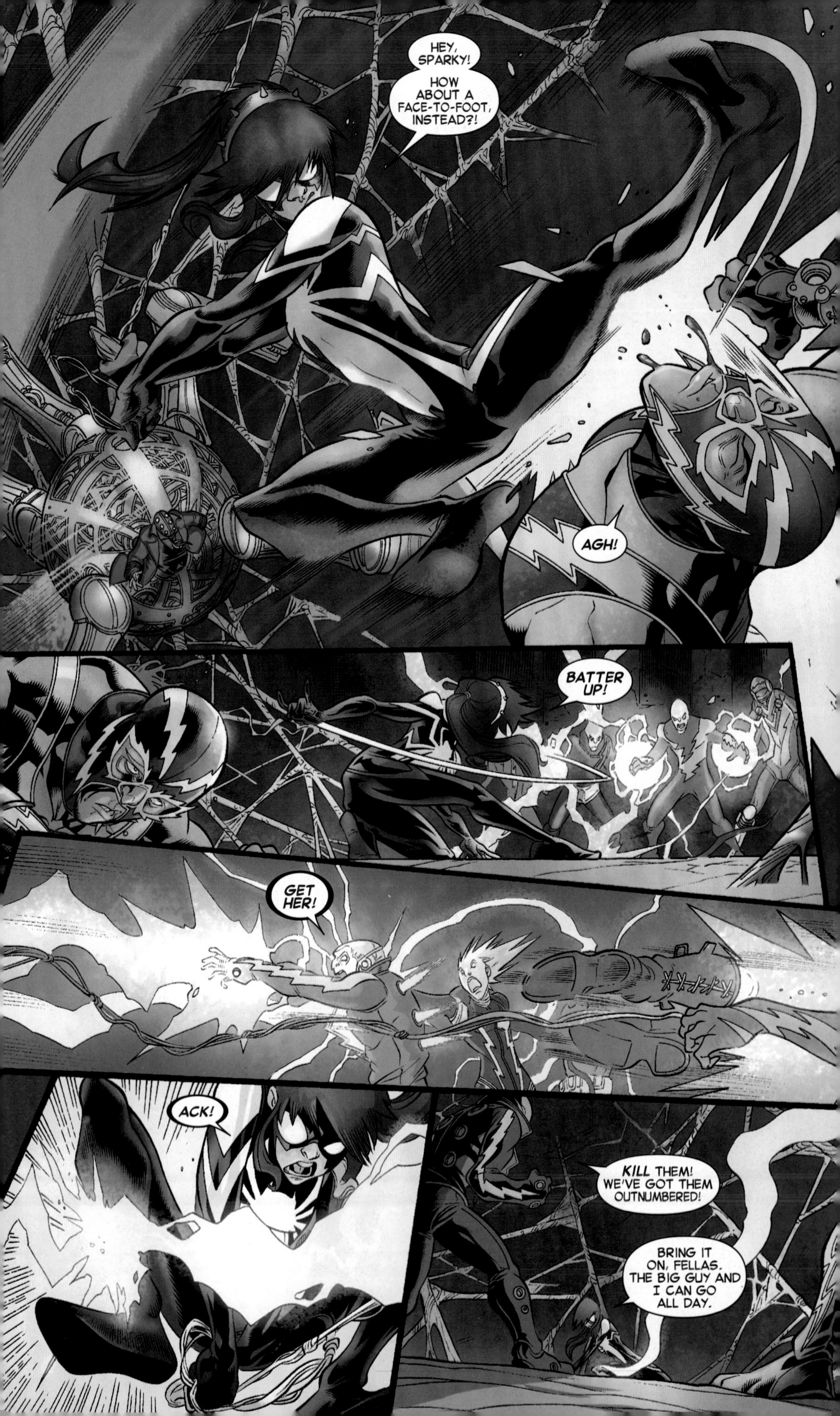
HEY, SPARKY!
HOW ABOUT A FACE-TO-FOOT, INSTEAD?!
AGH!
BATTER UP!
GET HER!
ACK!
KILL THEM! WE'VE GOT THEM OUTNUMBERED!
BRING IT ON, FELLAS. THE BIG GUY AND I CAN GO ALL DAY.

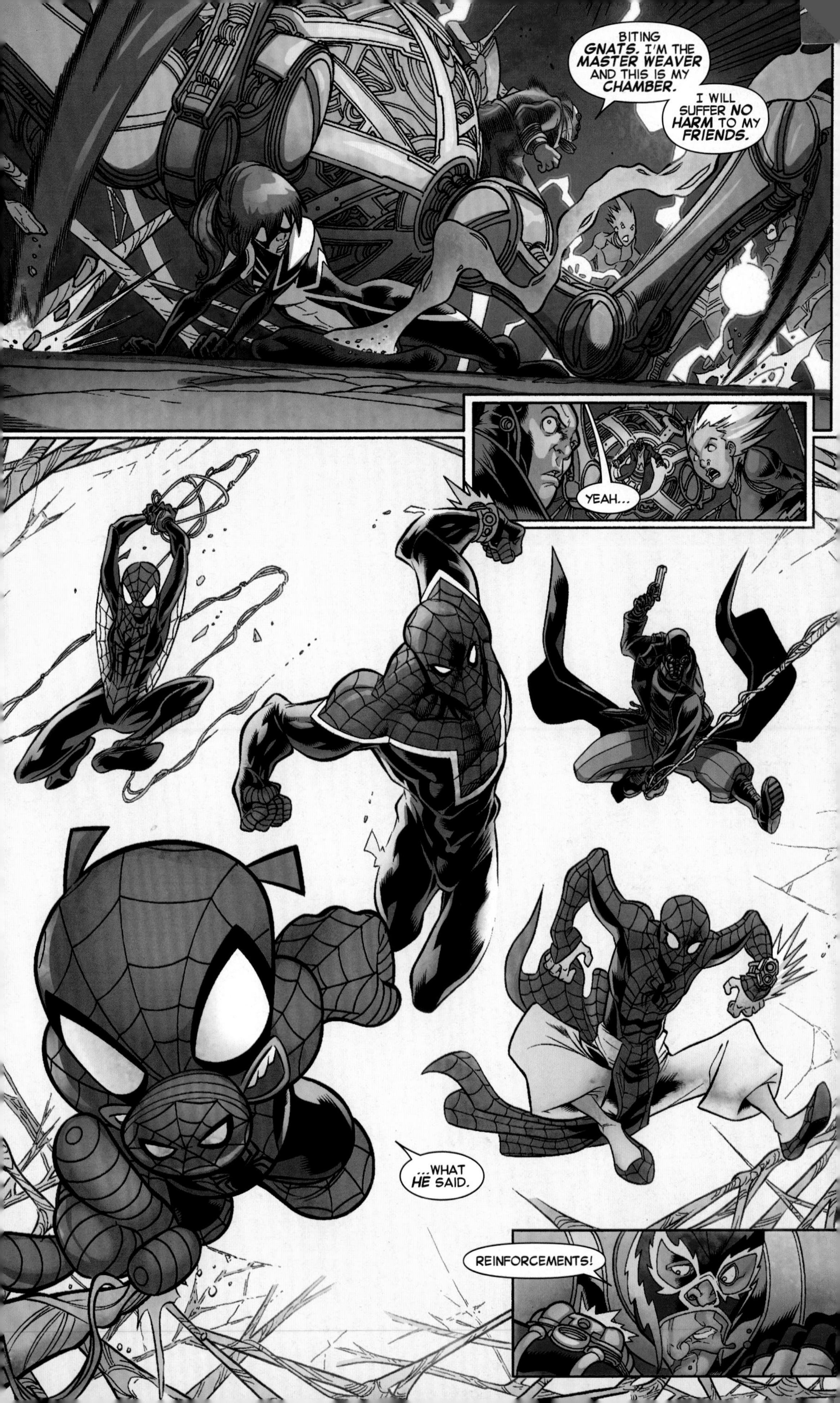
BITING GNATS. I'M THE MASTER WEAVER AND THIS IS MY CHAMBER.
I WILL SUFFER NO HARM TO MY FRIENDS.
YEAH...
...WHAT HE SAID.
REINFORCEMENTS!

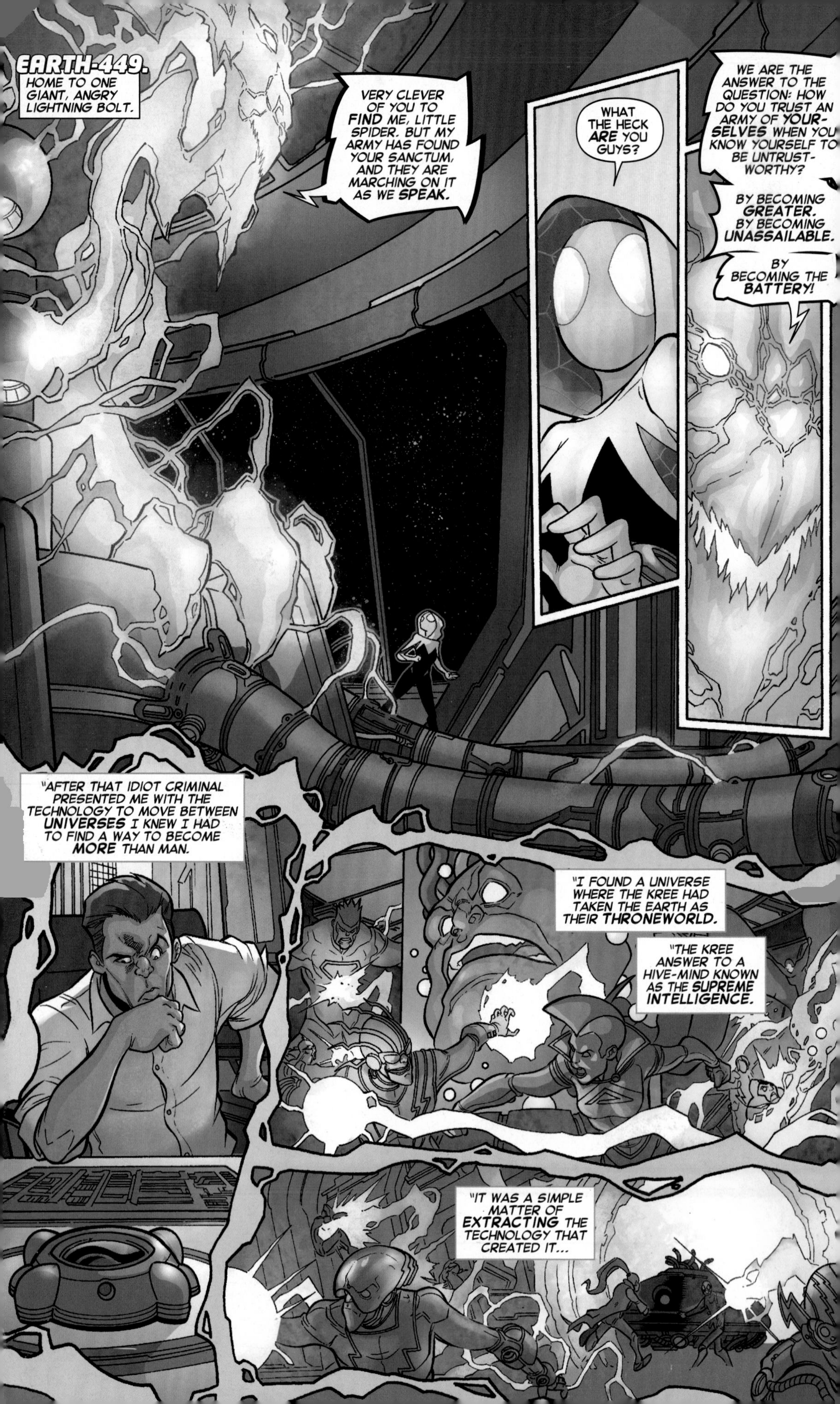
EARTH-449.
HOME TO ONE GIANT, ANGRY LIGHTNING BOLT.
VERY CLEVER OF YOU TO FIND ME, LITTLE SPIDER. BUT MY ARMY HAS FOUND YOUR SANCTUM, AND THEY ARE MARCHING ON IT AS WE SPEAK.
WHAT THE HECK ARE YOU GUYS?
WE ARE THE ANSWER TO THE QUESTION: HOW DO YOU TRUST AN ARMY OF YOURSELVES WHEN YOU KNOW YOURSELF TO BE UNTRUSTWORTHY?
BY BECOMING GREATER. BY BECOMING UNASSAILABLE.
BY BECOMING THE BATTERY!
"AFTER THAT IDIOT CRIMINAL PRESENTED ME WITH THE TECHNOLOGY TO MOVE BETWEEN UNIVERSES I KNEW I HAD TO FIND A WAY TO BECOME MORE THAN MAN.
"I FOUND A UNIVERSE WHERE THE KREE HAD TAKEN THE EARTH AS THEIR THRONEWORLD.
"THE KREE ANSWER TO A HIVE-MIND KNOWN AS THE SUPREME INTELLIGENCE.
"IT WAS A SIMPLE MATTER OF EXTRACTING THE TECHNOLOGY THAT CREATED IT...

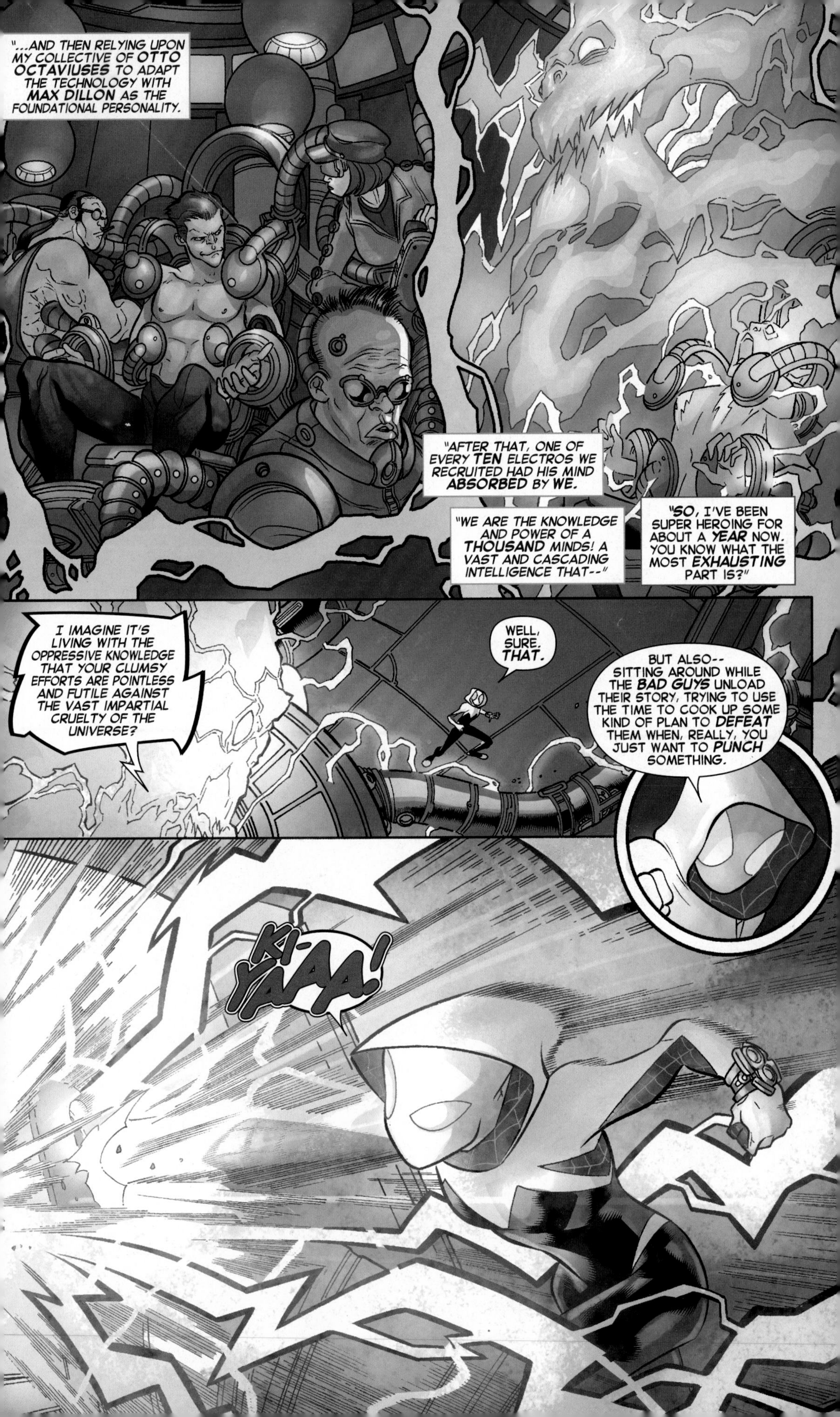
"...AND THEN RELYING UPON MY COLLECTIVE OF OTTO OCTAVIUSES TO ADAPT THE TECHNOLOGY WITH MAX DILLON AS THE FOUNDATIONAL PERSONALITY.
"AFTER THAT, ONE OF EVERY TEN ELECTROS WE RECRUITED HAD HIS MIND ABSORBED BY WE.
"WE ARE THE KNOWLEDGE AND POWER OF A THOUSAND MINDS! A VAST AND CASCADING INTELLIGENCE THAT--"
"SO, I'VE BEEN SUPER HEROING FOR ABOUT A YEAR NOW. YOU KNOW WHAT THE MOST EXHAUSTING PART IS?"
I IMAGINE IT'S LIVING WITH THE OPPRESSIVE KNOWLEDGE THAT YOUR CLUMSY EFFORTS ARE POINTLESS AND FUTILE AGAINST THE VAST IMPARTIAL CRUELTY OF THE UNIVERSE?
WELL, SURE. THAT.
BUT ALSO-- SITTING AROUND WHILE THE BAD GUYS UNLOAD THEIR STORY, TRYING TO USE THE TIME TO COOK UP SOME KIND OF PLAN TO DEFEAT THEM WHEN, REALLY, YOU JUST WANT TO PUNCH SOMETHING.
KI-YAAA!

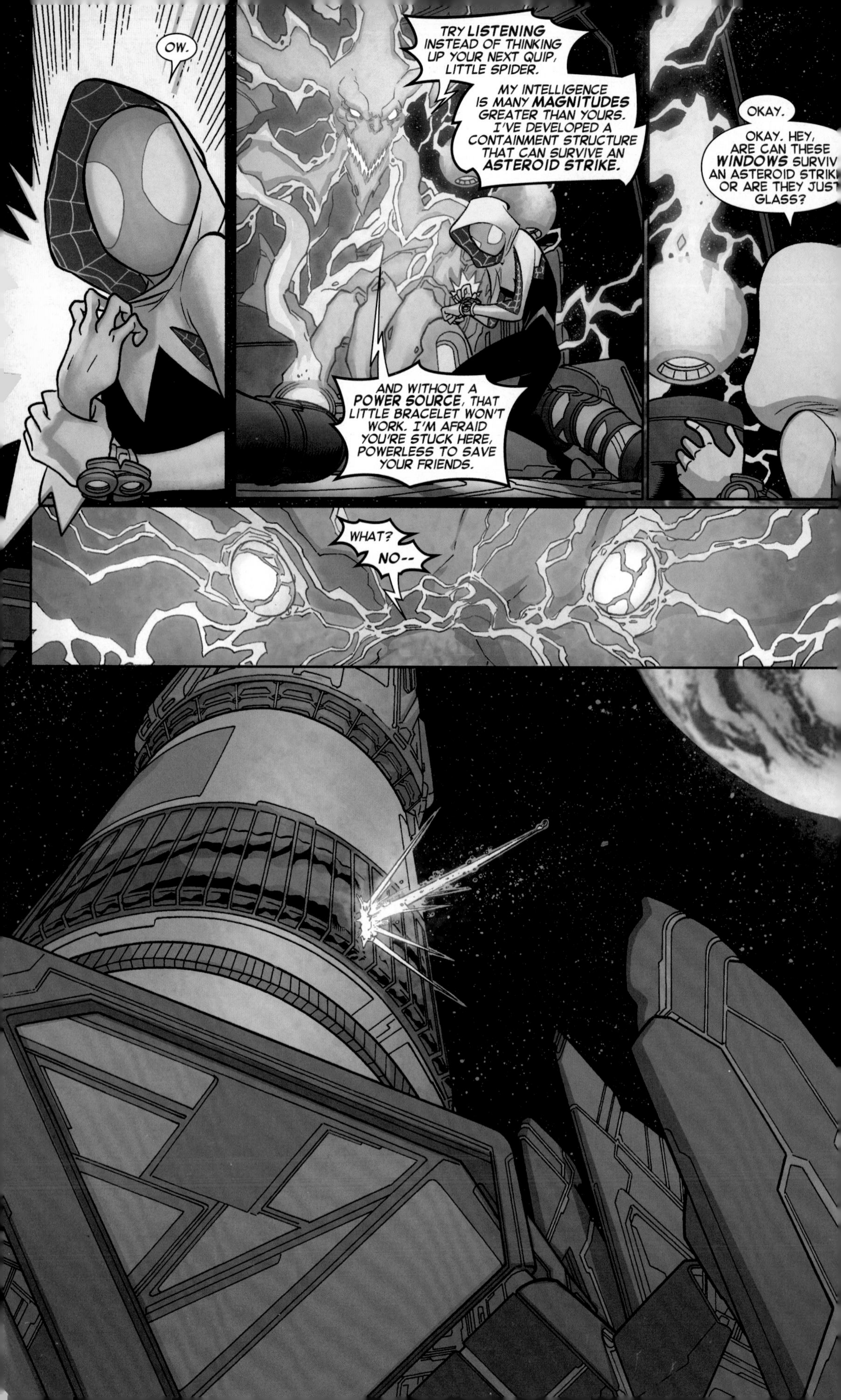
OW.
TRY LISTENING INSTEAD OF THINKING UP YOUR NEXT QUIP, LITTLE SPIDER.
MY INTELLIGENCE IS MANY MAGNITUDES GREATER THAN YOURS. I'VE DEVELOPED A CONTAINMENT STRUCTURE THAT CAN SURVIVE AN ASTEROID STRIKE.
AND WITHOUT A POWER SOURCE, THAT LITTLE BRACELET WON'T WORK. I'M AFRAID YOU'RE STUCK HERE, POWERLESS TO SAVE YOUR FRIENDS.
OKAY.
OKAY. HEY, ARE CAN THESE WINDOWS SURVIV AN ASTEROID STRIK OR ARE THEY JUST GLASS?
WHAT?
NO--

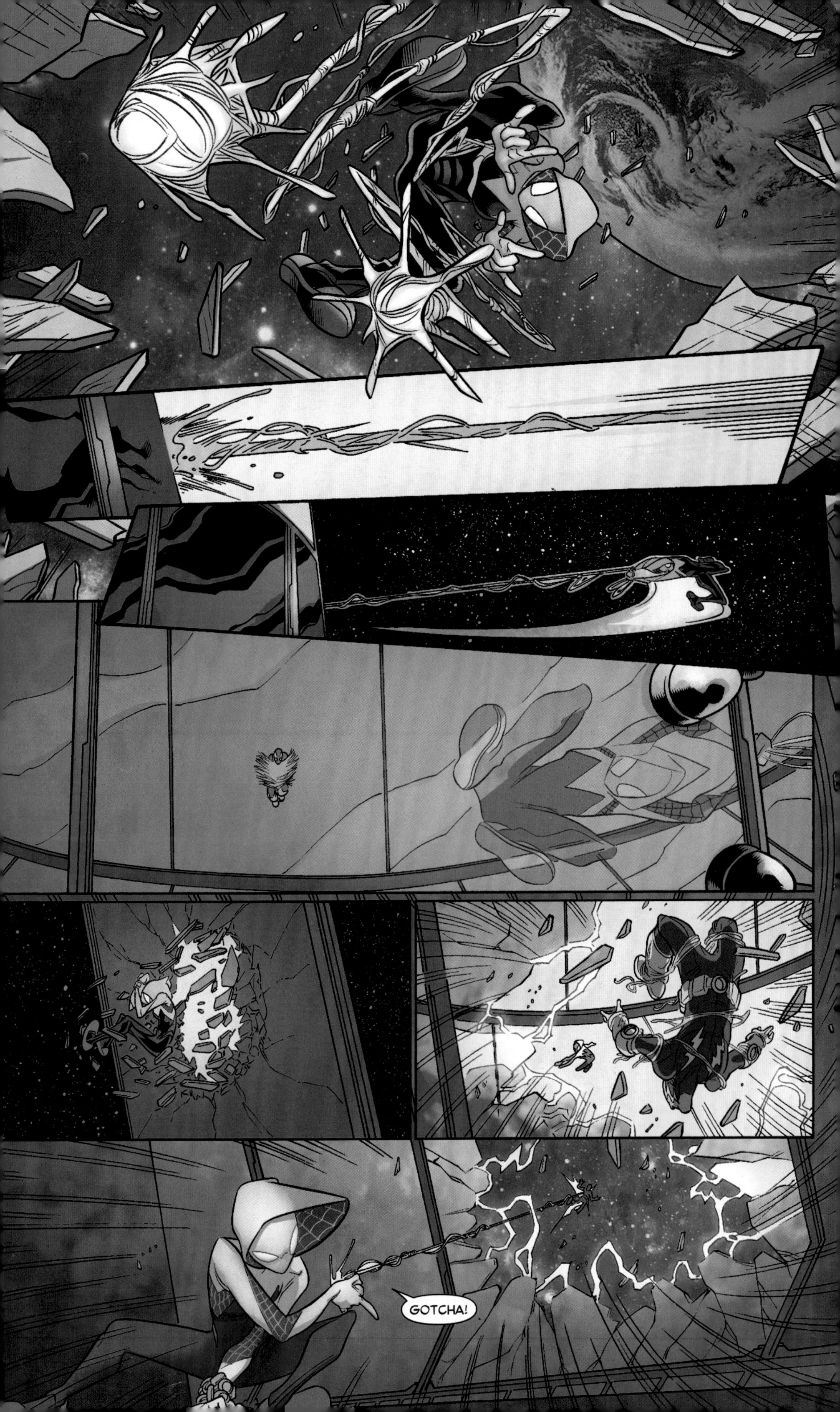
GOTCHA!

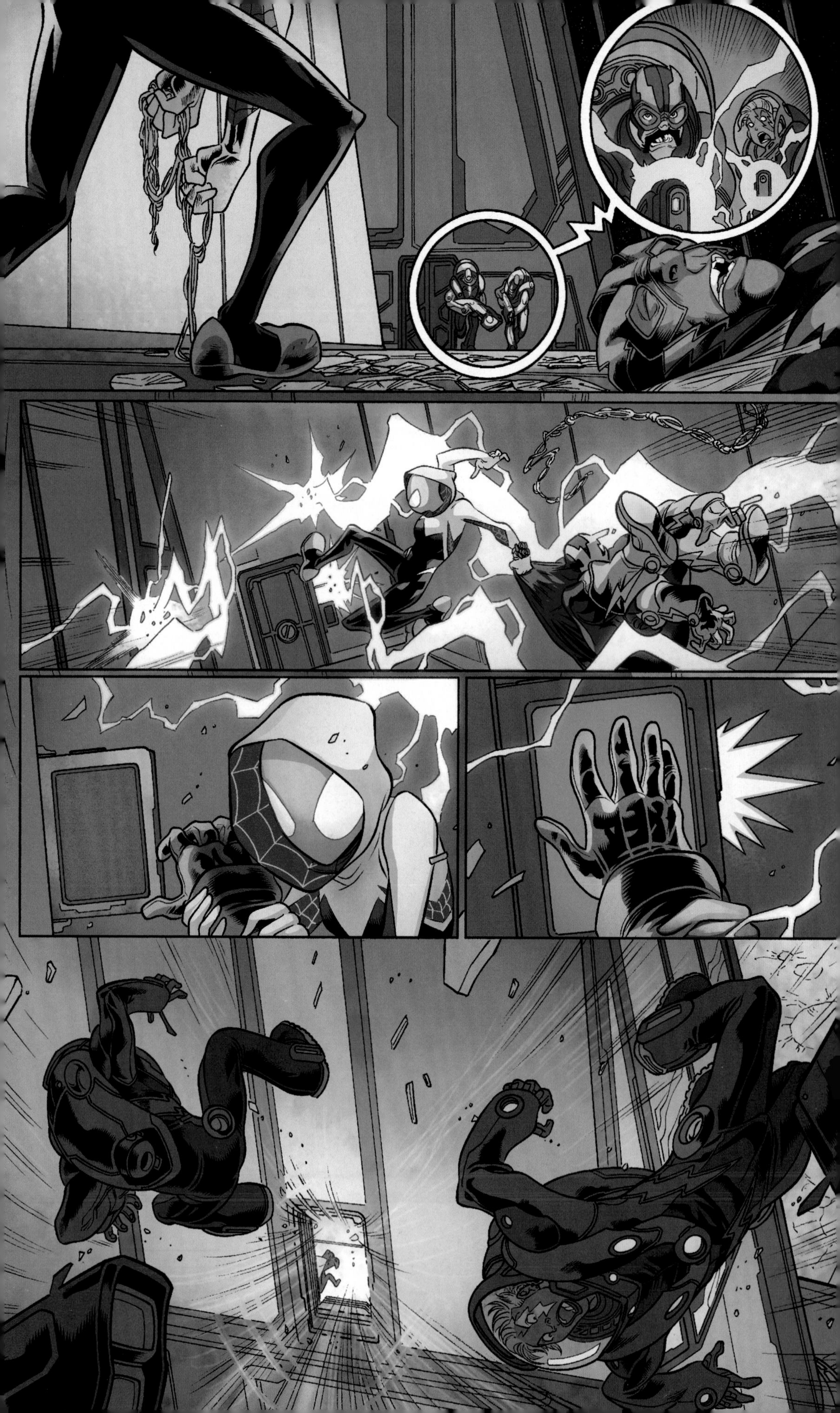

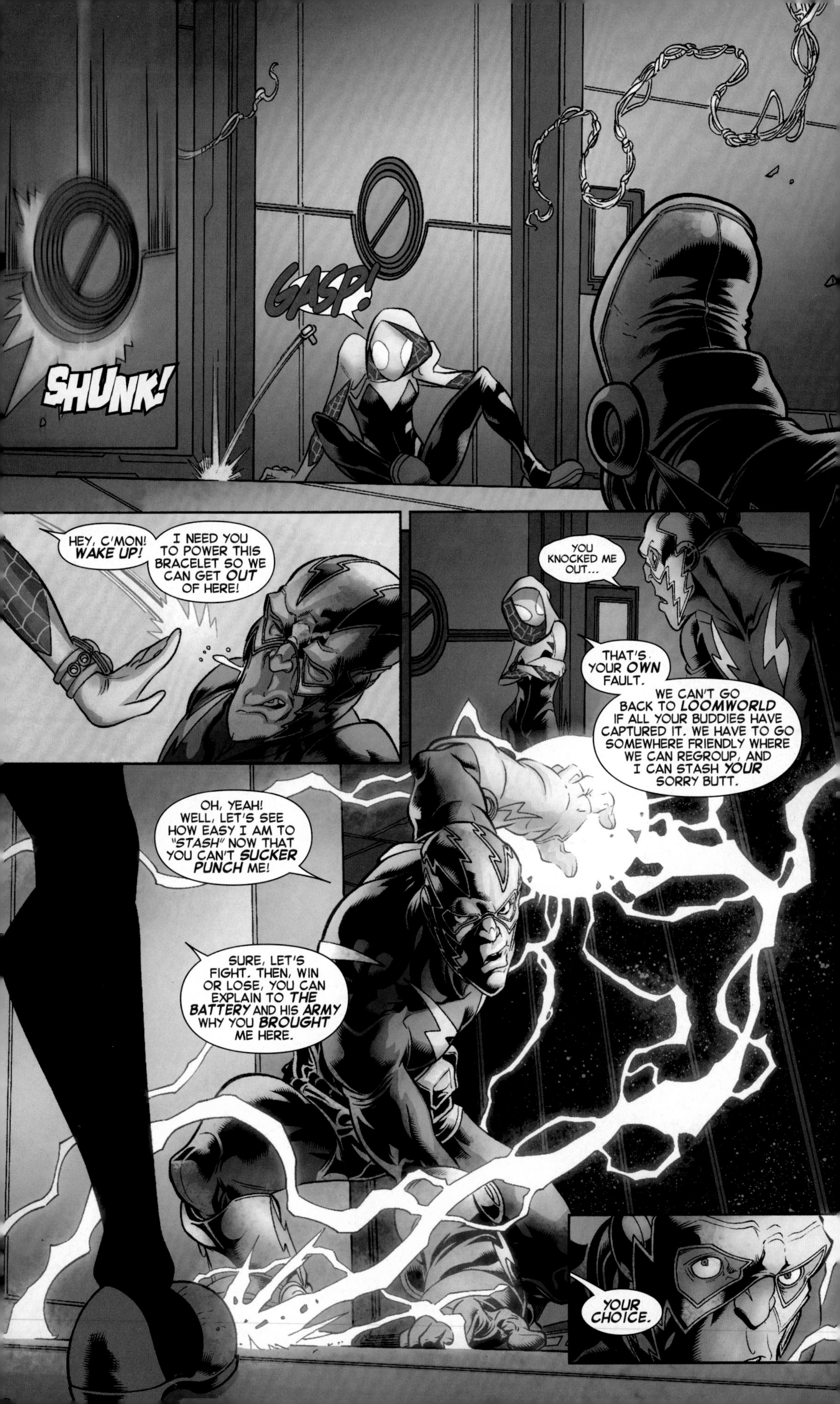

SHUNK!
GASP!
HEY, C'MON! WAKE UP!
I NEED YOU TO POWER THIS BRACELET SO WE CAN GET OUT OF HERE!
YOU KNOCKED ME OUT...
THAT'S YOUR OWN FAULT.
WE CAN'T GO BACK TO LOOMWORLD IF ALL YOUR BUDDIES HAVE CAPTURED IT. WE HAVE TO GO SOMEWHERE FRIENDLY WHERE WE CAN REGROUP, AND I CAN STASH YOUR SORRY BUTT.
OH, YEAH! WELL, LET'S SEE HOW EASY I AM TO "STASH" NOW THAT YOU CAN'T SUCKER PUNCH ME!
SURE, LET'S FIGHT. THEN, WIN OR LOSE, YOU CAN EXPLAIN TO THE BATTERY AND HIS ARMY WHY YOU BROUGHT ME HERE.
YOUR CHOICE.

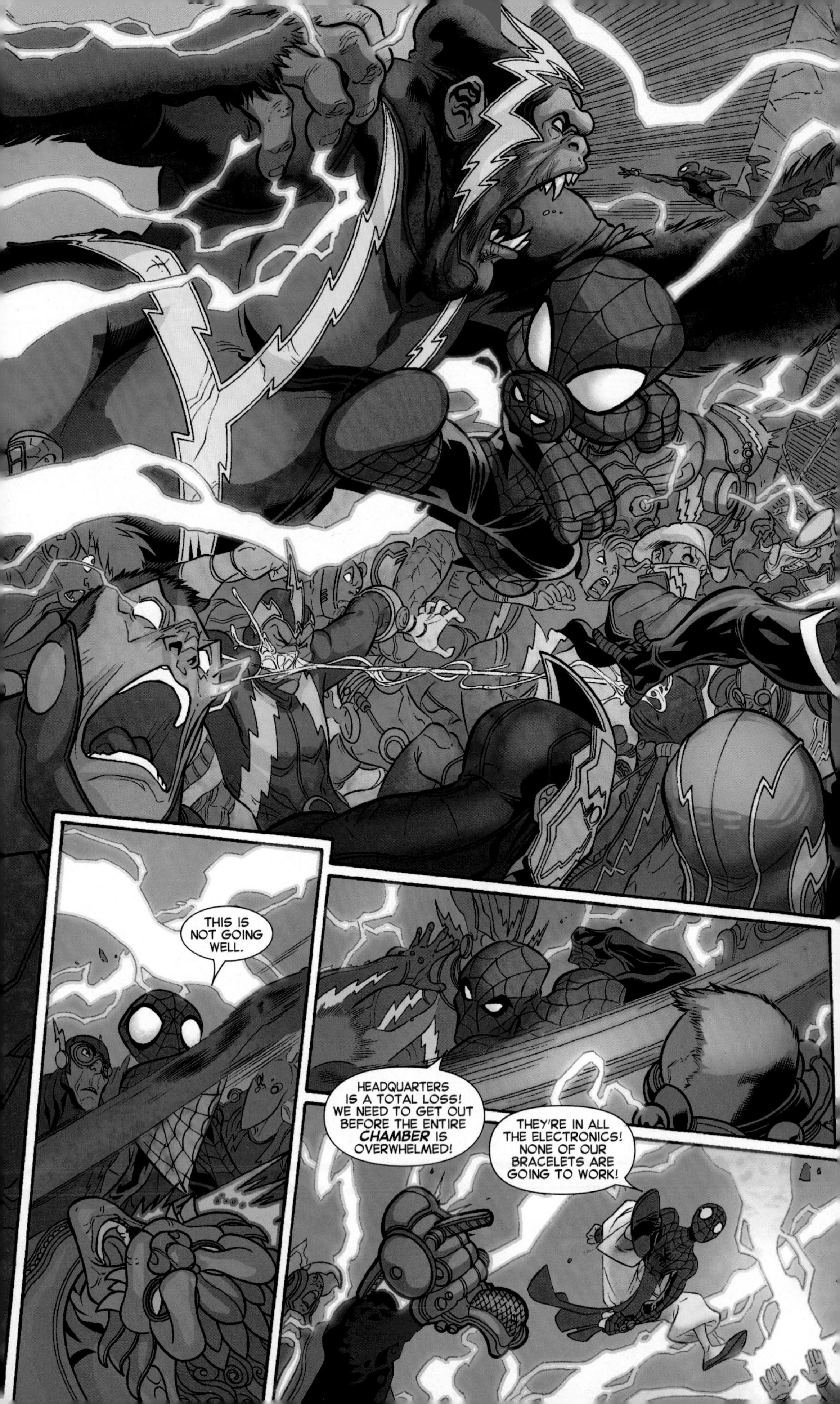

THIS IS NOT GOING WELL.
HEADQUARTERS IS A TOTAL LOSS! WE NEED TO GET OUT BEFORE THE ENTIRE CHAMBER IS OVERWHELMED!
THEY'RE IN ALL THE ELECTRONICS! NONE OF OUR BRACELETS ARE GOING TO WORK!

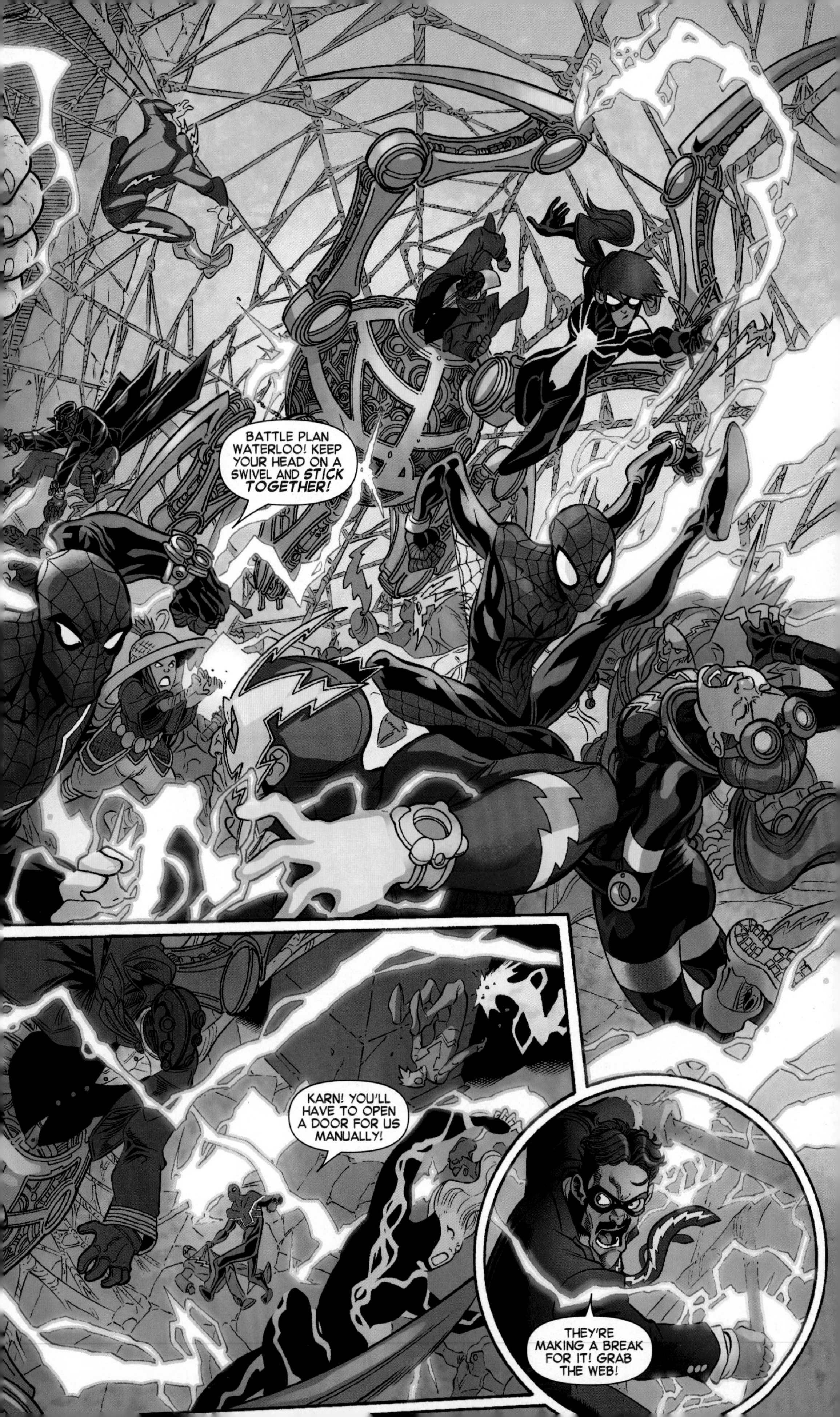
BATTLE PLAN WATERLOO! KEEP YOUR HEAD ON A SWIVEL AND STICK TOGETHER!
KARN! YOU'LL HAVE TO OPEN A DOOR FOR US MANUALLY!
THEY'RE MAKING A BREAK FOR IT! GRAB THE WEB!

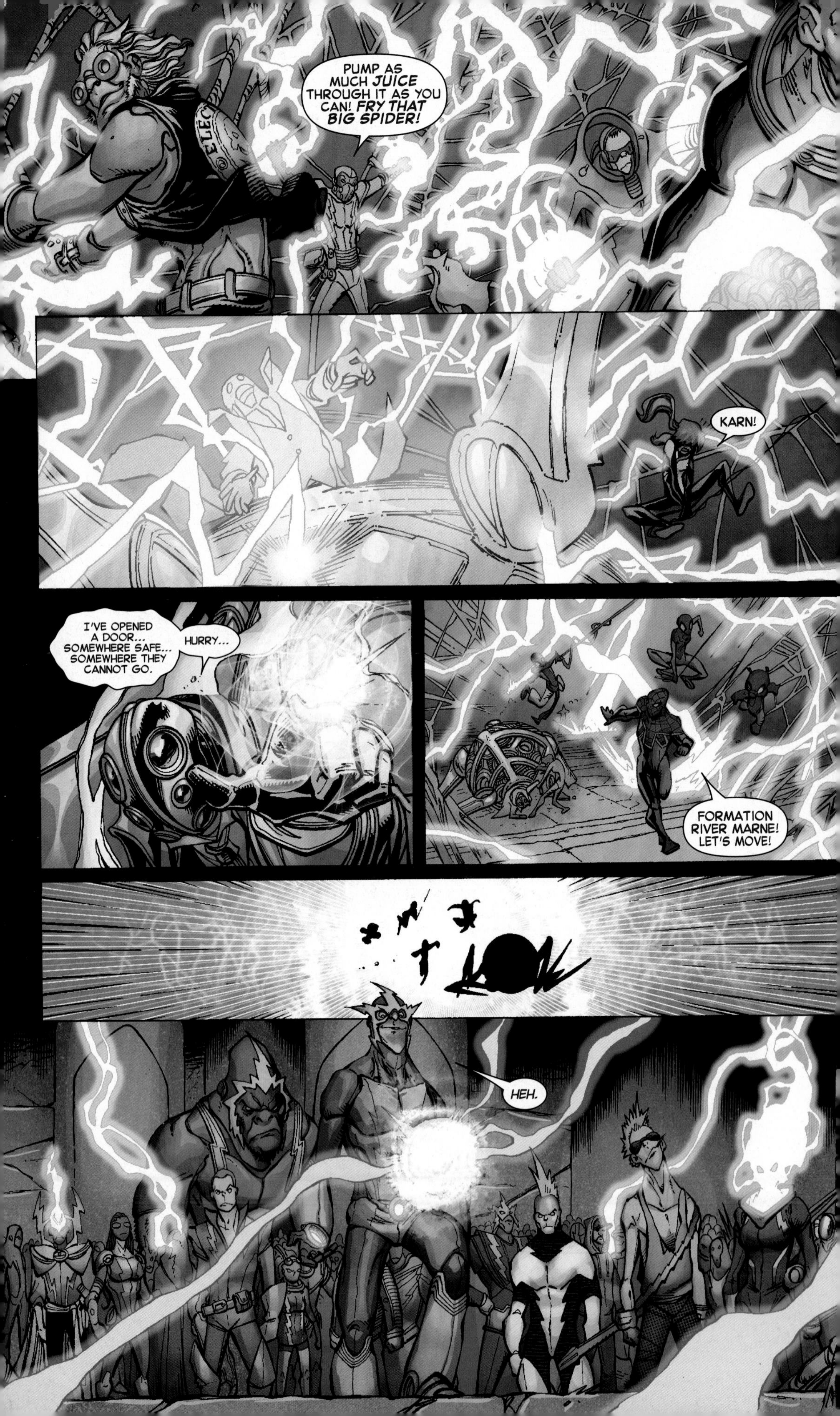
PUMP AS MUCH JUICE THROUGH IT AS YOU CAN! FRY THAT BIG SPIDER!
KARN!
I'VE OPENED A DOOR... SOMEWHERE SAFE... SOMEWHERE THEY CANNOT GO.
HURRY...
FORMATION RIVER MARNE! LET'S MOVE!
HEH.

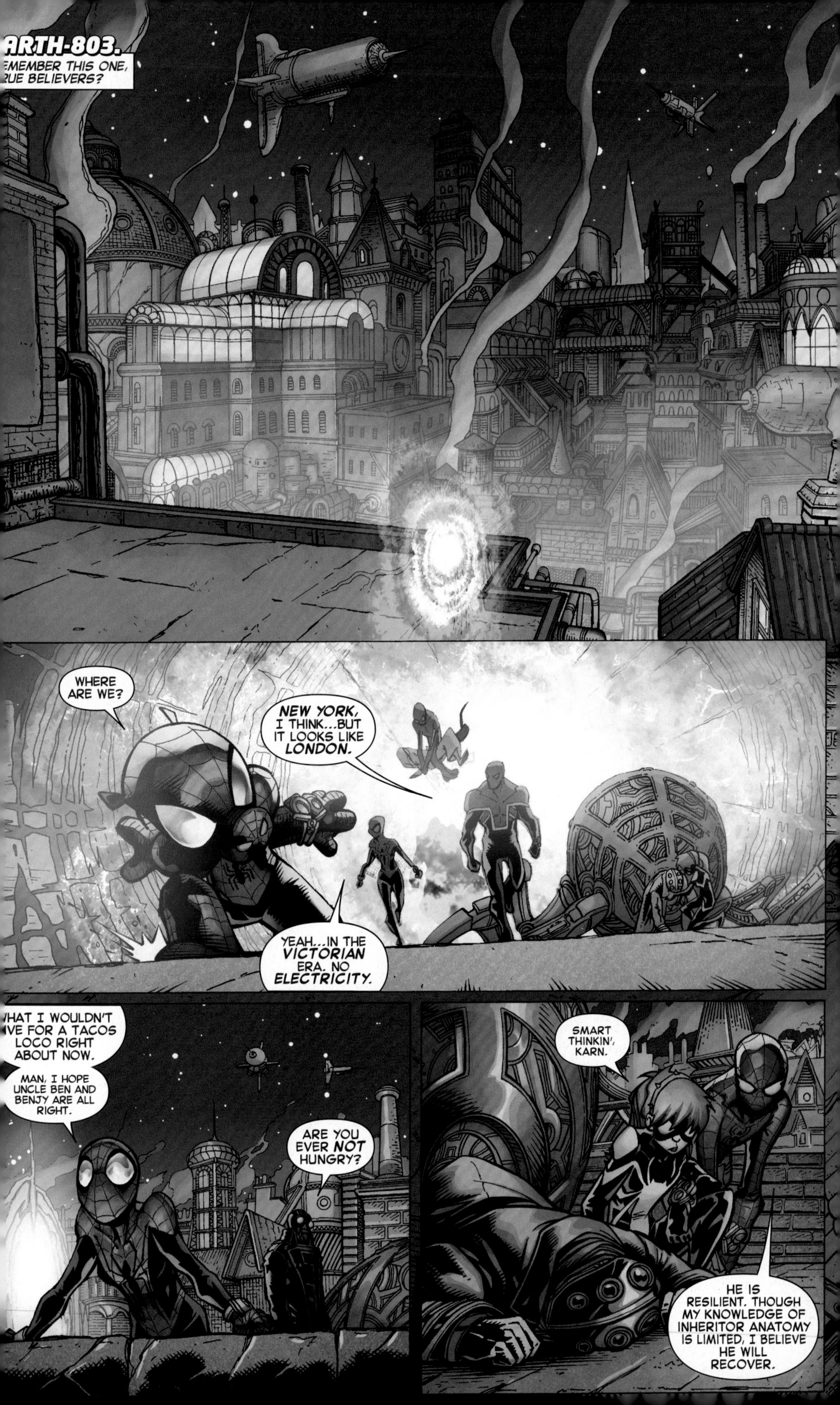
ARTH-803.
EMEMBER THIS ONE,
RUE BELIEVERS?
WHERE ARE WE?
NEW YORK, I THINK...BUT IT LOOKS LIKE LONDON.
YEAH...IN THE VICTORIAN ERA. NO ELECTRICITY.
HAT I WOULDN'T
IVE FOR A TACOS LOCO RIGHT ABOUT NOW.
MAN, I HOPE UNCLE BEN AND BENJY ARE ALL RIGHT.
ARE YOU EVER NOT HUNGRY?
SMART THINKIN', KARN.
HE IS RESILIENT. THOUGH MY KNOWLEDGE OF INHERITOR ANATOMY IS LIMITED, I BELIEVE HE WILL RECOVER.

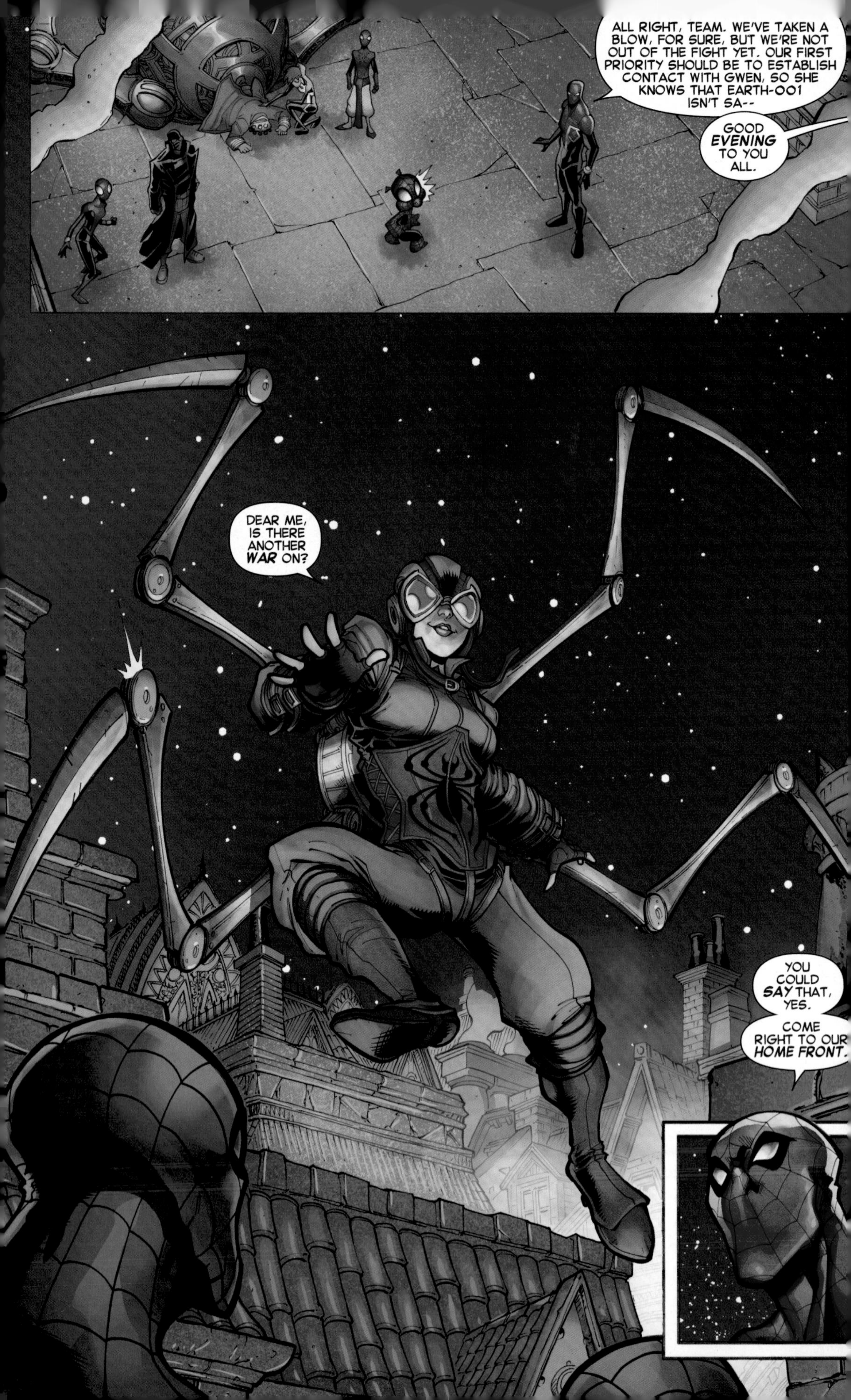
ALL RIGHT, TEAM. WE'VE TAKEN A BLOW, FOR SURE, BUT WE'RE NOT OUT OF THE FIGHT YET. OUR FIRST PRIORITY SHOULD BE TO ESTABLISH CONTACT WITH GWEN, SO SHE KNOWS THAT EARTH-001 ISN'T SA--
GOOD EVENING TO YOU ALL.
DEAR ME, IS THERE ANOTHER WAR ON?
YOU COULD SAY THAT, YES.
COME RIGHT TO OUR HOME FRONT.

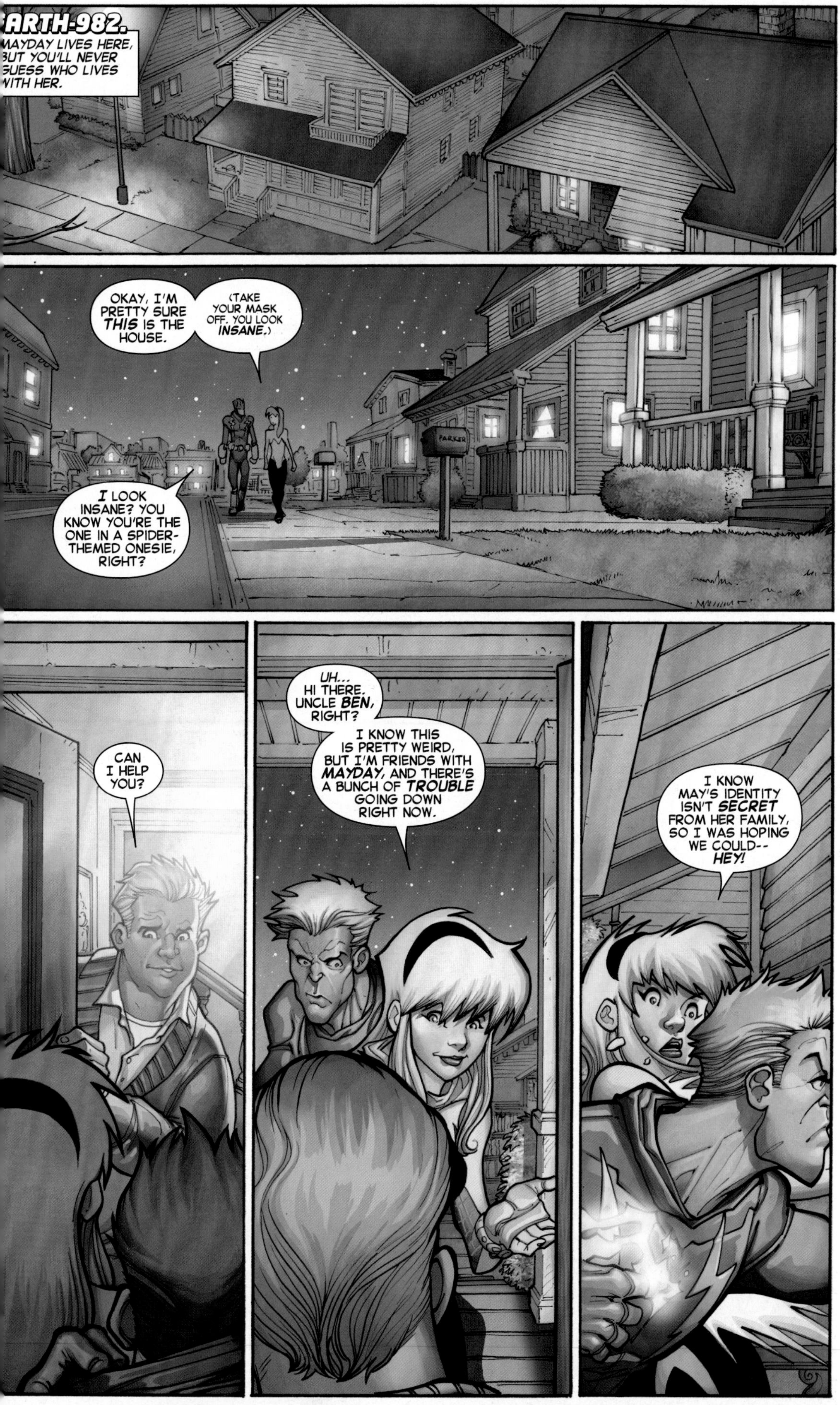
ARTH-982.
MAYDAY LIVES HERE, BUT YOU'LL NEVER GUESS WHO LIVES WITH HER.
OKAY, I'M PRETTY SURE THIS IS THE HOUSE.
(TAKE YOUR MASK OFF. YOU LOOK INSANE.)
I LOOK INSANE? YOU KNOW YOU'RE THE ONE IN A SPIDER-THEMED ONESIE, RIGHT?
PARKER
CAN I HELP YOU?
UH... HI THERE. UNCLE BEN, RIGHT?
I KNOW THIS IS PRETTY WEIRD, BUT I'M FRIENDS WITH MAYDAY, AND THERE'S A BUNCH OF TROUBLE GOING DOWN RIGHT NOW.
I KNOW MAY'S IDENTITY ISN'T SECRET FROM HER FAMILY, SO I WAS HOPING WE COULD-- HEY!

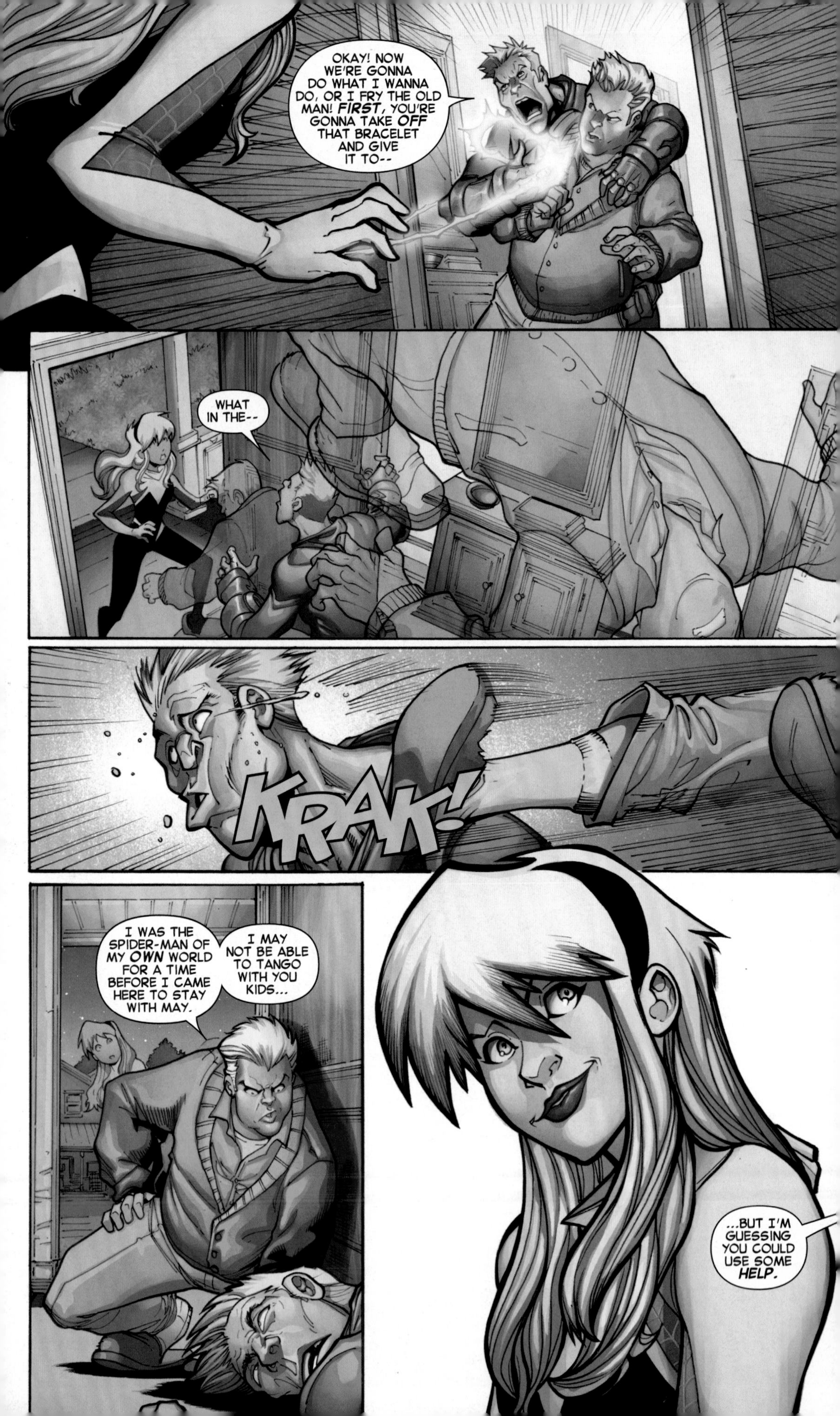
OKAY! NOW WE'RE GONNA DO WHAT I WANNA DO, OR I FRY THE OLD MAN! FIRST, YOU'RE GONNA TAKE OFF THAT BRACELET AND GIVE IT TO--
WHAT IN THE--
KRAK!
I WAS THE SPIDER-MAN OF MY OWN WORLD FOR A TIME BEFORE I CAME HERE TO STAY WITH MAY.
I MAY NOT BE ABLE TO TANGO WITH YOU KIDS...
...BUT I'M GUESSING YOU COULD USE SOME HELP.

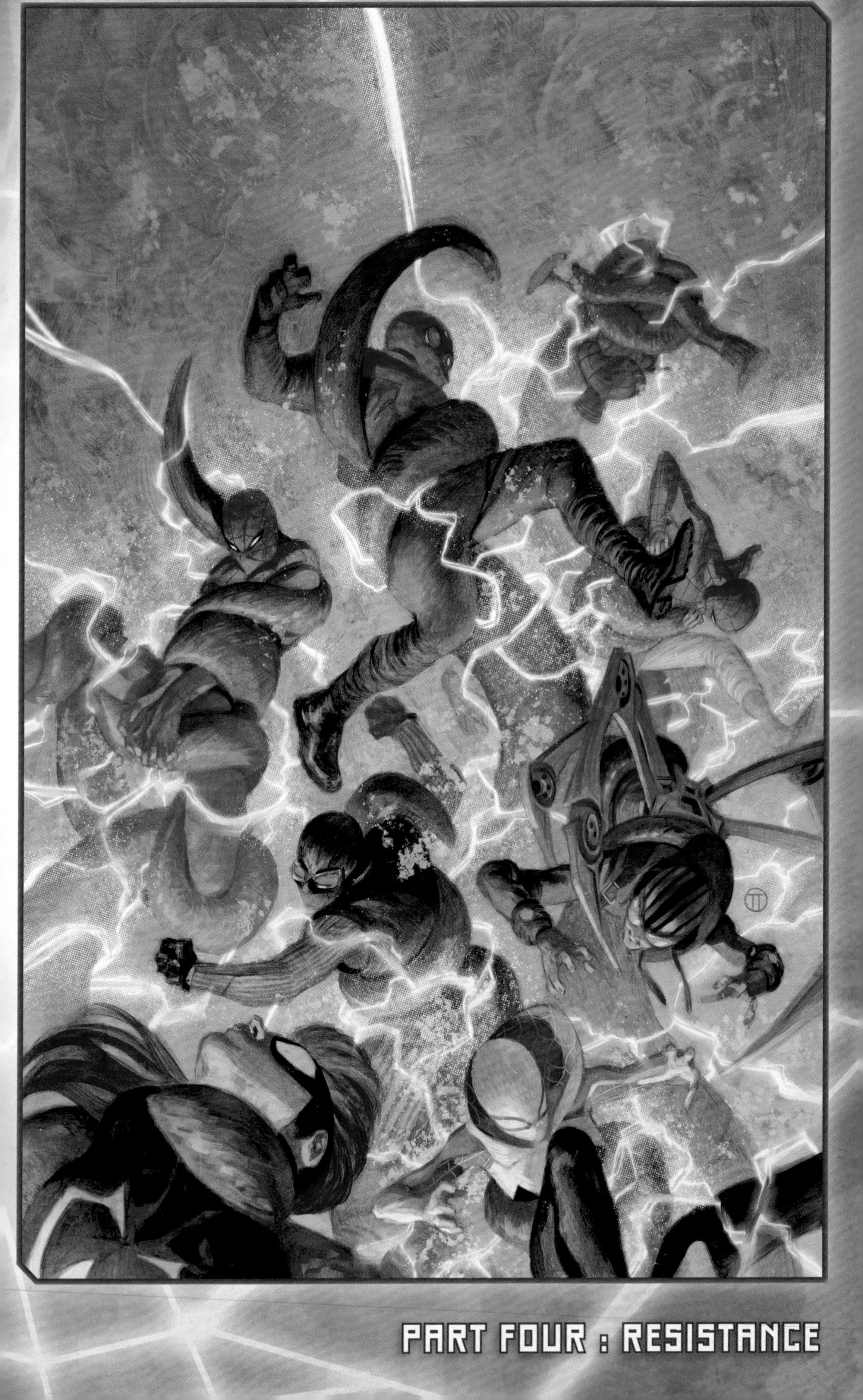

PART FOUR : RESISTANCE

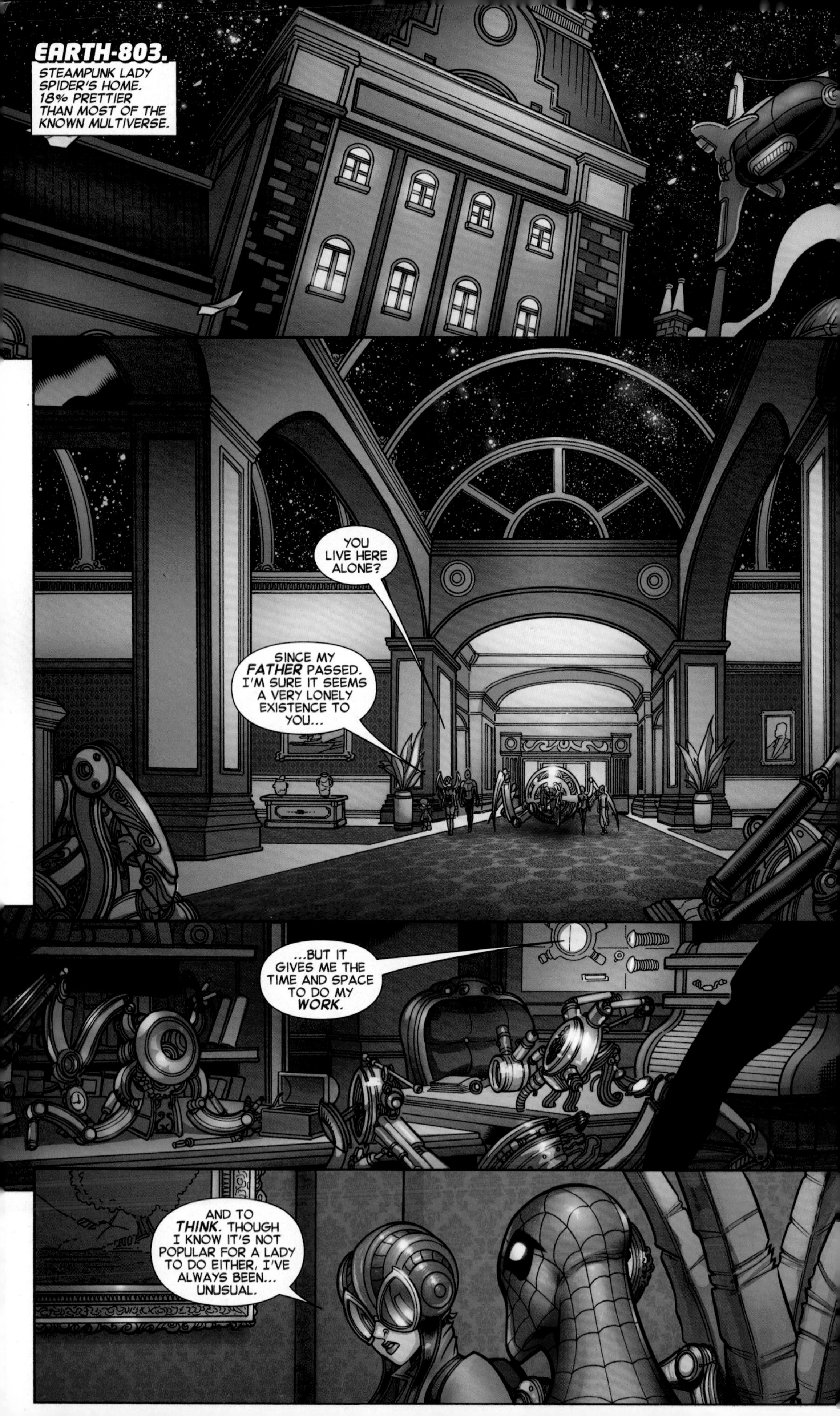
EARTH-803.
STEAMPUNK LADY SPIDER'S HOME. 18% PRETTIER THAN MOST OF THE KNOWN MULTIVERSE.
YOU LIVE HERE ALONE?
SINCE MY FATHER PASSED. I'M SURE IT SEEMS A VERY LONELY EXISTENCE TO YOU...
...BUT IT GIVES ME THE TIME AND SPACE TO DO MY WORK.
AND TO THINK. THOUGH I KNOW IT'S NOT POPULAR FOR A LADY TO DO EITHER, I'VE ALWAYS BEEN... UNUSUAL.

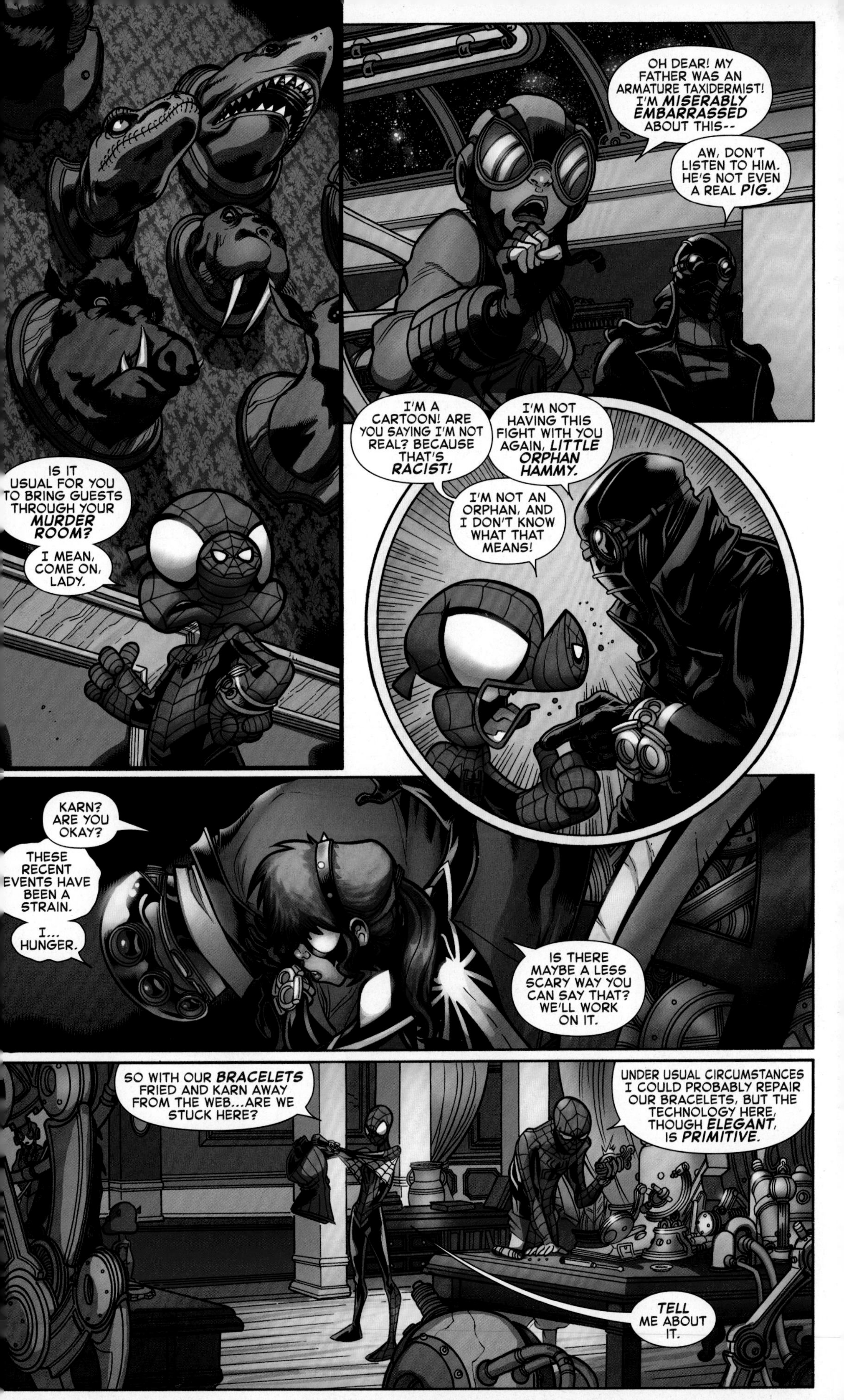
OH DEAR! MY FATHER WAS AN ARMATURE TAXIDERMIST! I'M MISERABLY EMBARRASSED ABOUT THIS--
AW, DON'T LISTEN TO HIM. HE'S NOT EVEN A REAL PIG.
IS IT USUAL FOR YOU TO BRING GUESTS THROUGH YOUR MURDER ROOM?
I MEAN, COME ON, LADY.
I'M A CARTOON! ARE YOU SAYING I'M NOT REAL? BECAUSE THAT'S RACIST!
I'M NOT HAVING THIS FIGHT WITH YOU AGAIN, LITTLE ORPHAN HAMMY.
I'M NOT AN ORPHAN, AND I DON'T KNOW WHAT THAT MEANS!
KARN? ARE YOU OKAY?
THESE RECENT EVENTS HAVE BEEN A STRAIN.
I... HUNGER.
IS THERE MAYBE A LESS SCARY WAY YOU CAN SAY THAT? WE'LL WORK ON IT.
SO WITH OUR BRACELETS FRIED AND KARN AWAY FROM THE WEB...ARE WE STUCK HERE?
UNDER USUAL CIRCUMSTANCES I COULD PROBABLY REPAIR OUR BRACELETS, BUT THE TECHNOLOGY HERE, THOUGH ELEGANT, IS PRIMITIVE.
TELL ME ABOUT IT.

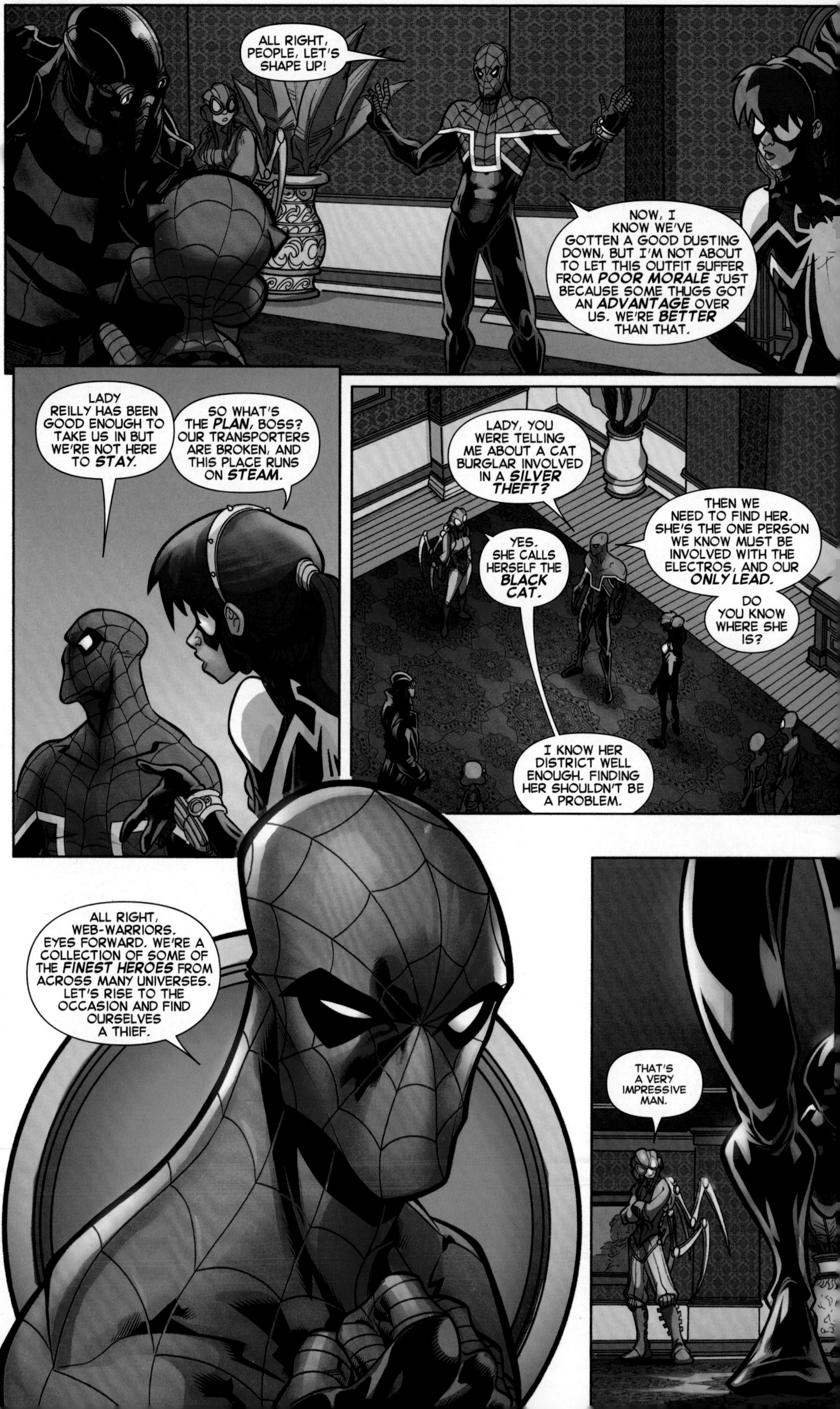
ALL RIGHT, PEOPLE, LET'S SHAPE UP!
NOW, I KNOW WE'VE GOTTEN A GOOD DUSTING DOWN, BUT I'M NOT ABOUT TO LET THIS OUTFIT SUFFER FROM POOR MORALE JUST BECAUSE SOME THUGS GOT AN ADVANTAGE OVER US. WE'RE BETTER THAN THAT.
LADY REILLY HAS BEEN GOOD ENOUGH TO TAKE US IN BUT WE'RE NOT HERE TO STAY.
SO WHAT'S THE PLAN, BOSS? OUR TRANSPORTERS ARE BROKEN, AND THIS PLACE RUNS ON STEAM.
LADY, YOU WERE TELLING ME ABOUT A CAT BURGLAR INVOLVED IN A SILVER THEFT?
YES. SHE CALLS HERSELF THE BLACK CAT.
THEN WE NEED TO FIND HER. SHE'S THE ONE PERSON WE KNOW MUST BE INVOLVED WITH THE ELECTROS, AND OUR ONLY LEAD.
DO YOU KNOW WHERE SHE IS?
I KNOW HER DISTRICT WELL ENOUGH. FINDING HER SHOULDN'T BE A PROBLEM.
ALL RIGHT, WEB-WARRIORS. EYES FORWARD. WE'RE A COLLECTION OF SOME OF THE FINEST HEROES FROM ACROSS MANY UNIVERSES. LET'S RISE TO THE OCCASION AND FIND OURSELVES A THIEF.
THAT'S A VERY IMPRESSIVE MAN.

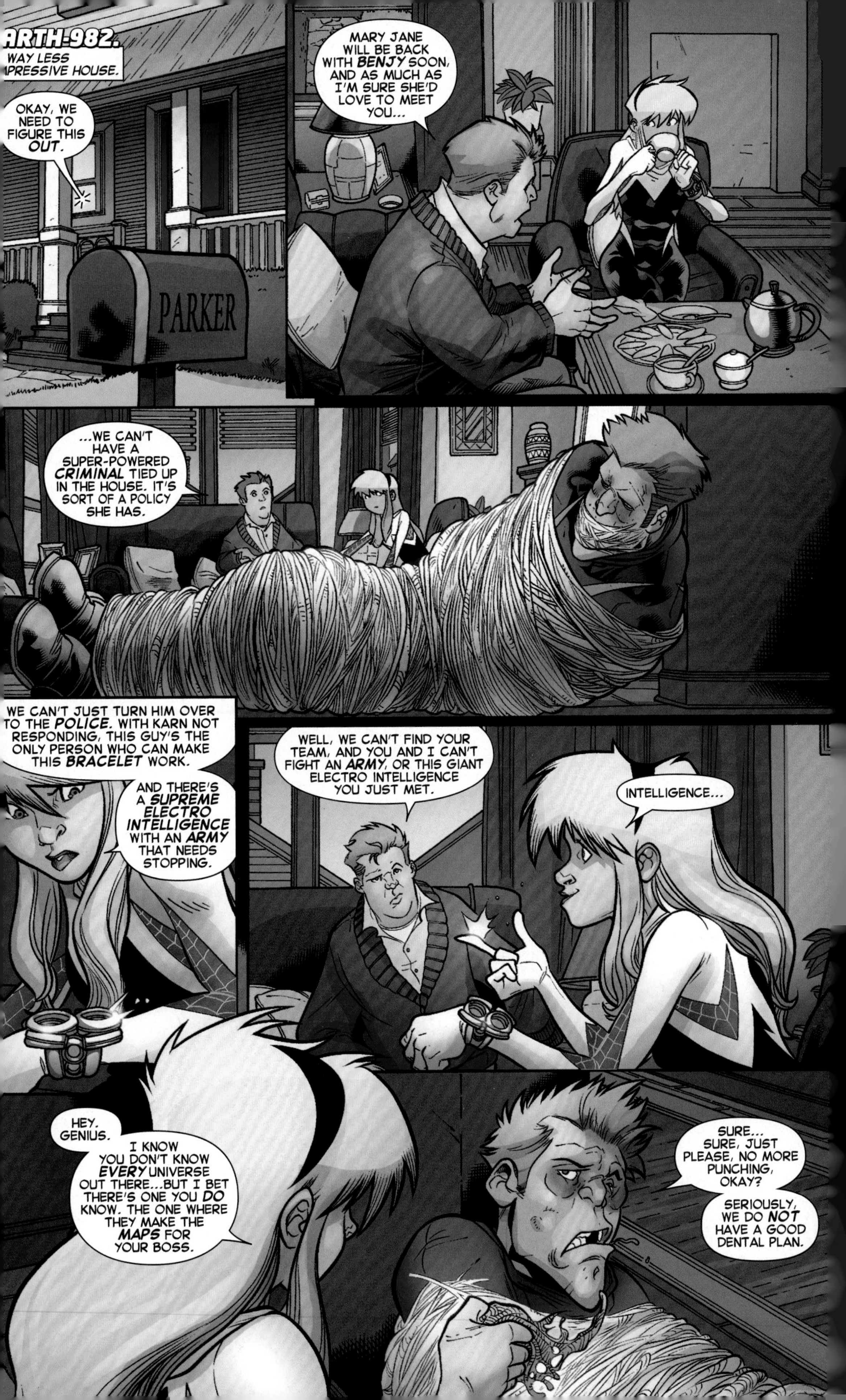

ARTH-982.
WAY LESS
IMPRESSIVE HOUSE.
OKAY, WE NEED TO FIGURE THIS OUT.
PARKER
MARY JANE WILL BE BACK WITH BENJY SOON, AND AS MUCH AS I'M SURE SHE'D LOVE TO MEET YOU...
...WE CAN'T HAVE A SUPER-POWERED CRIMINAL TIED UP IN THE HOUSE. IT'S SORT OF A POLICY SHE HAS.
WE CAN'T JUST TURN HIM OVER TO THE POLICE. WITH KARN NOT RESPONDING, THIS GUY'S THE ONLY PERSON WHO CAN MAKE THIS BRACELET WORK.
AND THERE'S A SUPREME ELECTRO INTELLIGENCE WITH AN ARMY THAT NEEDS STOPPING.
WELL, WE CAN'T FIND YOUR TEAM, AND YOU AND I CAN'T FIGHT AN ARMY, OR THIS GIANT ELECTRO INTELLIGENCE YOU JUST MET.
INTELLIGENCE...
HEY. GENIUS.
I KNOW YOU DON'T KNOW EVERY UNIVERSE OUT THERE...BUT I BET THERE'S ONE YOU DO KNOW. THE ONE WHERE THEY MAKE THE MAPS FOR YOUR BOSS.
SURE... SURE, JUST PLEASE, NO MORE PUNCHING, OKAY?
SERIOUSLY, WE DO NOT HAVE A GOOD DENTAL PLAN.

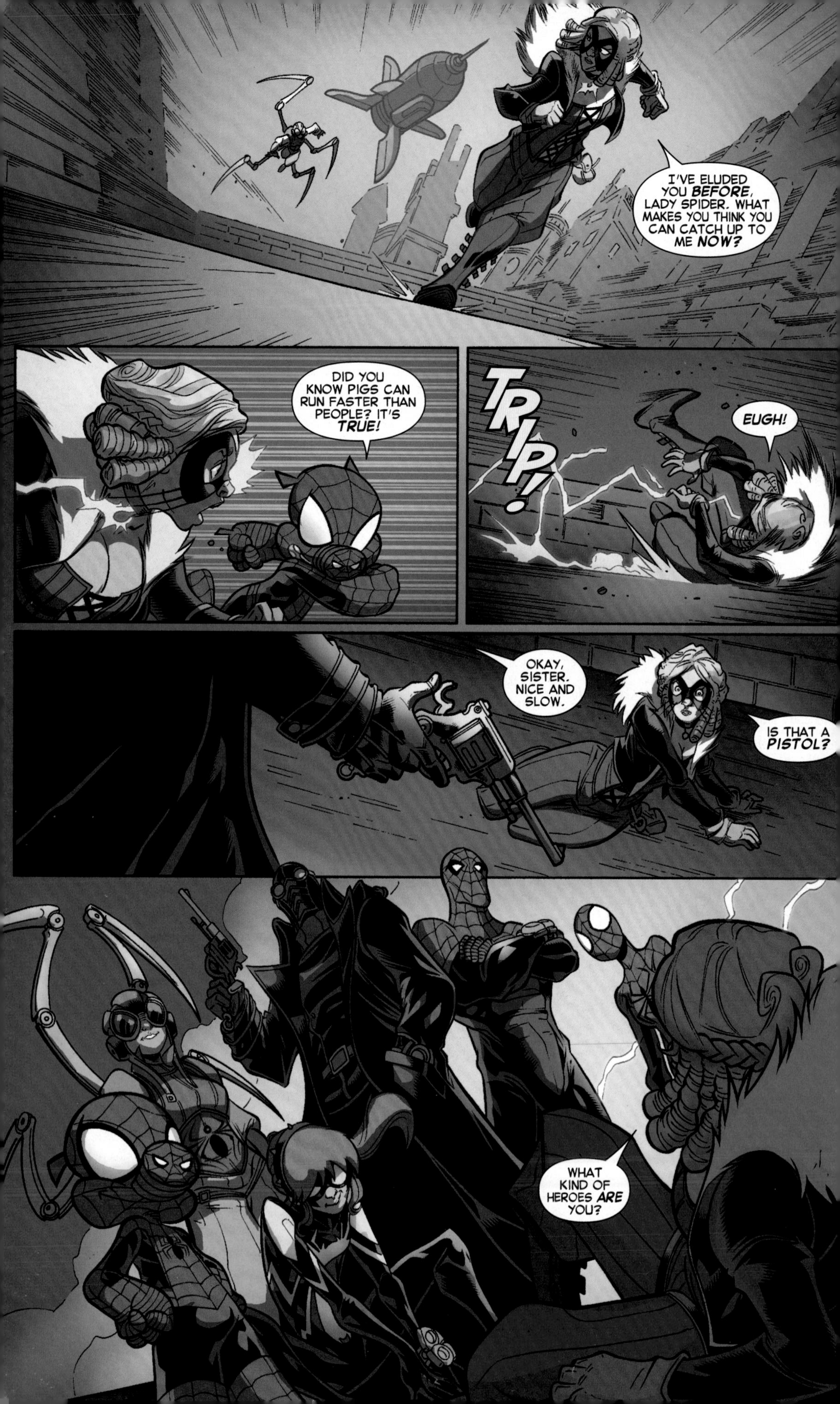
I'VE ELUDED YOU BEFORE, LADY SPIDER. WHAT MAKES YOU THINK YOU CAN CATCH UP TO ME NOW?
DID YOU KNOW PIGS CAN RUN FASTER THAN PEOPLE? IT'S TRUE!
TRIP!
EUGH!
OKAY, SISTER. NICE AND SLOW.
IS THAT A PISTOL?
WHAT KIND OF HEROES ARE YOU?

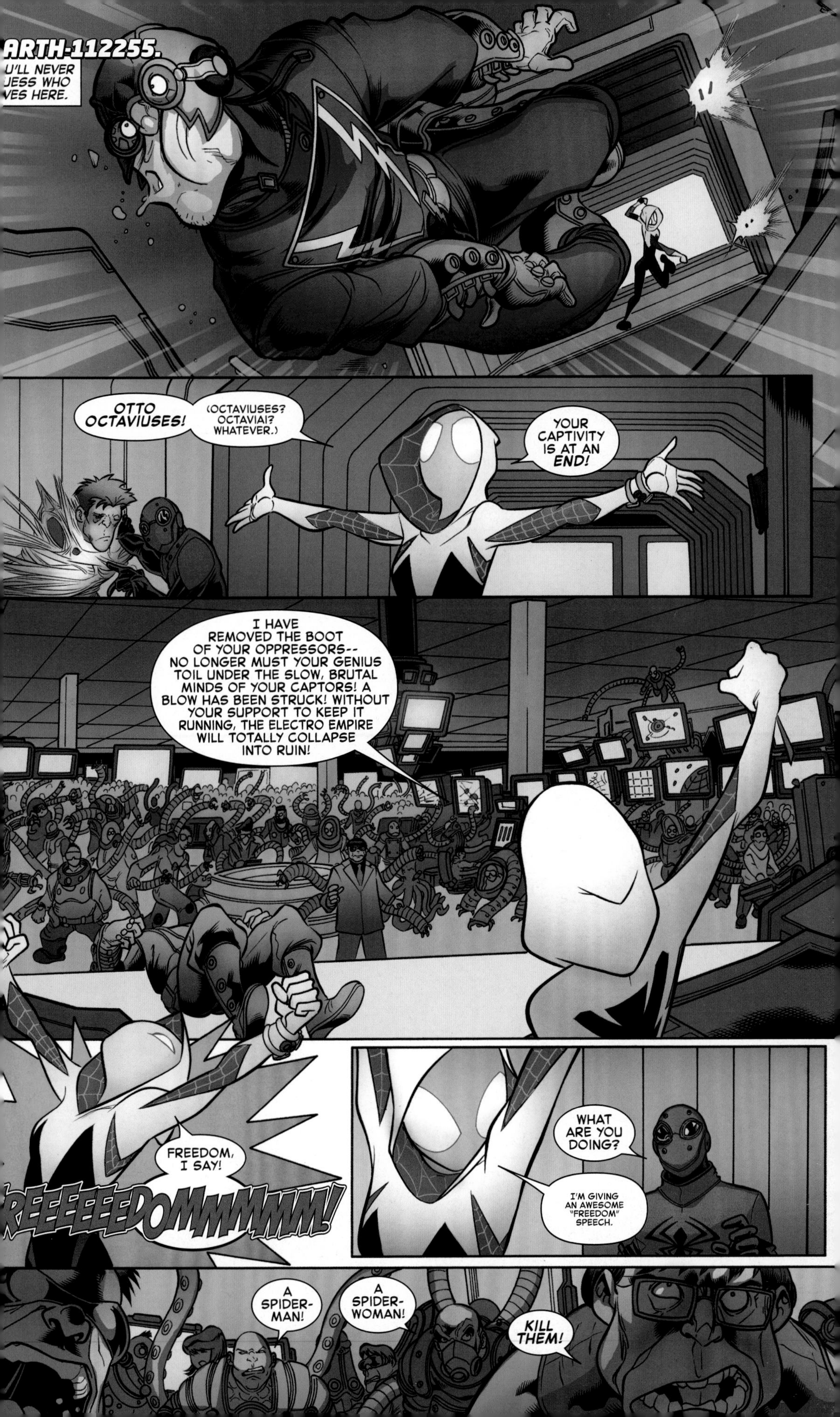
ARTH-112255.
U'LL NEVER JESS WHO VES HERE.
OTTO OCTAVIUSES!
(OCTAVIUSES? OCTAVIAI? WHATEVER.)
YOUR CAPTIVITY IS AT AN END!
I HAVE REMOVED THE BOOT OF YOUR OPPRESSORS-- NO LONGER MUST YOUR GENIUS TOIL UNDER THE SLOW, BRUTAL MINDS OF YOUR CAPTORS! A BLOW HAS BEEN STRUCK! WITHOUT YOUR SUPPORT TO KEEP IT RUNNING, THE ELECTRO EMPIRE WILL TOTALLY COLLAPSE INTO RUIN!
FREEDOM, I SAY!
REEEEEEEDOMMMMMM!
WHAT ARE YOU DOING?
I'M GIVING AN AWESOME "FREEDOM" SPEECH.
A SPIDER-MAN!
A SPIDER-WOMAN!
KILL THEM!

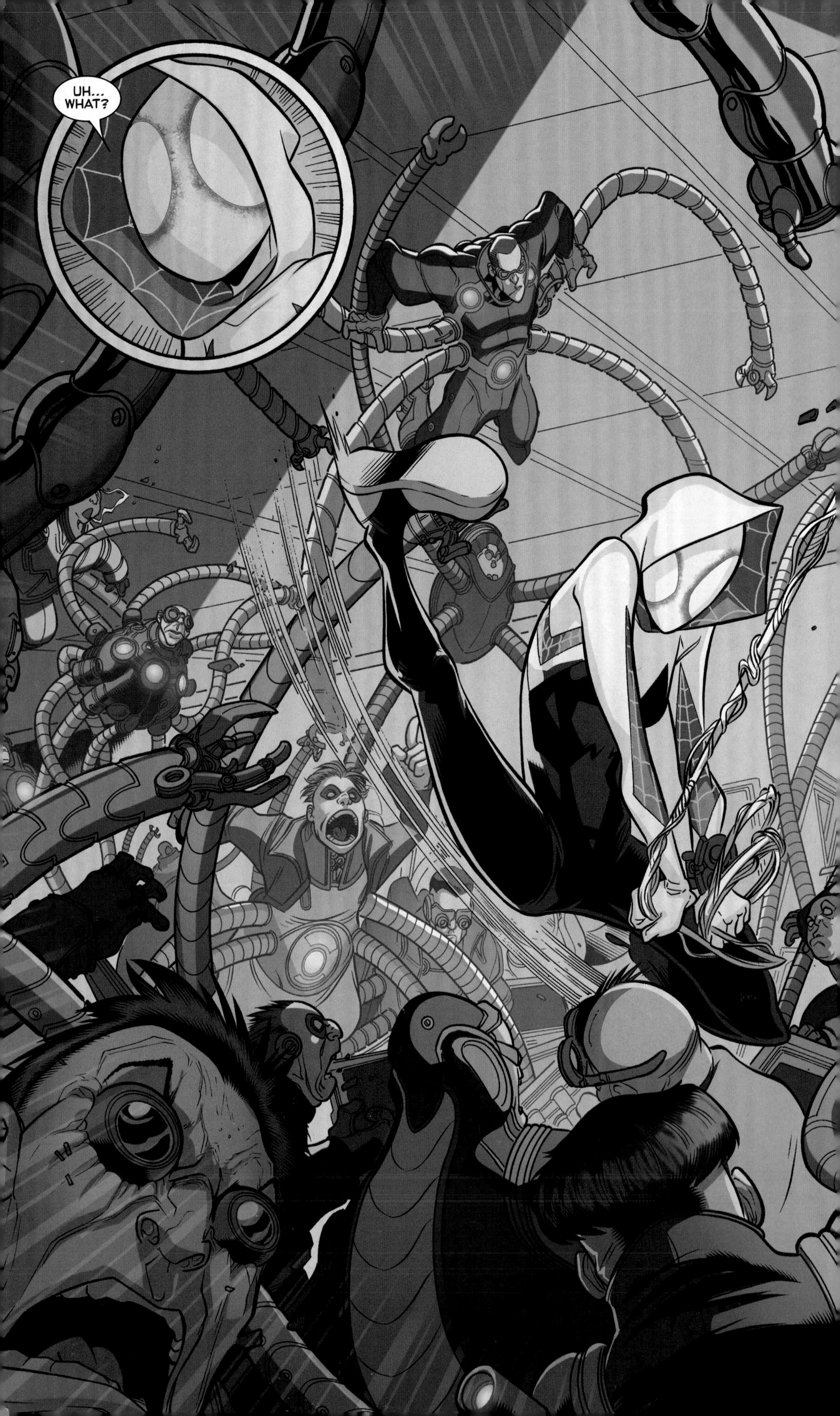
UH... WHAT?

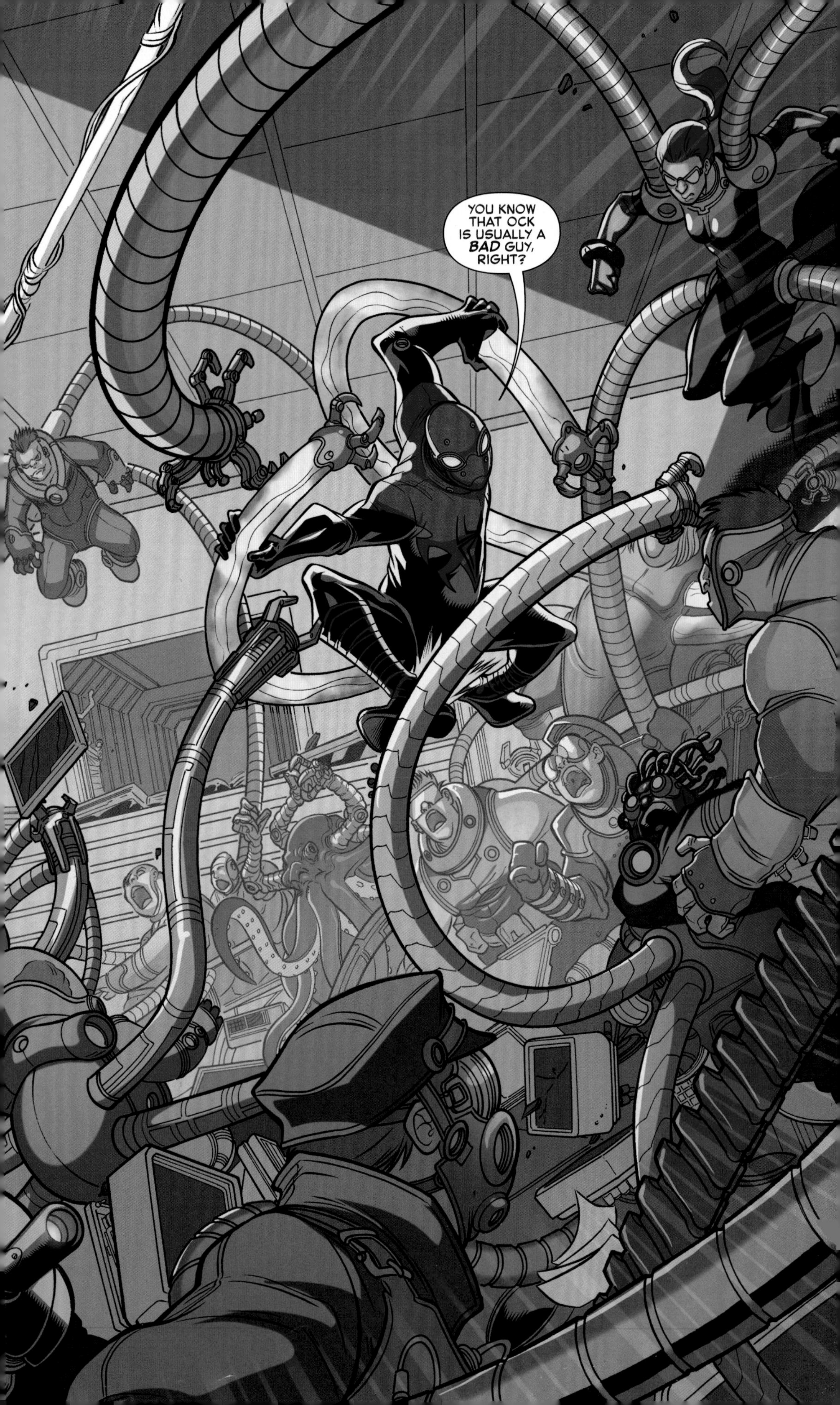
YOU KNOW THAT OCK IS USUALLY A BAD GUY, RIGHT?

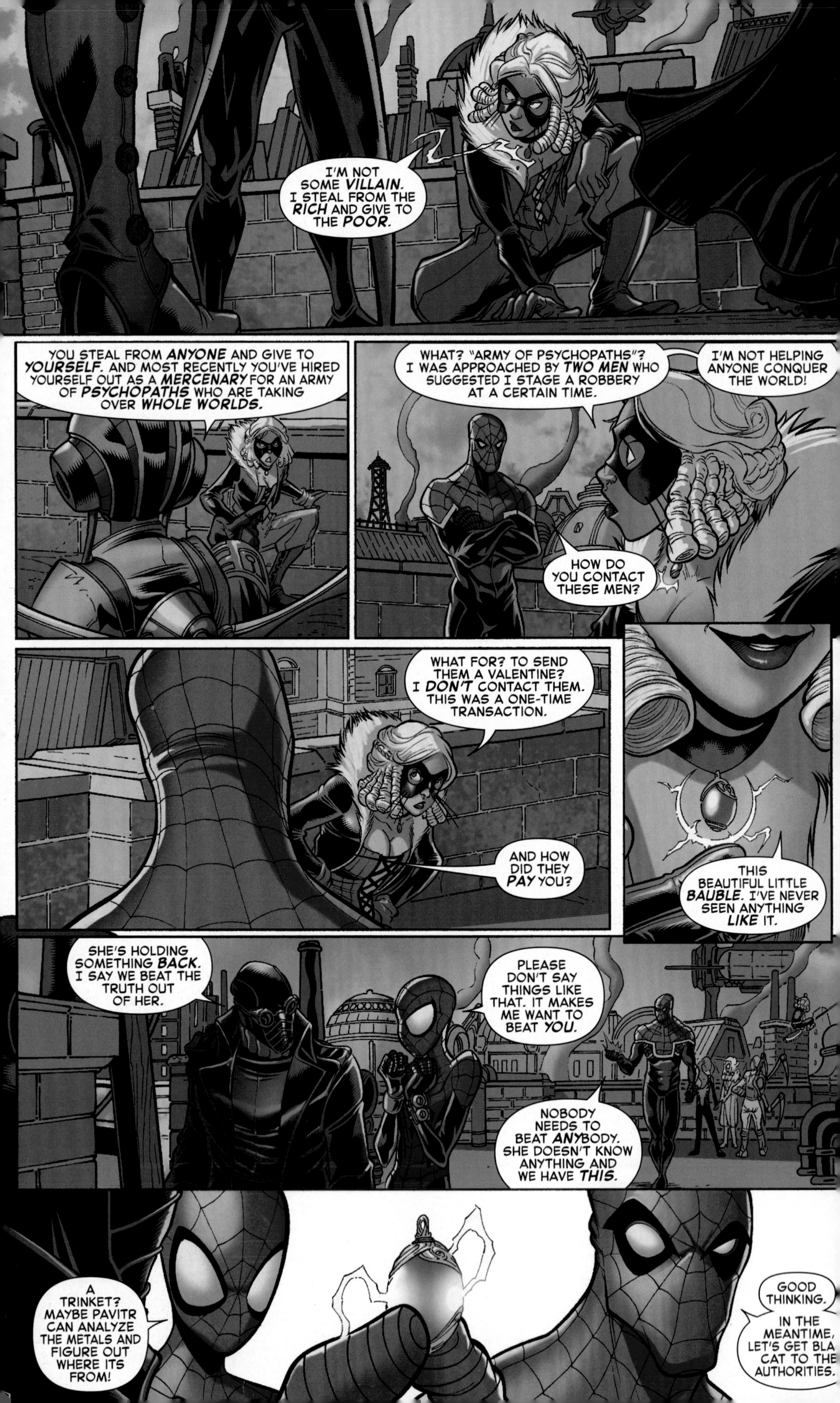
I'M NOT SOME VILLAIN. I STEAL FROM THE RICH AND GIVE TO THE POOR.
YOU STEAL FROM ANYONE AND GIVE TO YOURSELF. AND MOST RECENTLY YOU'VE HIRED YOURSELF OUT AS A MERCENARY FOR AN ARMY OF PSYCHOPATHS WHO ARE TAKING OVER WHOLE WORLDS.
WHAT? "ARMY OF PSYCHOPATHS"? I WAS APPROACHED BY TWO MEN WHO SUGGESTED I STAGE A ROBBERY AT A CERTAIN TIME.
I'M NOT HELPING ANYONE CONQUER THE WORLD!
HOW DO YOU CONTACT THESE MEN?
WHAT FOR? TO SEND THEM A VALENTINE? I DON'T CONTACT THEM. THIS WAS A ONE-TIME TRANSACTION.
AND HOW DID THEY PAY YOU?
THIS BEAUTIFUL LITTLE BAUBLE. I'VE NEVER SEEN ANYTHING LIKE IT.
SHE'S HOLDING SOMETHING BACK. I SAY WE BEAT THE TRUTH OUT OF HER.
PLEASE DON'T SAY THINGS LIKE THAT. IT MAKES ME WANT TO BEAT YOU.
NOBODY NEEDS TO BEAT ANYBODY. SHE DOESN'T KNOW ANYTHING AND WE HAVE THIS.
A TRINKET? MAYBE PAVITR CAN ANALYZE THE METALS AND FIGURE OUT WHERE ITS FROM!
GOOD THINKING.
IN THE MEANTIME, LET'S GET BLA CAT TO THE AUTHORITIES.

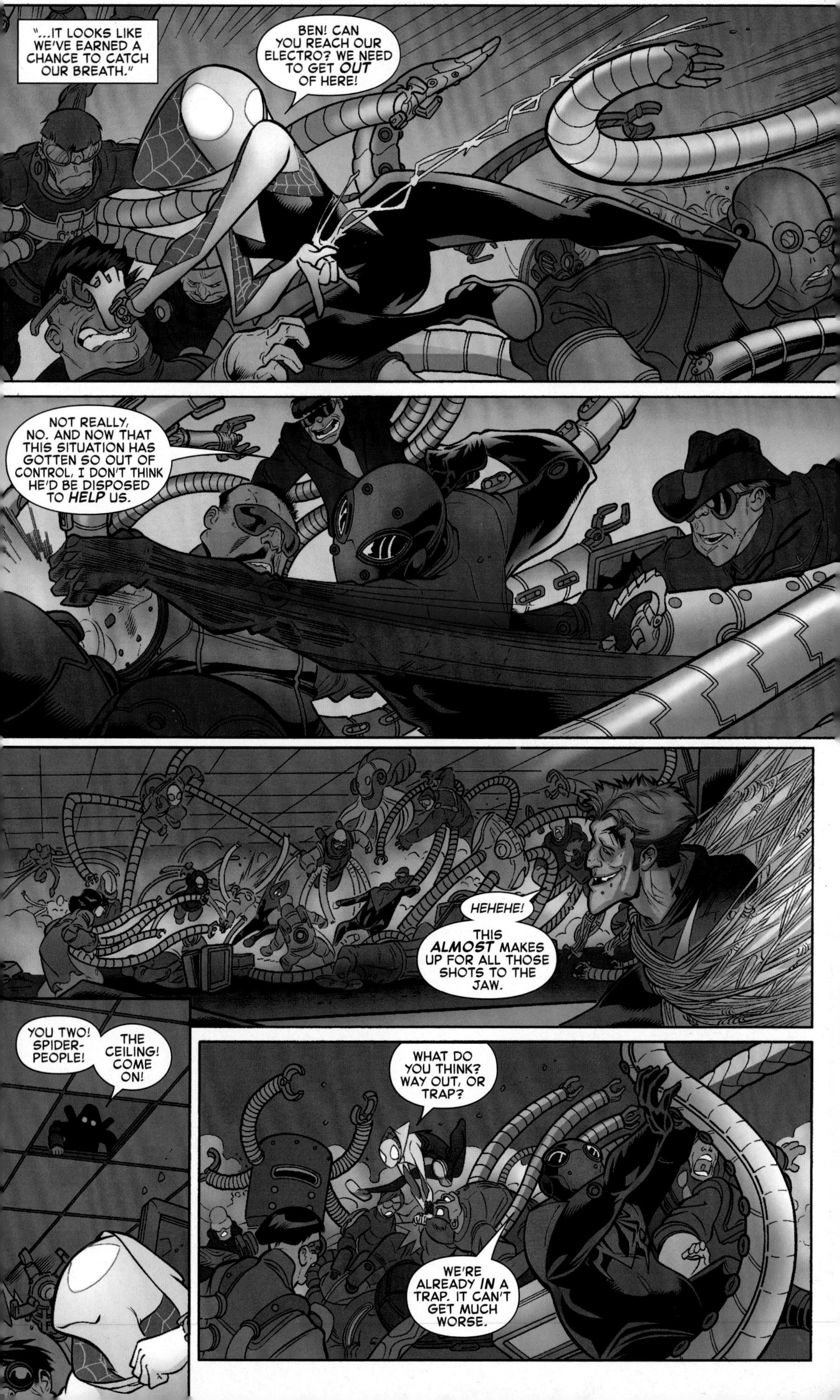
"...IT LOOKS LIKE WE'VE EARNED A CHANCE TO CATCH OUR BREATH."
BEN! CAN YOU REACH OUR ELECTRO? WE NEED TO GET *OUT* OF HERE!
NOT REALLY, NO. AND NOW THAT THIS SITUATION HAS GOTTEN SO OUT OF CONTROL, I DON'T THINK HE'D BE DISPOSED TO *HELP* US.
HEHEHE!
THIS *ALMOST* MAKES UP FOR ALL THOSE SHOTS TO THE JAW.
YOU TWO! SPIDER-PEOPLE!
THE CEILING! COME ON!
WHAT DO YOU THINK? WAY OUT, OR TRAP?
WE'RE ALREADY *IN* A TRAP. IT CAN'T GET MUCH WORSE.

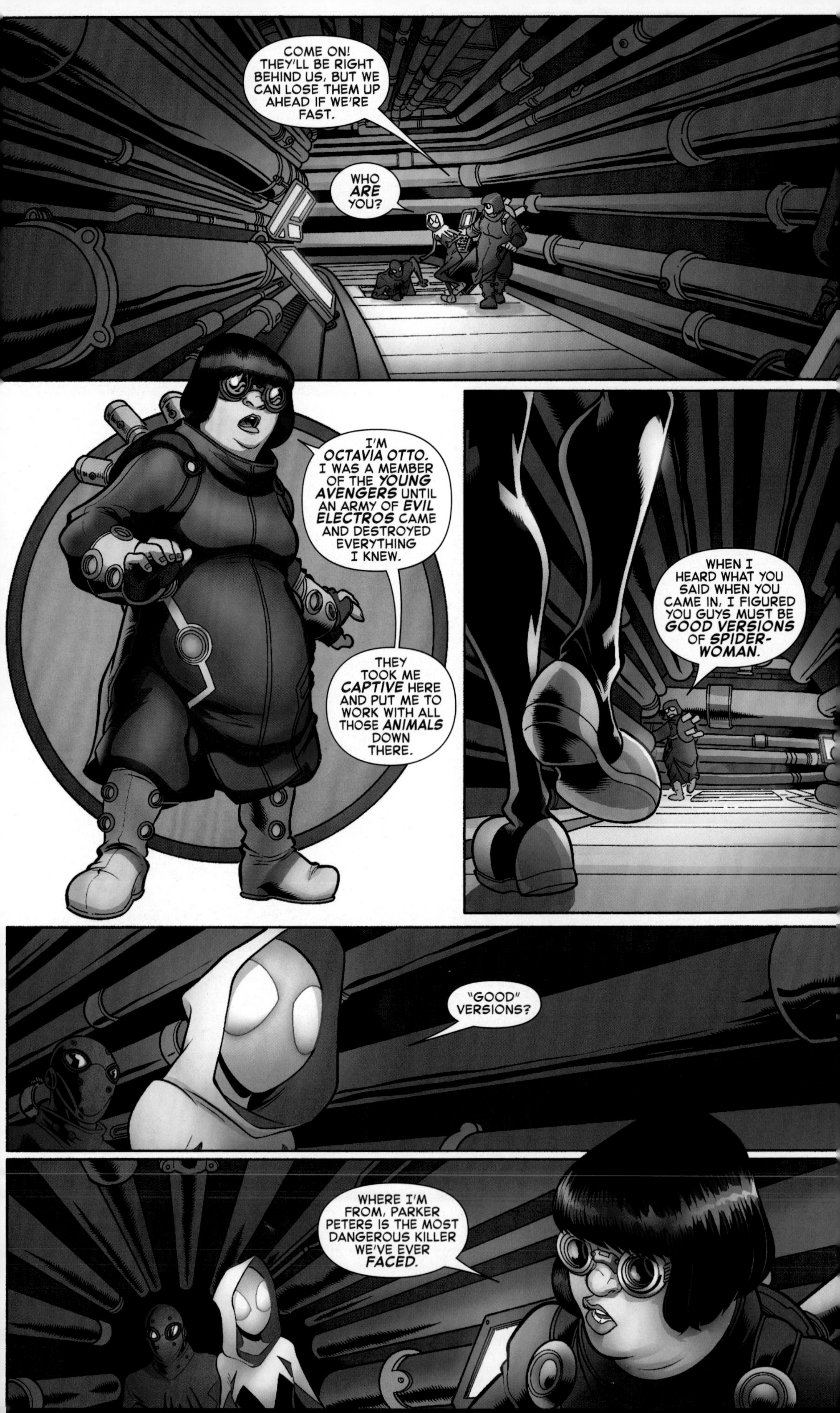
COME ON! THEY'LL BE RIGHT BEHIND US, BUT WE CAN LOSE THEM UP AHEAD IF WE'RE FAST.
WHO ARE YOU?
I'M OCTAVIA OTTO. I WAS A MEMBER OF THE YOUNG AVENGERS UNTIL AN ARMY OF EVIL ELECTROS CAME AND DESTROYED EVERYTHING I KNEW.
THEY TOOK ME CAPTIVE HERE AND PUT ME TO WORK WITH ALL THOSE ANIMALS DOWN THERE.
WHEN I HEARD WHAT YOU SAID WHEN YOU CAME IN, I FIGURED YOU GUYS MUST BE GOOD VERSIONS OF SPIDER-WOMAN.
"GOOD" VERSIONS?
WHERE I'M FROM, PARKER PETERS IS THE MOST DANGEROUS KILLER WE'VE EVER FACED.

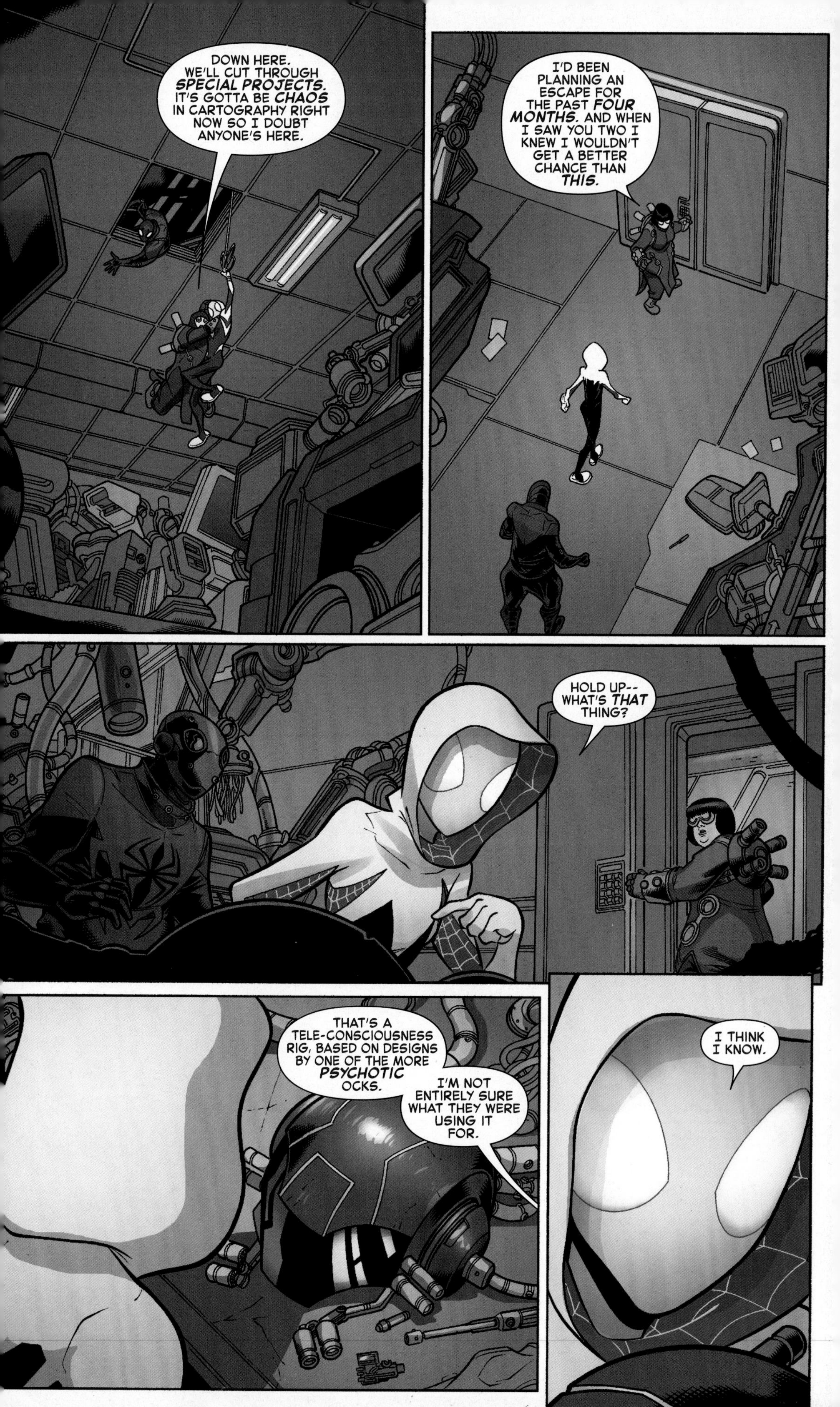
DOWN HERE. WE'LL CUT THROUGH SPECIAL PROJECTS. IT'S GOTTA BE CHAOS IN CARTOGRAPHY RIGHT NOW SO I DOUBT ANYONE'S HERE.
I'D BEEN PLANNING AN ESCAPE FOR THE PAST FOUR MONTHS. AND WHEN I SAW YOU TWO I KNEW I WOULDN'T GET A BETTER CHANCE THAN THIS.
HOLD UP-- WHAT'S THAT THING?
THAT'S A TELE-CONSCIOUSNESS RIG, BASED ON DESIGNS BY ONE OF THE MORE PSYCHOTIC OCKS.
I'M NOT ENTIRELY SURE WHAT THEY WERE USING IT FOR.
I THINK I KNOW.

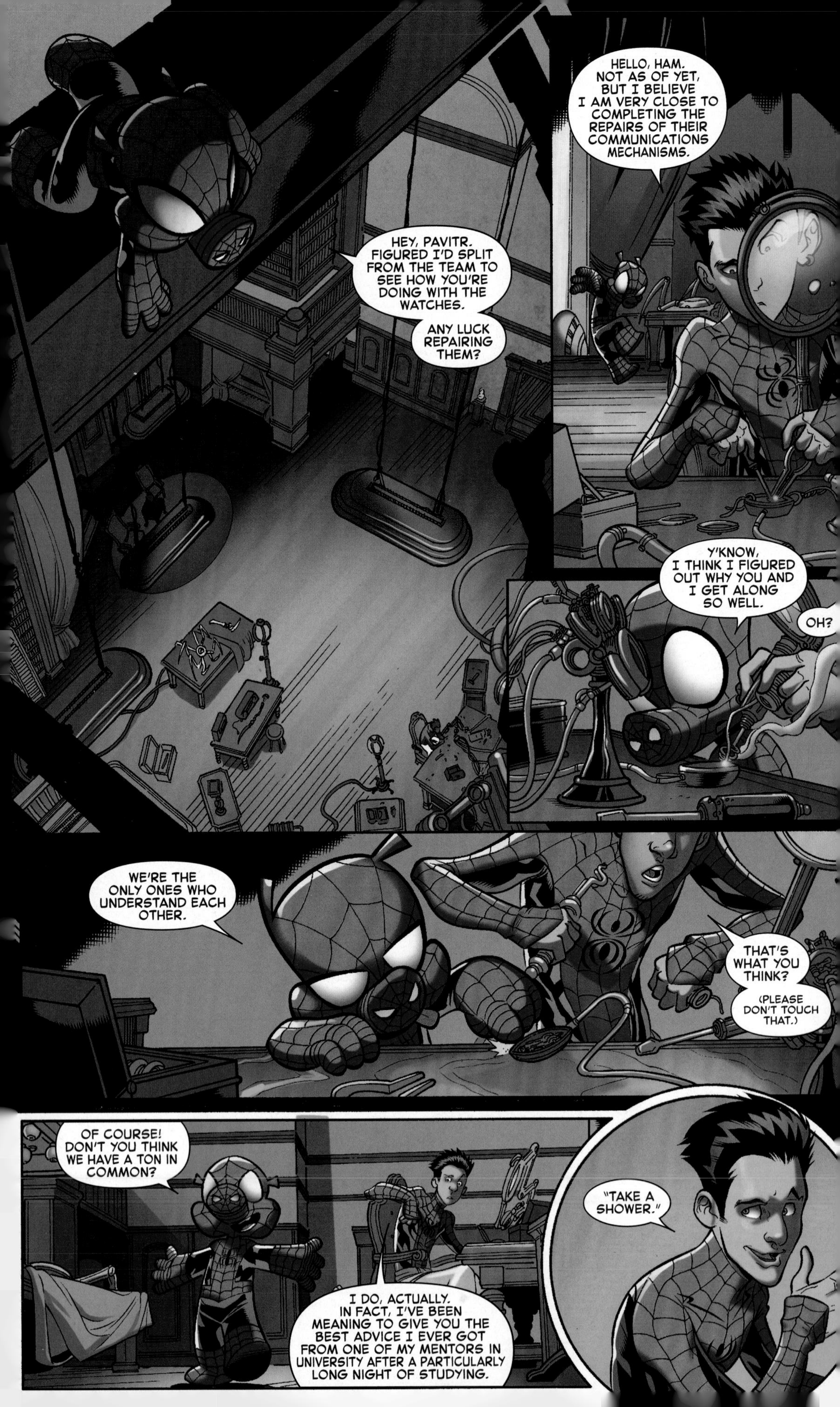
HEY, PAVITR. FIGURED I'D SPLIT FROM THE TEAM TO SEE HOW YOU'RE DOING WITH THE WATCHES.
ANY LUCK REPAIRING THEM?
HELLO, HAM. NOT AS OF YET, BUT I BELIEVE I AM VERY CLOSE TO COMPLETING THE REPAIRS OF THEIR COMMUNICATIONS MECHANISMS.
Y'KNOW, I THINK I FIGURED OUT WHY YOU AND I GET ALONG SO WELL.
OH?
WE'RE THE ONLY ONES WHO UNDERSTAND EACH OTHER.
THAT'S WHAT YOU THINK?
(PLEASE DON'T TOUCH THAT.)
OF COURSE! DON'T YOU THINK WE HAVE A TON IN COMMON?
I DO, ACTUALLY. IN FACT, I'VE BEEN MEANING TO GIVE YOU THE BEST ADVICE I EVER GOT FROM ONE OF MY MENTORS IN UNIVERSITY AFTER A PARTICULARLY LONG NIGHT OF STUDYING.
"TAKE A SHOWER."

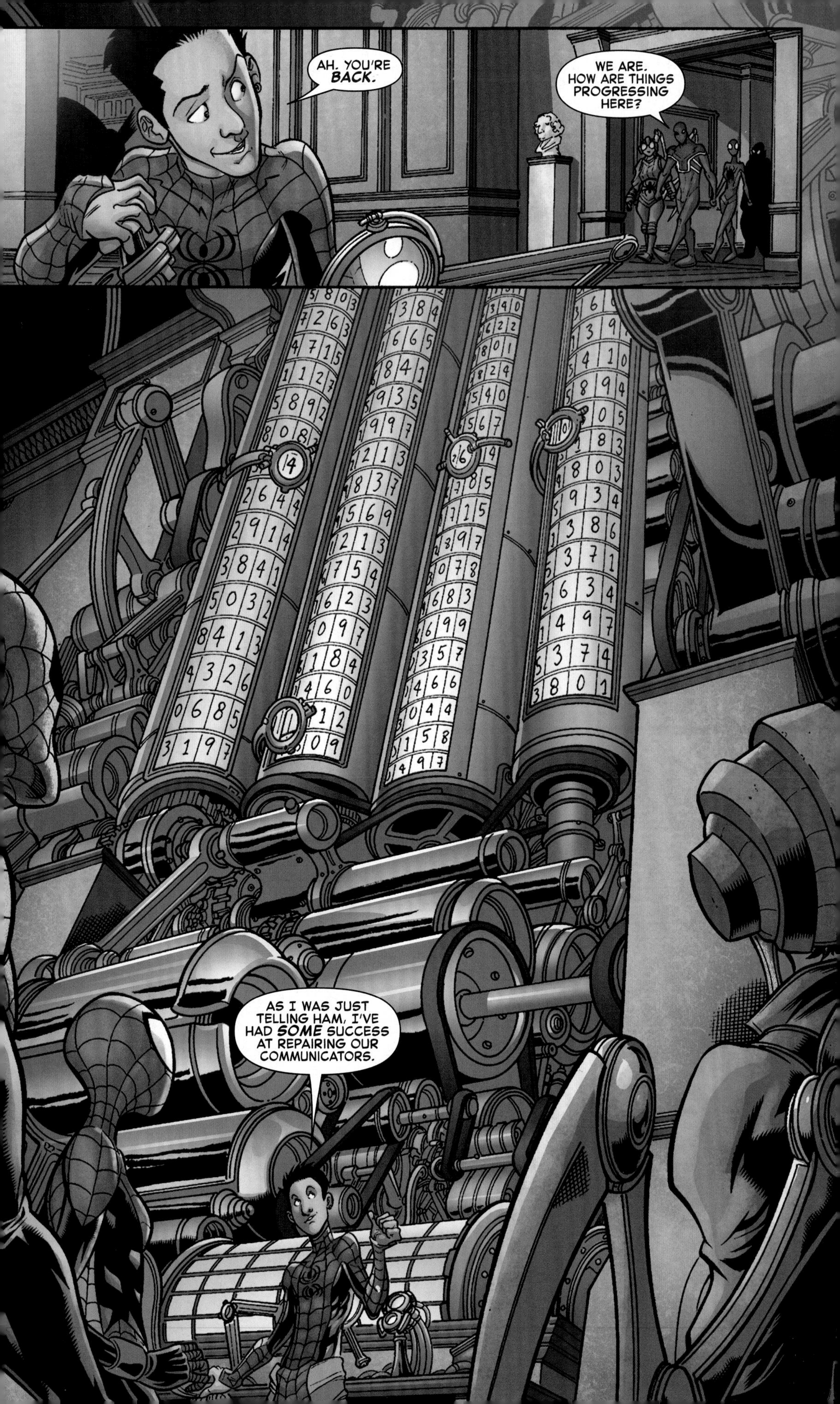
AH. YOU'RE BACK.
WE ARE. HOW ARE THINGS PROGRESSING HERE?
AS I WAS JUST TELLING HAM, I'VE HAD SOME SUCCESS AT REPAIRING OUR COMMUNICATORS.

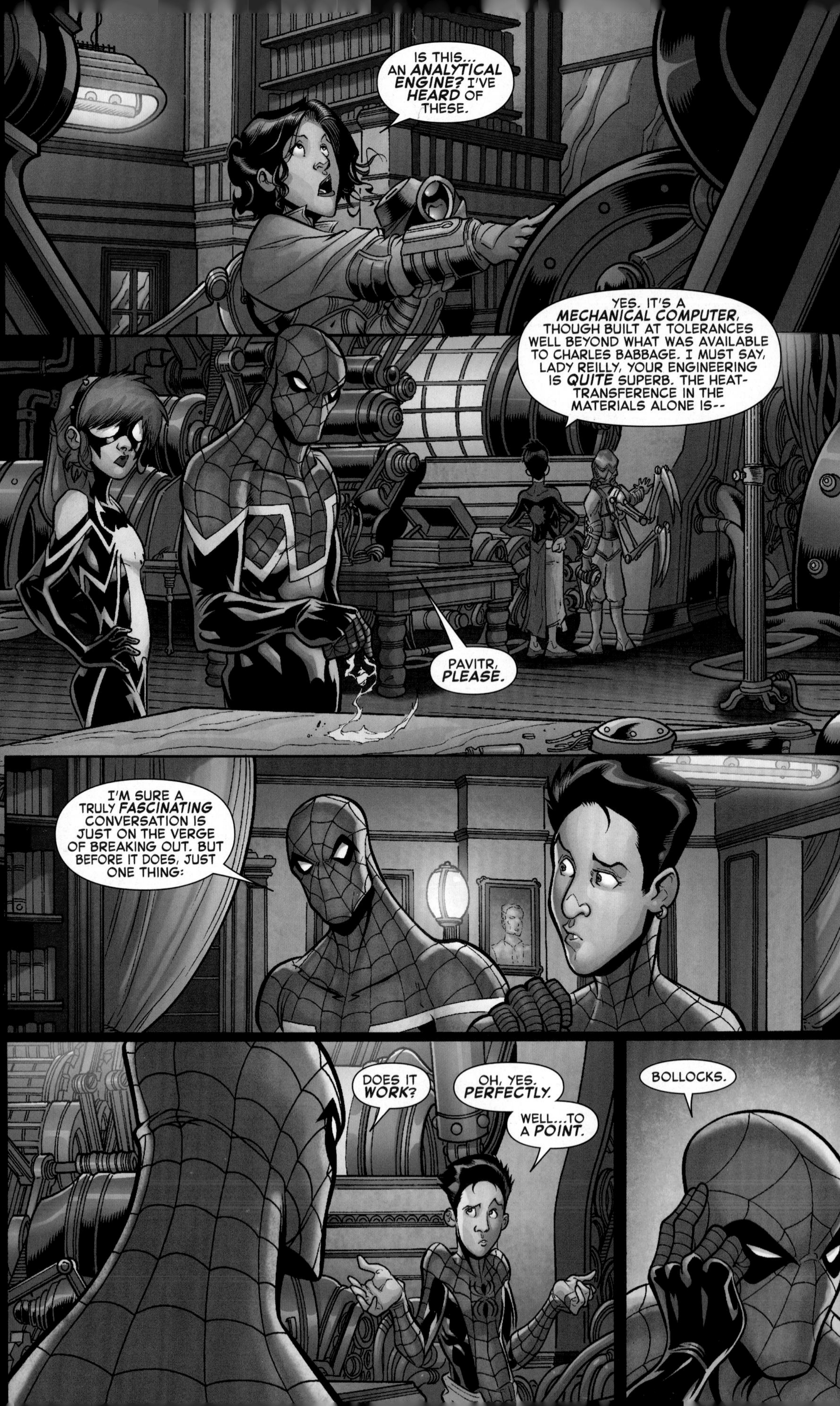
IS THIS... AN ANALYTICAL ENGINE? I'VE HEARD OF THESE.
YES. IT'S A MECHANICAL COMPUTER, THOUGH BUILT AT TOLERANCES WELL BEYOND WHAT WAS AVAILABLE TO CHARLES BABBAGE. I MUST SAY, LADY REILLY, YOUR ENGINEERING IS QUITE SUPERB. THE HEAT-TRANSFERENCE IN THE MATERIALS ALONE IS--
PAVITR, PLEASE.
I'M SURE A TRULY FASCINATING CONVERSATION IS JUST ON THE VERGE OF BREAKING OUT. BUT BEFORE IT DOES, JUST ONE THING:
DOES IT WORK?
OH, YES. PERFECTLY.
WELL...TO A POINT.
BOLLOCKS.

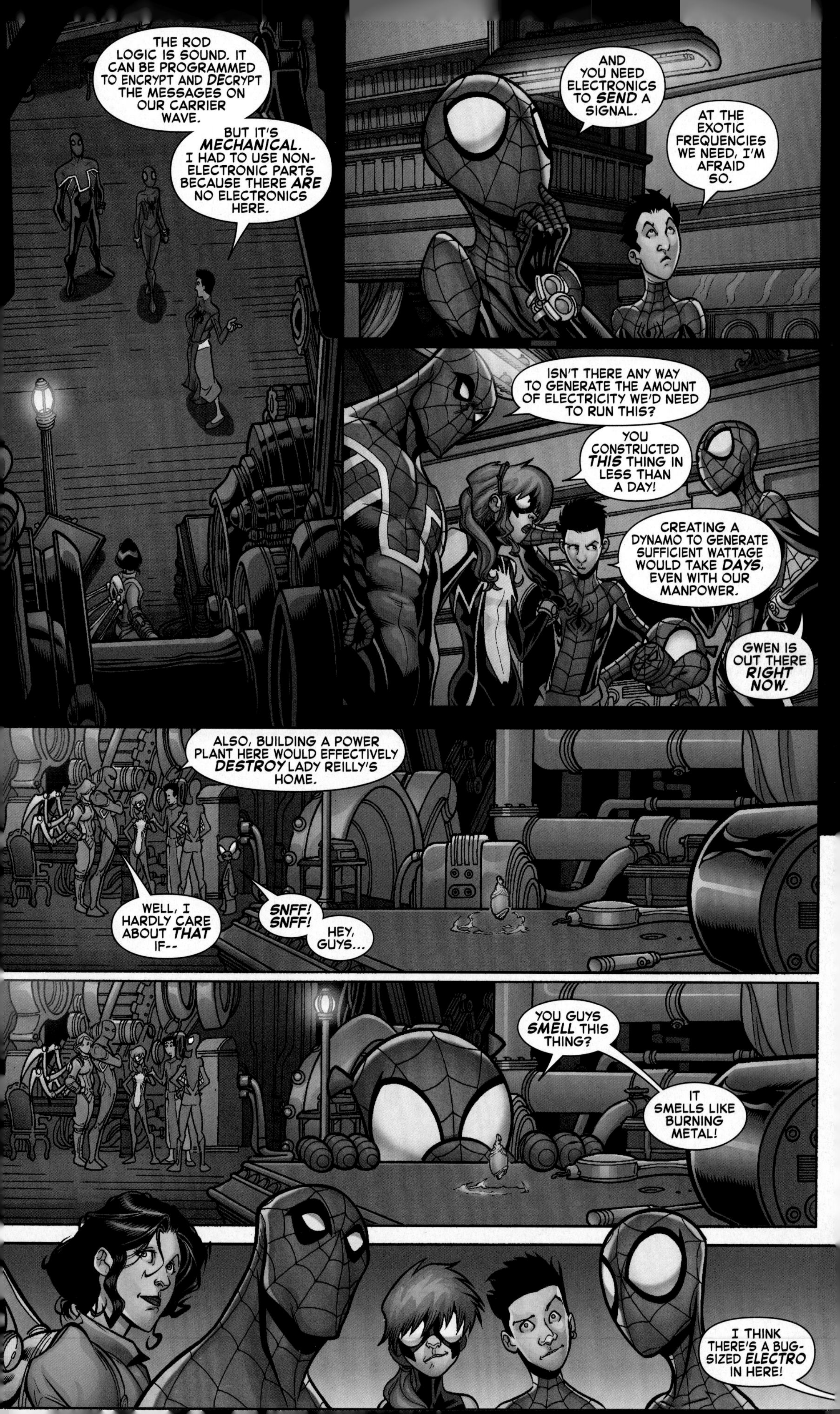
THE ROD LOGIC IS SOUND. IT CAN BE PROGRAMMED TO ENCRYPT AND DECRYPT THE MESSAGES ON OUR CARRIER WAVE.
BUT IT'S MECHANICAL. I HAD TO USE NON-ELECTRONIC PARTS BECAUSE THERE ARE NO ELECTRONICS HERE.
AND YOU NEED ELECTRONICS TO SEND A SIGNAL.
AT THE EXOTIC FREQUENCIES WE NEED, I'M AFRAID SO.
ISN'T THERE ANY WAY TO GENERATE THE AMOUNT OF ELECTRICITY WE'D NEED TO RUN THIS?
YOU CONSTRUCTED THIS THING IN LESS THAN A DAY!
CREATING A DYNAMO TO GENERATE SUFFICIENT WATTAGE WOULD TAKE DAYS, EVEN WITH OUR MANPOWER.
GWEN IS OUT THERE RIGHT NOW.
ALSO, BUILDING A POWER PLANT HERE WOULD EFFECTIVELY DESTROY LADY REILLY'S HOME.
WELL, I HARDLY CARE ABOUT THAT IF--
SNFF! SNFF!
HEY, GUYS...
YOU GUYS SMELL THIS THING?
IT SMELLS LIKE BURNING METAL!
I THINK THERE'S A BUG-SIZED ELECTRO IN HERE!

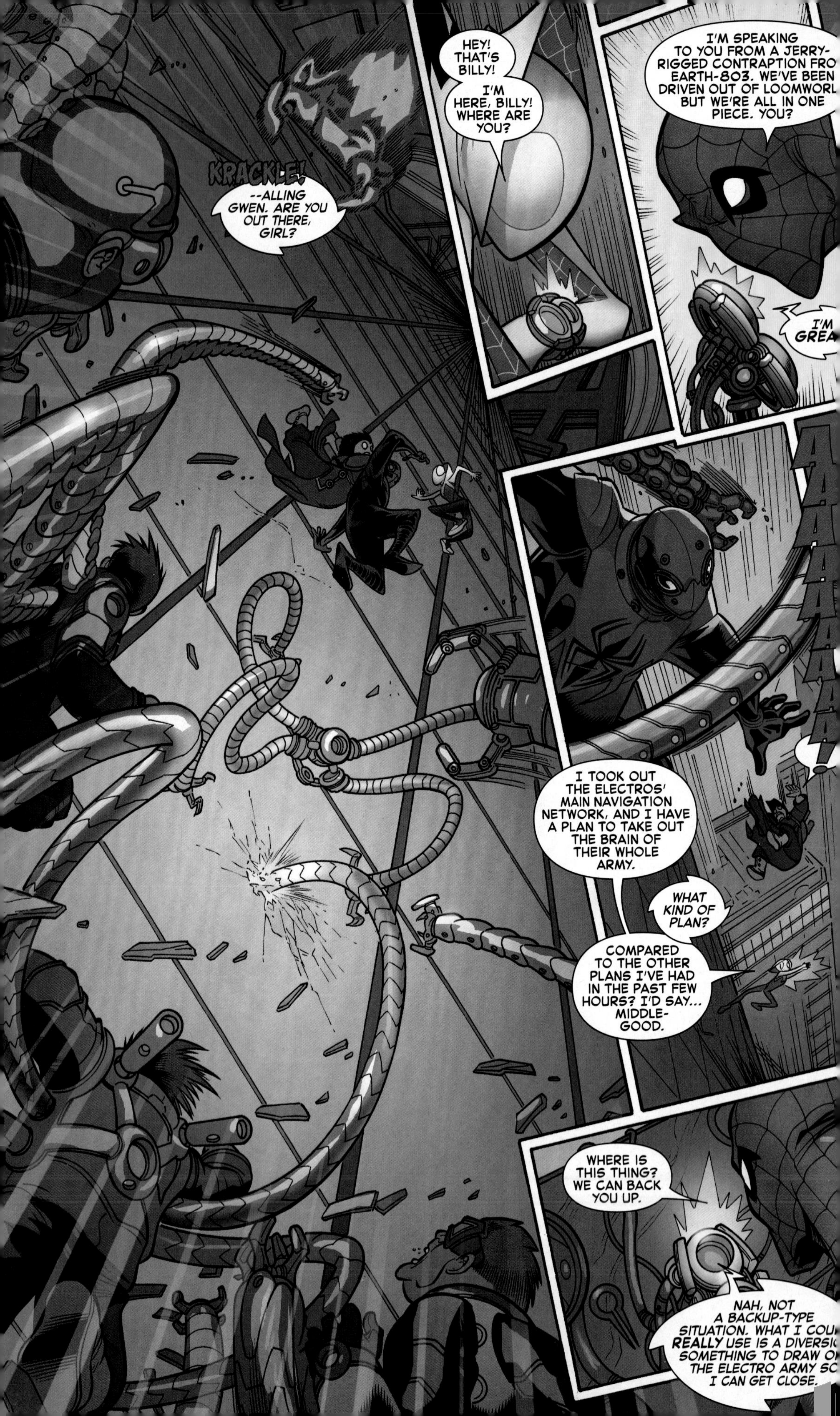
KRACKLE!
--ALLING GWEN. ARE YOU OUT THERE, GIRL?
HEY! THAT'S BILLY!
I'M HERE, BILLY! WHERE ARE YOU?
I'M SPEAKING TO YOU FROM A JERRY-RIGGED CONTRAPTION FRO EARTH-803. WE'VE BEEN DRIVEN OUT OF LOOMWORL BUT WE'RE ALL IN ONE PIECE. YOU?
I'M GREA
I TOOK OUT THE ELECTROS' MAIN NAVIGATION NETWORK, AND I HAVE A PLAN TO TAKE OUT THE BRAIN OF THEIR WHOLE ARMY.
WHAT KIND OF PLAN?
COMPARED TO THE OTHER PLANS I'VE HAD IN THE PAST FEW HOURS? I'D SAY... MIDDLE-GOOD.
WHERE IS THIS THING? WE CAN BACK YOU UP.
NAH, NOT A BACKUP-TYPE SITUATION. WHAT I COU REALLY USE IS A DIVERSI SOMETHING TO DRAW O THE ELECTRO ARMY SO I CAN GET CLOSE.

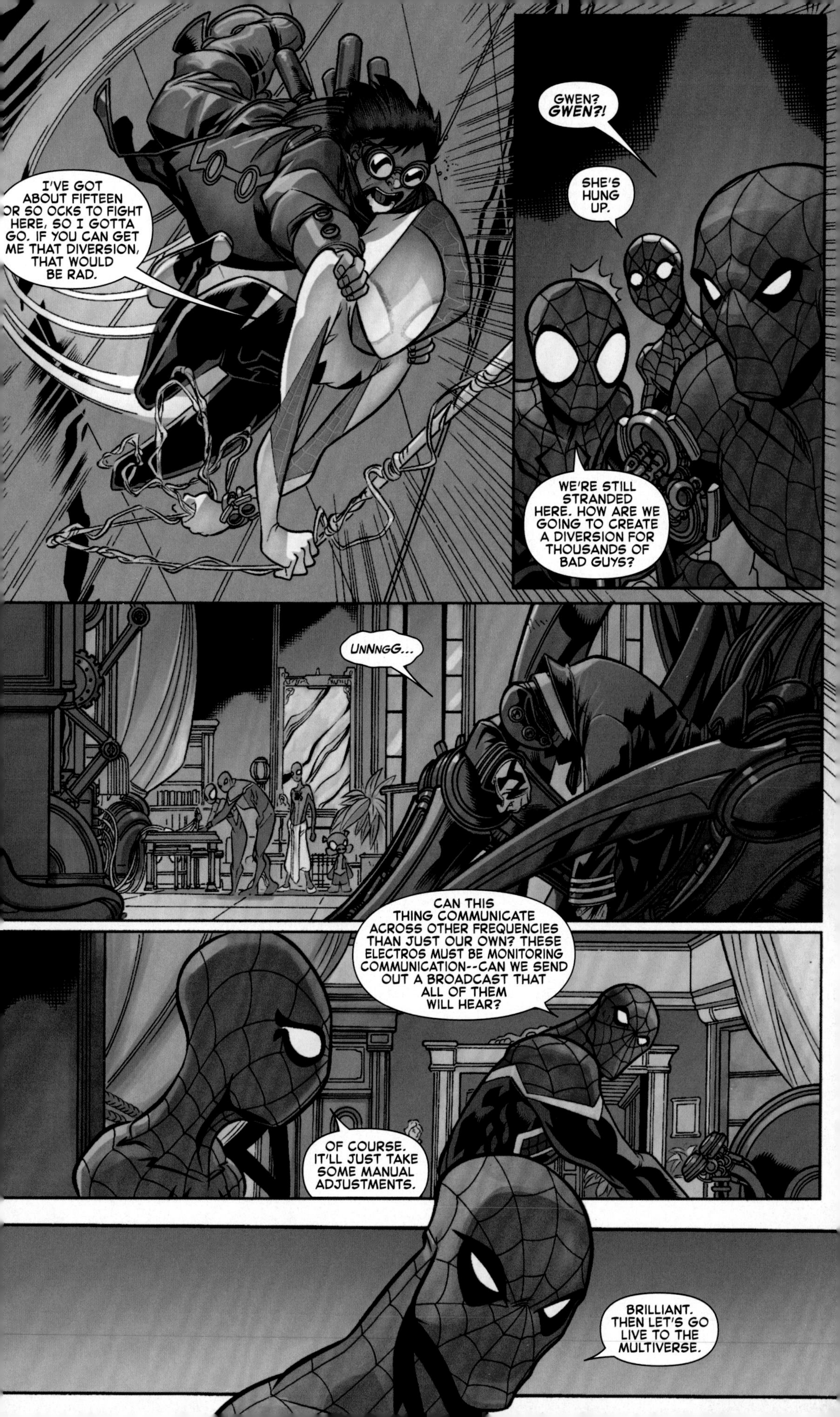
I'VE GOT ABOUT FIFTEEN OR SO OCKS TO FIGHT HERE, SO I GOTTA GO. IF YOU CAN GET ME THAT DIVERSION, THAT WOULD BE RAD.
GWEN? GWEN?!
SHE'S HUNG UP.
WE'RE STILL STRANDED HERE. HOW ARE WE GOING TO CREATE A DIVERSION FOR THOUSANDS OF BAD GUYS?
UNNNGG...
CAN THIS THING COMMUNICATE ACROSS OTHER FREQUENCIES THAN JUST OUR OWN? THESE ELECTROS MUST BE MONITORING COMMUNICATION--CAN WE SEND OUT A BROADCAST THAT ALL OF THEM WILL HEAR?
OF COURSE. IT'LL JUST TAKE SOME MANUAL ADJUSTMENTS.
BRILLIANT. THEN LET'S GO LIVE TO THE MULTIVERSE.

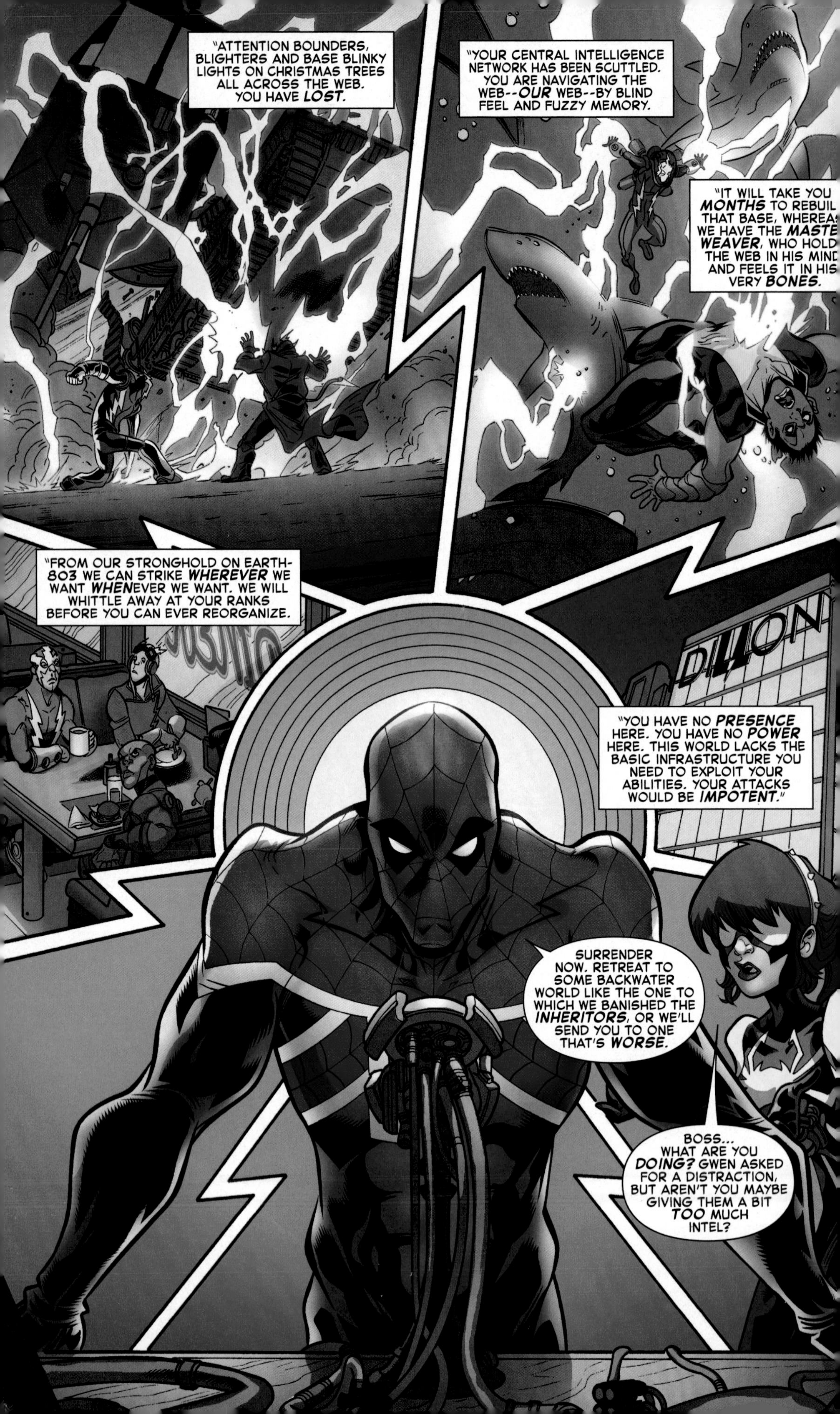
"ATTENTION BOUNDERS, BLIGHTERS AND BASE BLINKY LIGHTS ON CHRISTMAS TREES ALL ACROSS THE WEB. YOU HAVE LOST.
"YOUR CENTRAL INTELLIGENCE NETWORK HAS BEEN SCUTTLED. YOU ARE NAVIGATING THE WEB--OUR WEB--BY BLIND FEEL AND FUZZY MEMORY.
"IT WILL TAKE YOU MONTHS TO REBUIL THAT BASE, WHEREA WE HAVE THE MASTE WEAVER, WHO HOLD THE WEB IN HIS MINI AND FEELS IT IN HIS VERY BONES.
"FROM OUR STRONGHOLD ON EARTH-803 WE CAN STRIKE WHEREVER WE WANT WHENEVER WE WANT. WE WILL WHITTLE AWAY AT YOUR RANKS BEFORE YOU CAN EVER REORGANIZE.
DILLON
"YOU HAVE NO PRESENCE HERE. YOU HAVE NO POWER HERE. THIS WORLD LACKS THE BASIC INFRASTRUCTURE YOU NEED TO EXPLOIT YOUR ABILITIES. YOUR ATTACKS WOULD BE IMPOTENT."
SURRENDER NOW. RETREAT TO SOME BACKWATER WORLD LIKE THE ONE TO WHICH WE BANISHED THE INHERITORS, OR WE'LL SEND YOU TO ONE THAT'S WORSE.
BOSS... WHAT ARE YOU DOING? GWEN ASKED FOR A DISTRACTION, BUT AREN'T YOU MAYBE GIVING THEM A BIT TOO MUCH INTEL?

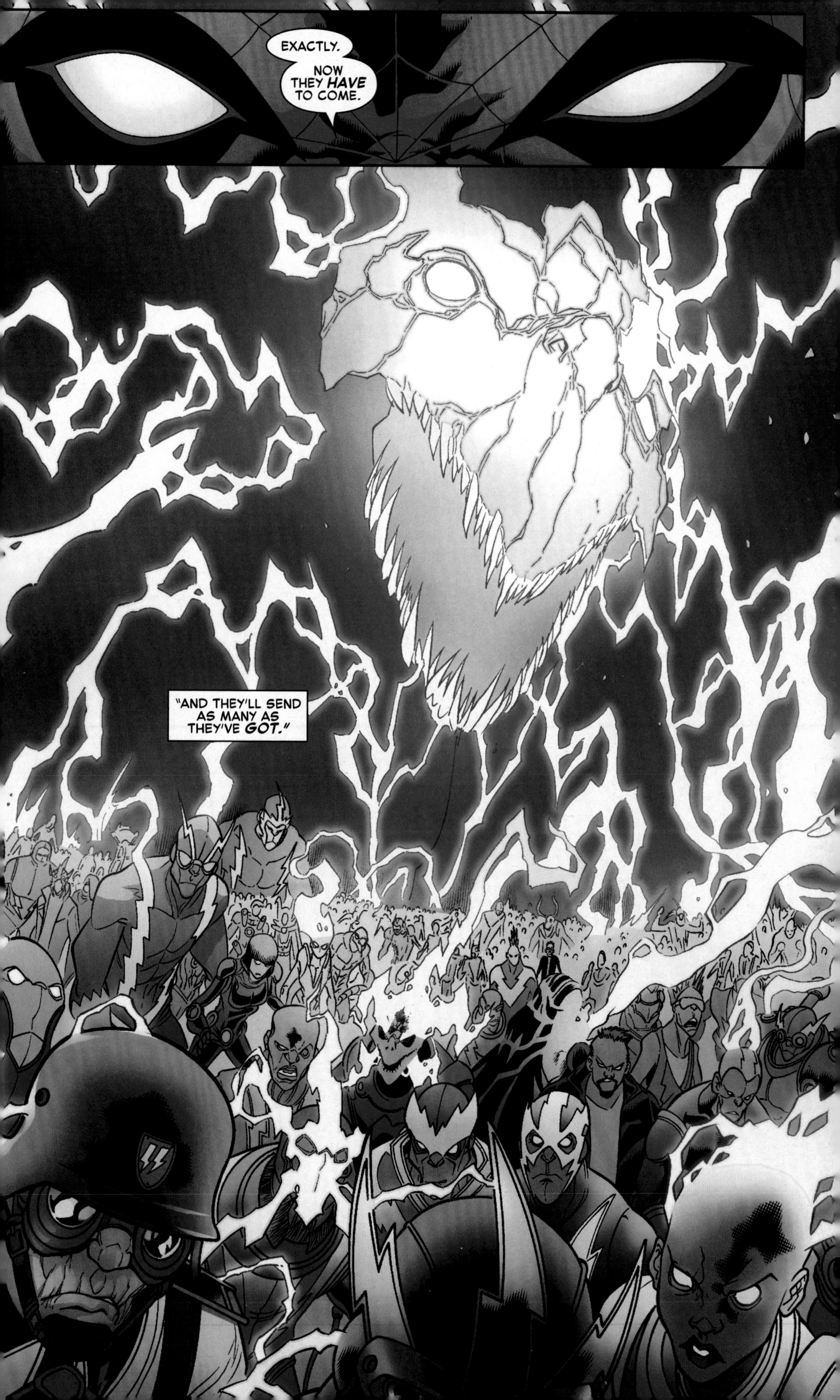
EXACTLY.
NOW THEY *HAVE* TO COME.
"AND THEY'LL SEND AS MANY AS THEY'VE *GOT*."

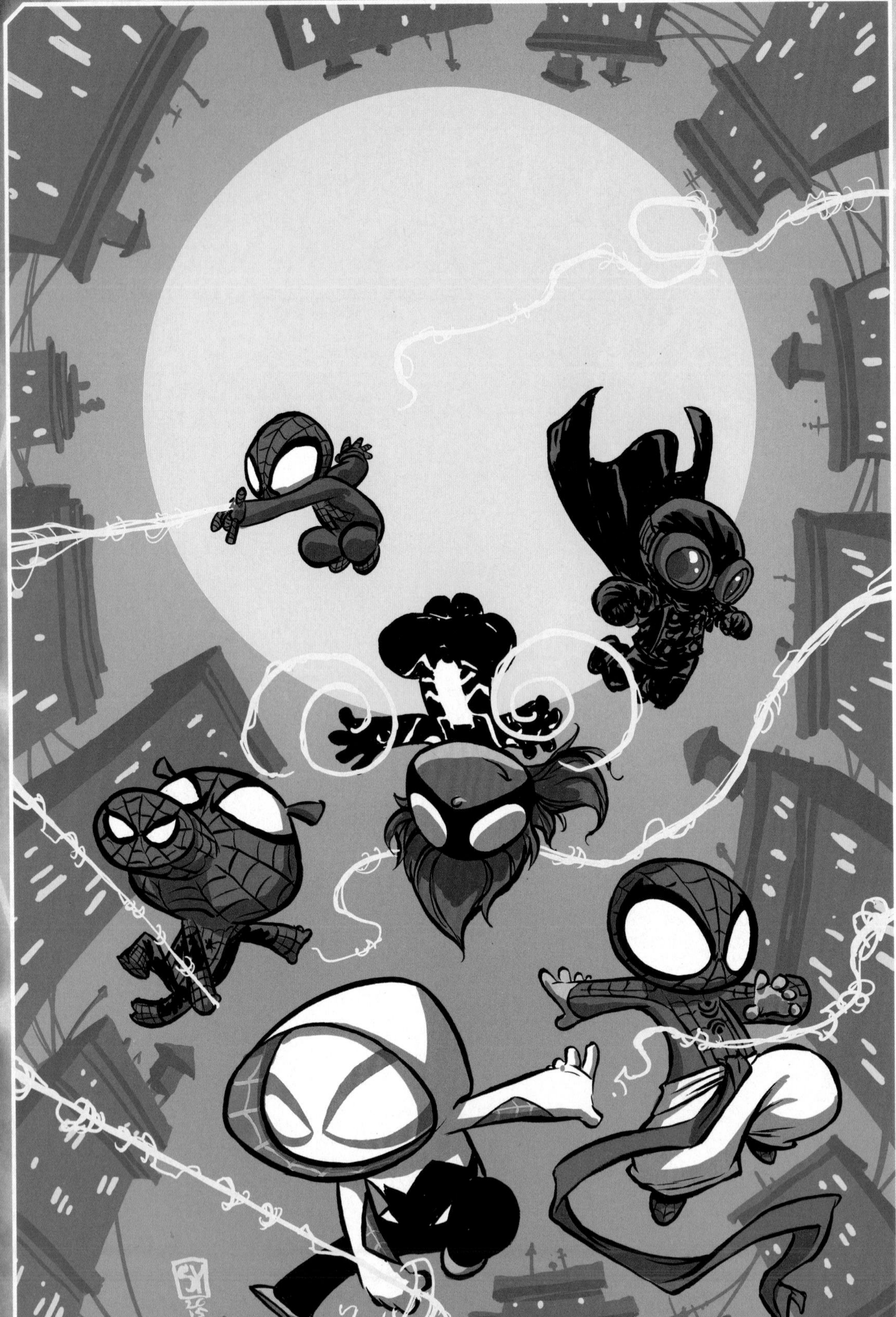

#1 VARIANT BY SKOTTIE YOUNG

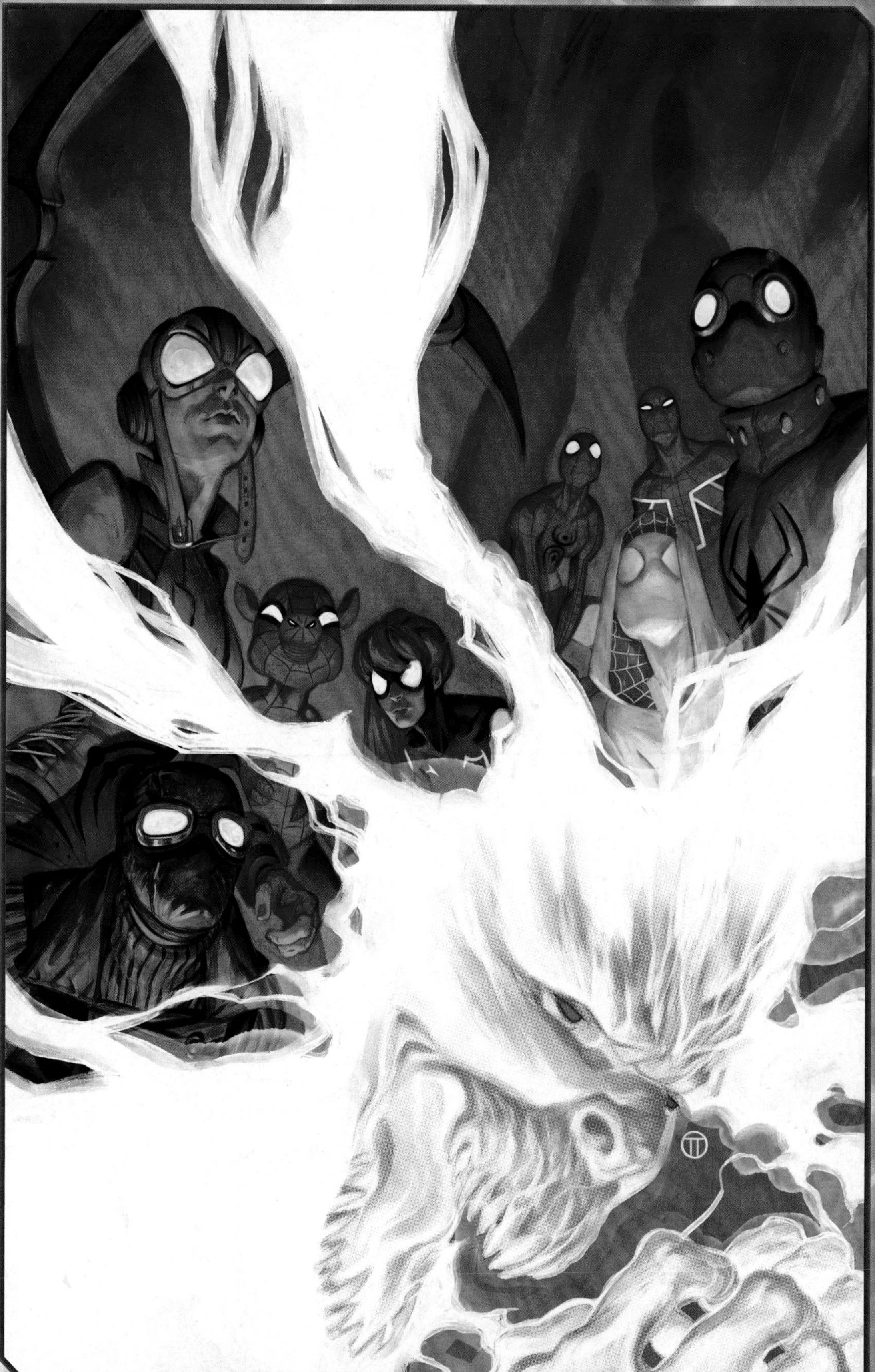

PART FIVE : INSULATION

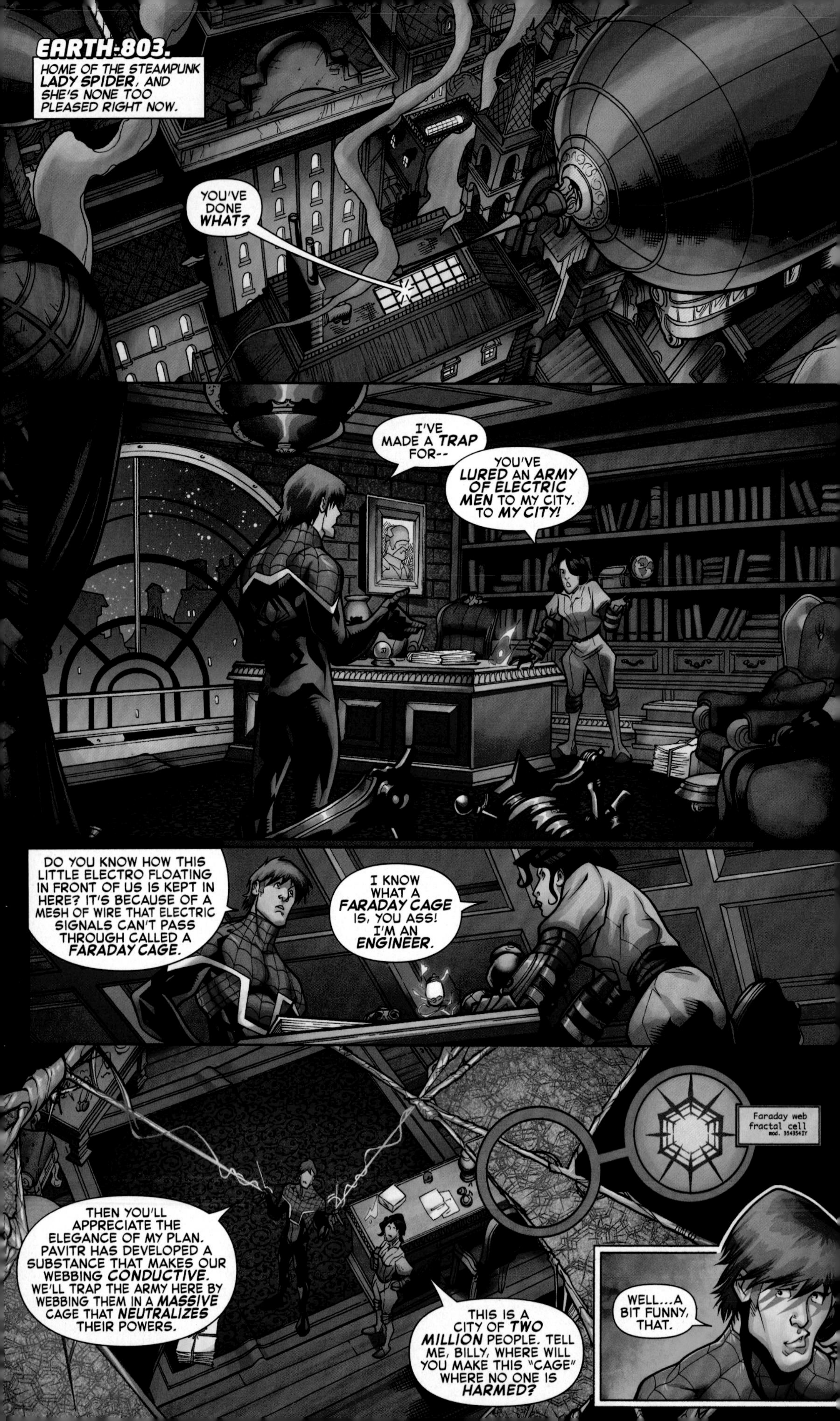
EARTH-803.
HOME OF THE STEAMPUNK LADY SPIDER, AND SHE'S NONE TOO PLEASED RIGHT NOW.
YOU'VE DONE WHAT?
I'VE MADE A TRAP FOR--
YOU'VE LURED AN ARMY OF ELECTRIC MEN TO MY CITY. TO MY CITY!
DO YOU KNOW HOW THIS LITTLE ELECTRO FLOATING IN FRONT OF US IS KEPT IN HERE? IT'S BECAUSE OF A MESH OF WIRE THAT ELECTRIC SIGNALS CAN'T PASS THROUGH CALLED A FARADAY CAGE.
I KNOW WHAT A FARADAY CAGE IS, YOU ASS! I'M AN ENGINEER.
Faraday web fractal cell
THEN YOU'LL APPRECIATE THE ELEGANCE OF MY PLAN. PAVITR HAS DEVELOPED A SUBSTANCE THAT MAKES OUR WEBBING CONDUCTIVE. WE'LL TRAP THE ARMY HERE BY WEBBING THEM IN A MASSIVE CAGE THAT NEUTRALIZES THEIR POWERS.
THIS IS A CITY OF TWO MILLION PEOPLE. TELL ME, BILLY, WHERE WILL YOU MAKE THIS "CAGE" WHERE NO ONE IS HARMED?
WELL...A BIT FUNNY, THAT.

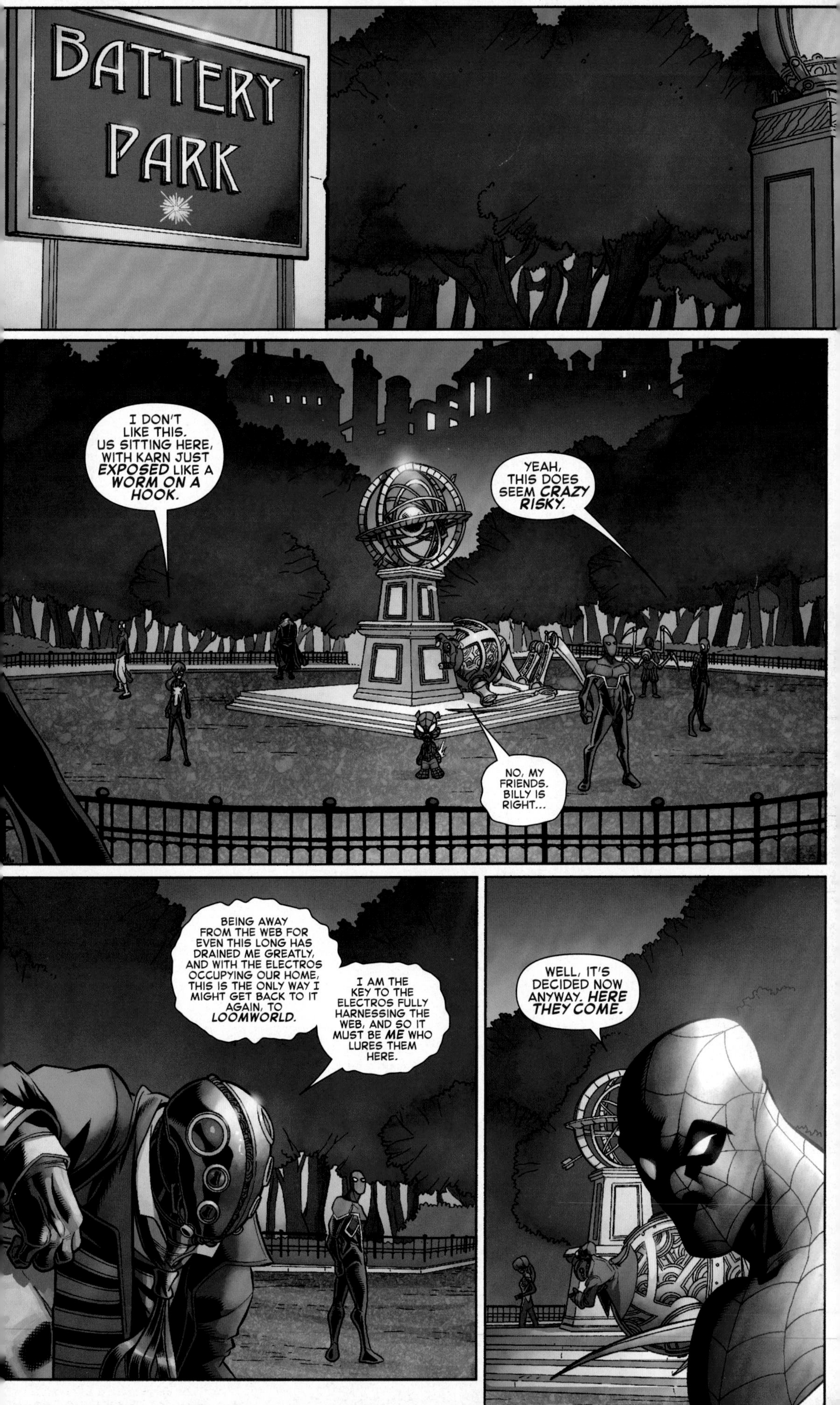
BATTERY PARK
I DON'T LIKE THIS. US SITTING HERE, WITH KARN JUST EXPOSED LIKE A WORM ON A HOOK.
YEAH, THIS DOES SEEM CRAZY RISKY.
NO, MY FRIENDS. BILLY IS RIGHT...
BEING AWAY FROM THE WEB FOR EVEN THIS LONG HAS DRAINED ME GREATLY, AND WITH THE ELECTROS OCCUPYING OUR HOME, THIS IS THE ONLY WAY I MIGHT GET BACK TO IT AGAIN, TO LOOMWORLD.
I AM THE KEY TO THE ELECTROS FULLY HARNESSING THE WEB, AND SO IT MUST BE ME WHO LURES THEM HERE.
WELL, IT'S DECIDED NOW ANYWAY. HERE THEY COME.

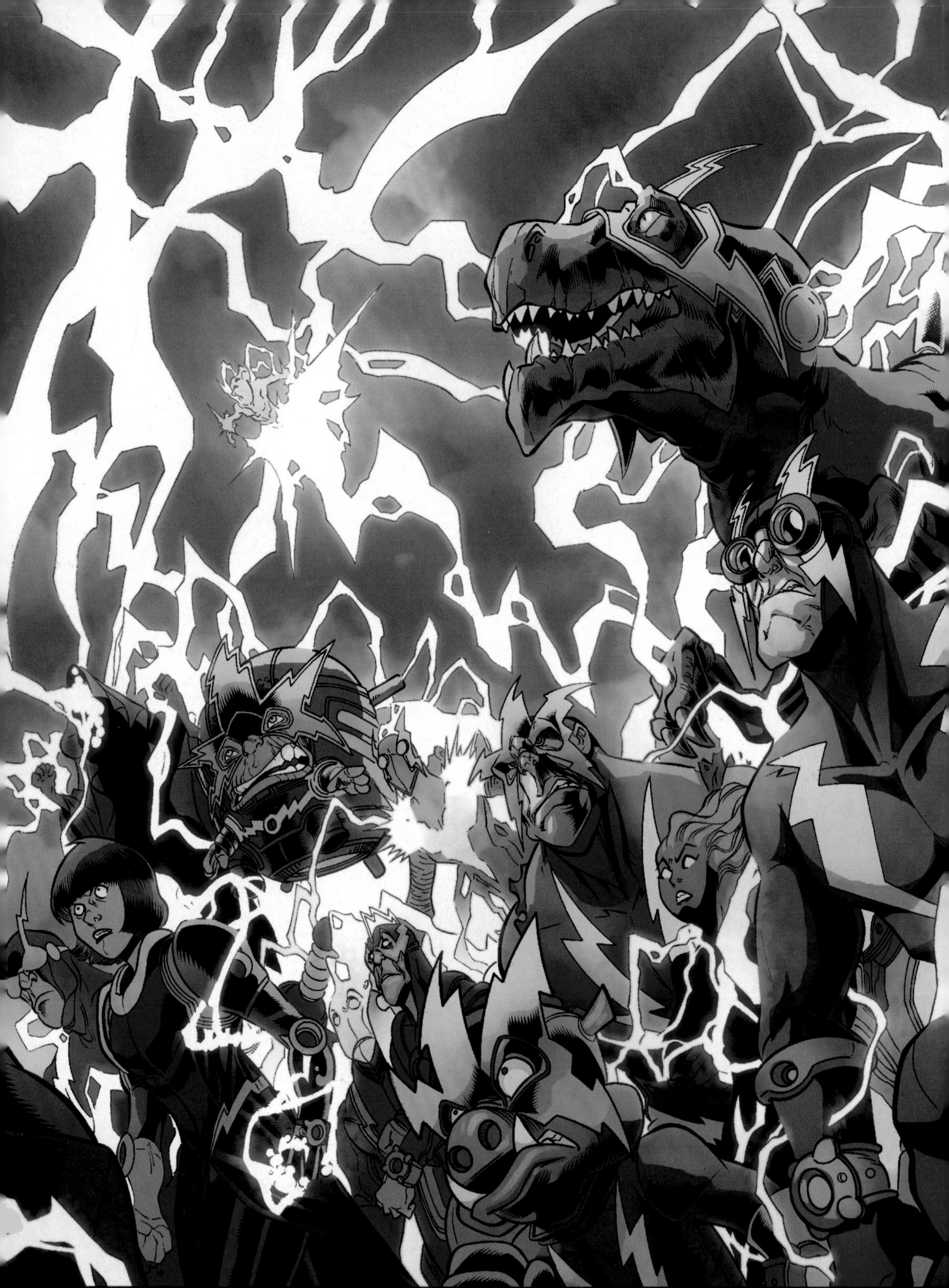

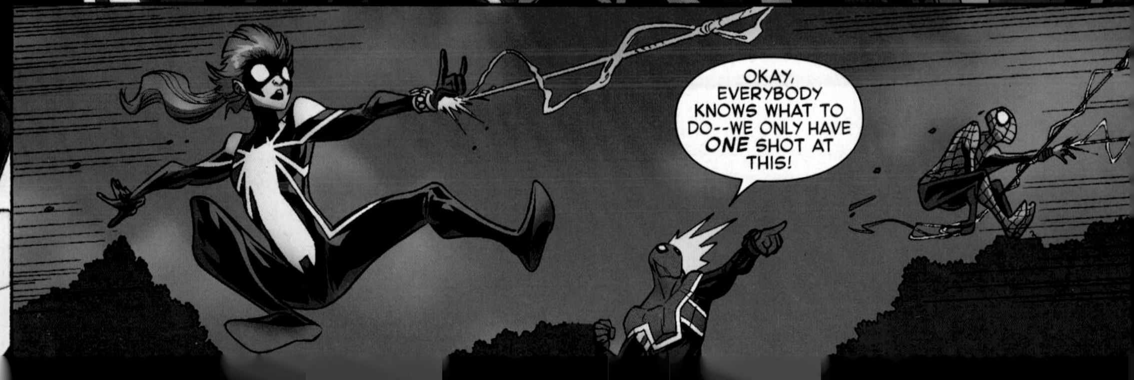
OKAY, EVERYBODY KNOWS WHAT TO DO--WE ONLY HAVE ONE SHOT AT THIS!

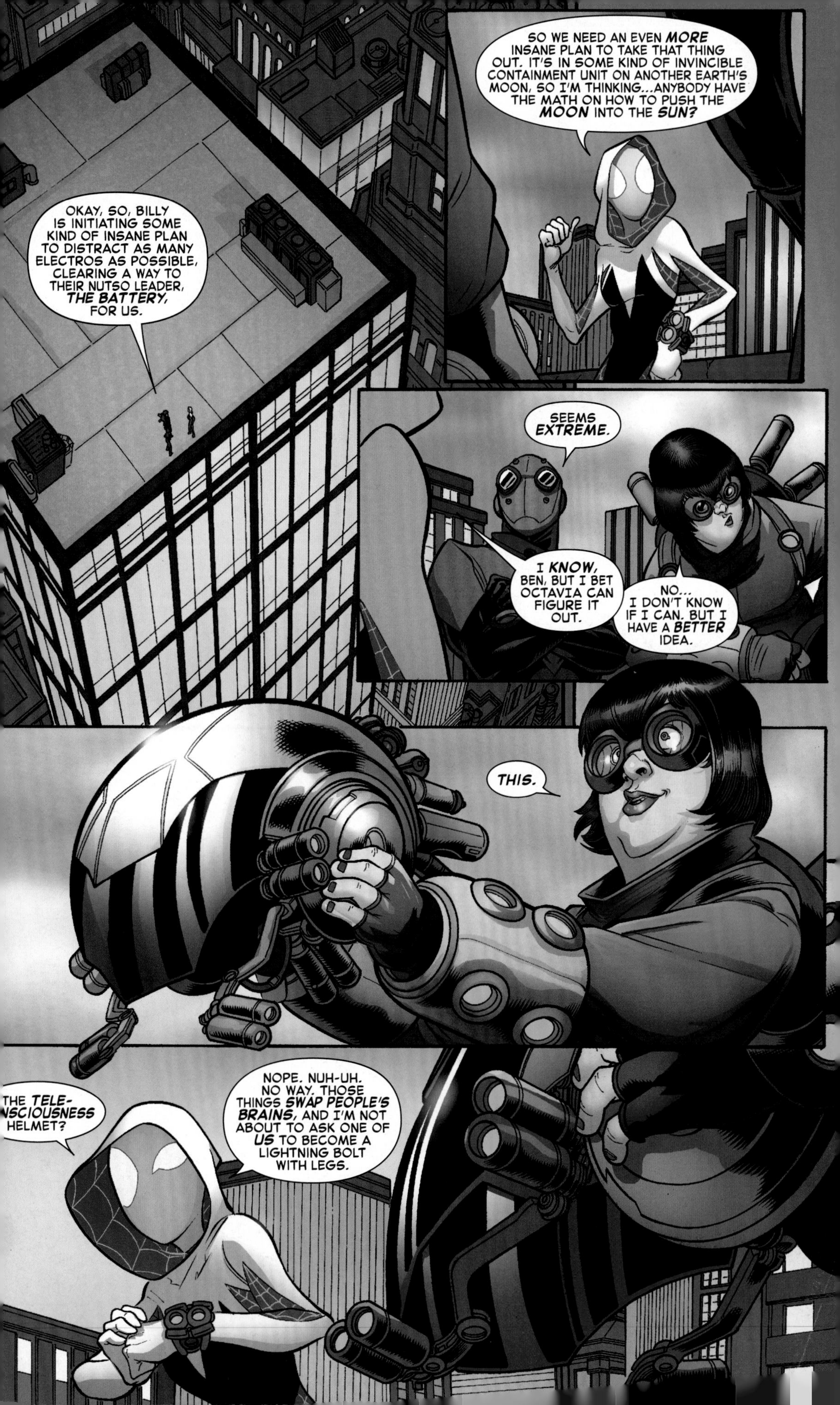

OKAY, SO, BILLY IS INITIATING SOME KIND OF INSANE PLAN TO DISTRACT AS MANY ELECTROS AS POSSIBLE, CLEARING A WAY TO THEIR NUTSO LEADER, THE BATTERY, FOR US.
SO WE NEED AN EVEN MORE INSANE PLAN TO TAKE THAT THING OUT. IT'S IN SOME KIND OF INVINCIBLE CONTAINMENT UNIT ON ANOTHER EARTH'S MOON, SO I'M THINKING...ANYBODY HAVE THE MATH ON HOW TO PUSH THE MOON INTO THE SUN?
SEEMS EXTREME.
I KNOW, BEN, BUT I BET OCTAVIA CAN FIGURE IT OUT.
NO... I DON'T KNOW IF I CAN. BUT I HAVE A BETTER IDEA.
THIS.
THE TELE-NSCIOUSNESS HELMET?
NOPE. NUH-UH. NO WAY. THOSE THINGS SWAP PEOPLE'S BRAINS, AND I'M NOT ABOUT TO ASK ONE OF US TO BECOME A LIGHTNING BOLT WITH LEGS.

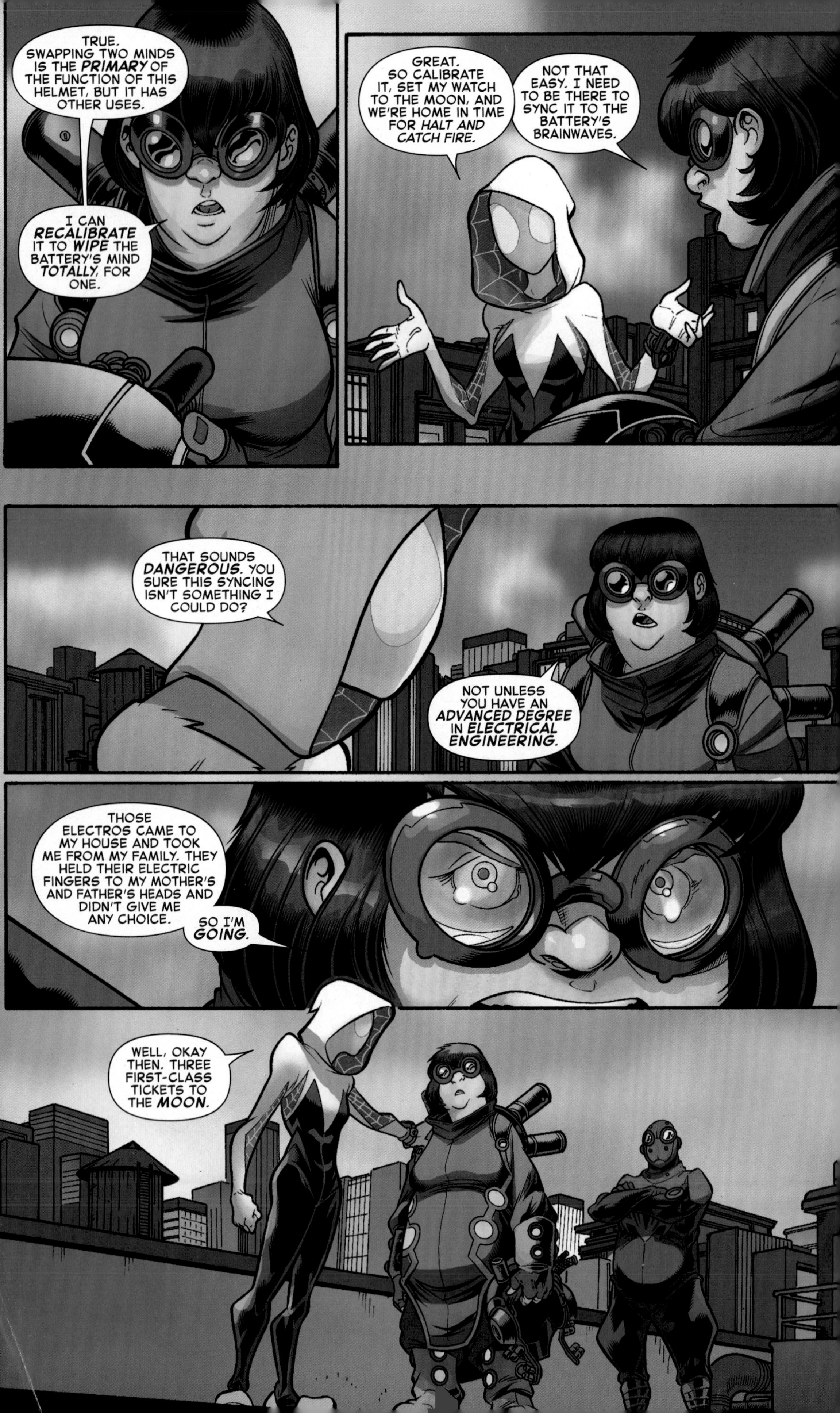
TRUE. SWAPPING TWO MINDS IS THE PRIMARY OF THE FUNCTION OF THIS HELMET, BUT IT HAS OTHER USES.
I CAN RECALIBRATE IT TO WIPE THE BATTERY'S MIND TOTALLY, FOR ONE.
GREAT. SO CALIBRATE IT, SET MY WATCH TO THE MOON, AND WE'RE HOME IN TIME FOR HALT AND CATCH FIRE.
NOT THAT EASY. I NEED TO BE THERE TO SYNC IT TO THE BATTERY'S BRAINWAVES.
THAT SOUNDS DANGEROUS. YOU SURE THIS SYNCING ISN'T SOMETHING I COULD DO?
NOT UNLESS YOU HAVE AN ADVANCED DEGREE IN ELECTRICAL ENGINEERING.
THOSE ELECTROS CAME TO MY HOUSE AND TOOK ME FROM MY FAMILY. THEY HELD THEIR ELECTRIC FINGERS TO MY MOTHER'S AND FATHER'S HEADS AND DIDN'T GIVE ME ANY CHOICE.
SO I'M GOING.
WELL, OKAY THEN. THREE FIRST-CLASS TICKETS TO THE MOON.

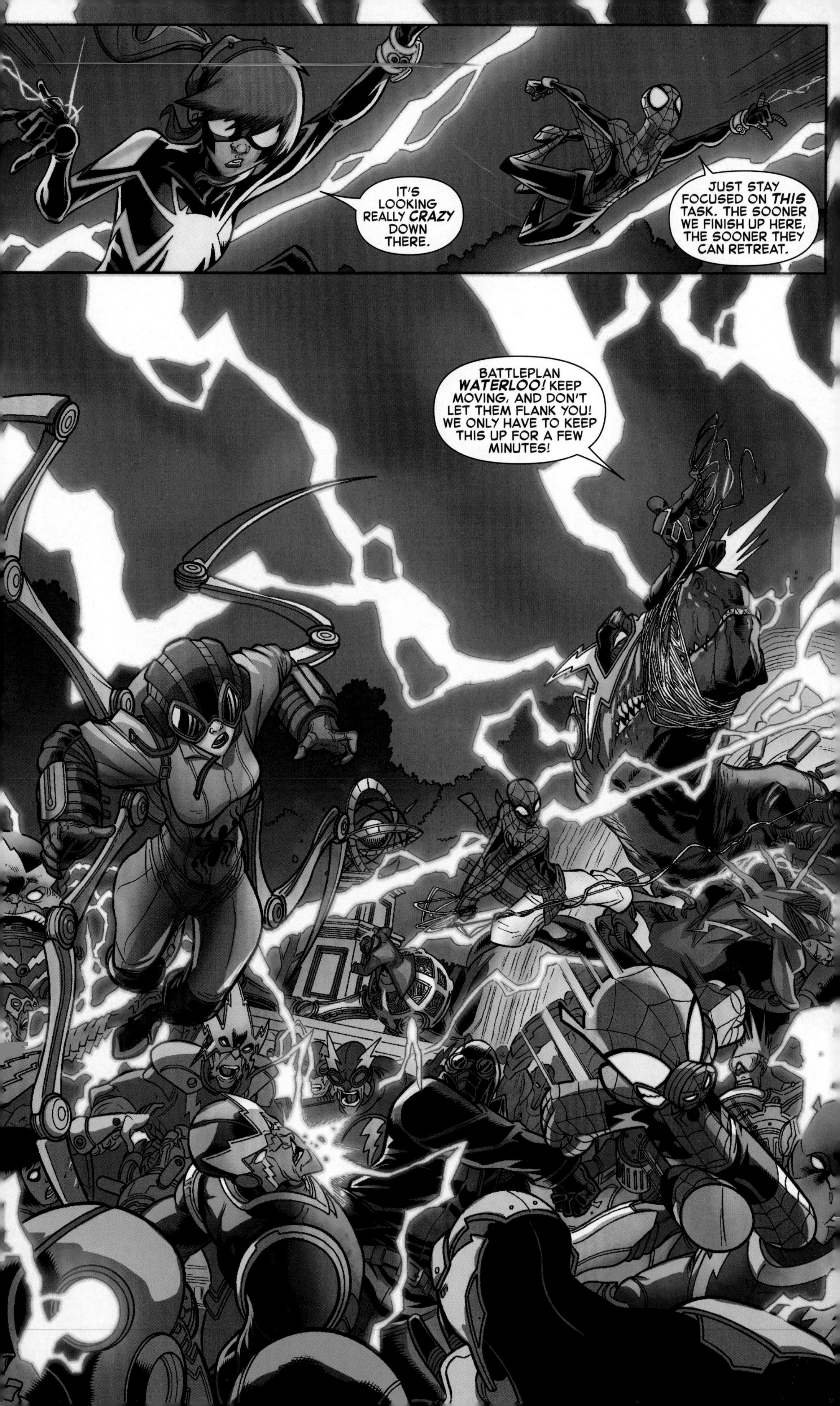
IT'S LOOKING REALLY CRAZY DOWN THERE.
JUST STAY FOCUSED ON THIS TASK. THE SOONER WE FINISH UP HERE, THE SOONER THEY CAN RETREAT.
BATTLEPLAN WATERLOO! KEEP MOVING, AND DON'T LET THEM FLANK YOU! WE ONLY HAVE TO KEEP THIS UP FOR A FEW MINUTES!

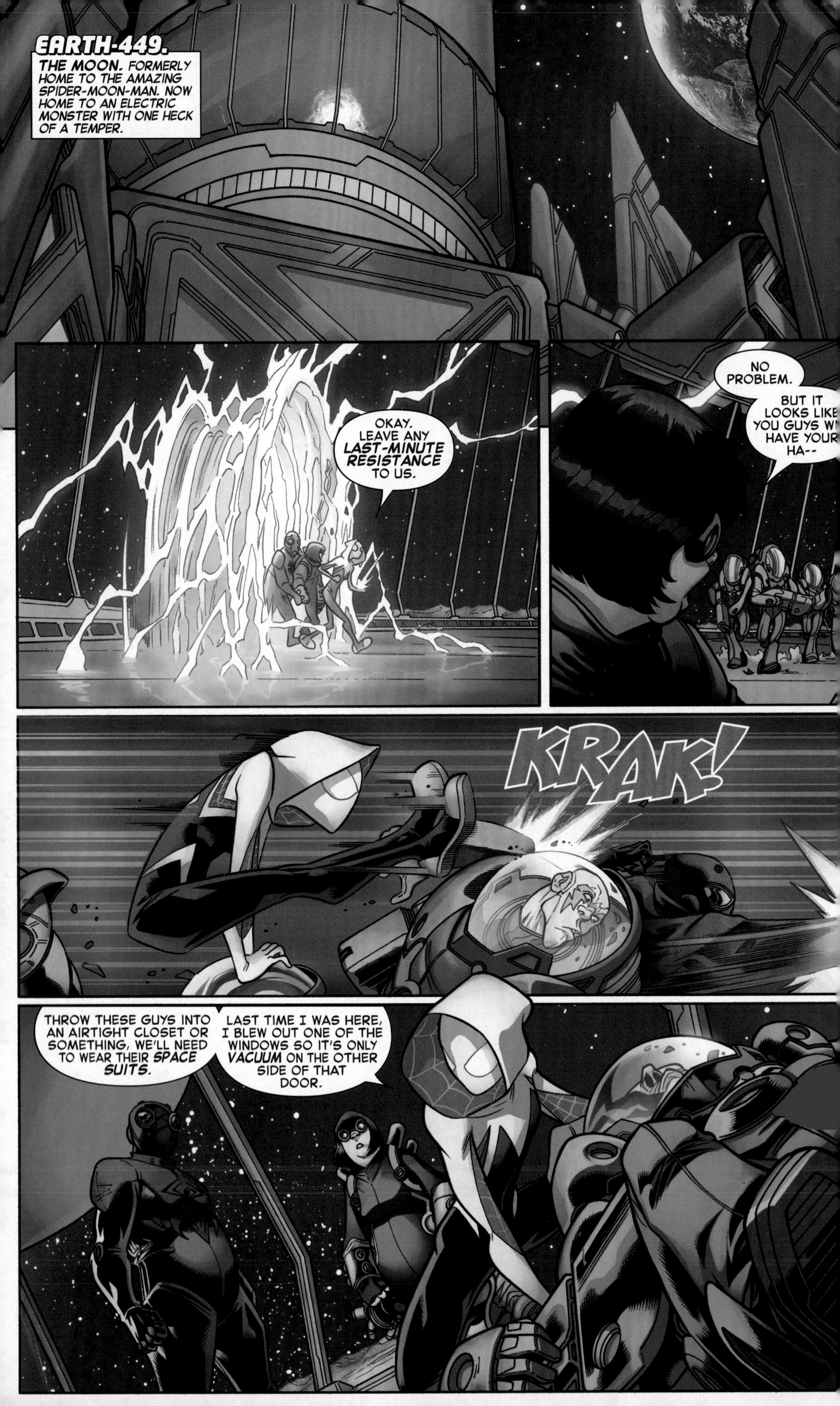
EARTH-449.
THE MOON. FORMERLY HOME TO THE AMAZING SPIDER-MOON-MAN. NOW HOME TO AN ELECTRIC MONSTER WITH ONE HECK OF A TEMPER.
OKAY. LEAVE ANY LAST-MINUTE RESISTANCE TO US.
NO PROBLEM.
BUT IT LOOKS LIKE YOU GUYS W HAVE YOUR HA--
KRAK!
THROW THESE GUYS INTO AN AIRTIGHT CLOSET OR SOMETHING, WE'LL NEED TO WEAR THEIR SPACE SUITS.
LAST TIME I WAS HERE, I BLEW OUT ONE OF THE WINDOWS SO IT'S ONLY VACUUM ON THE OTHER SIDE OF THAT DOOR.

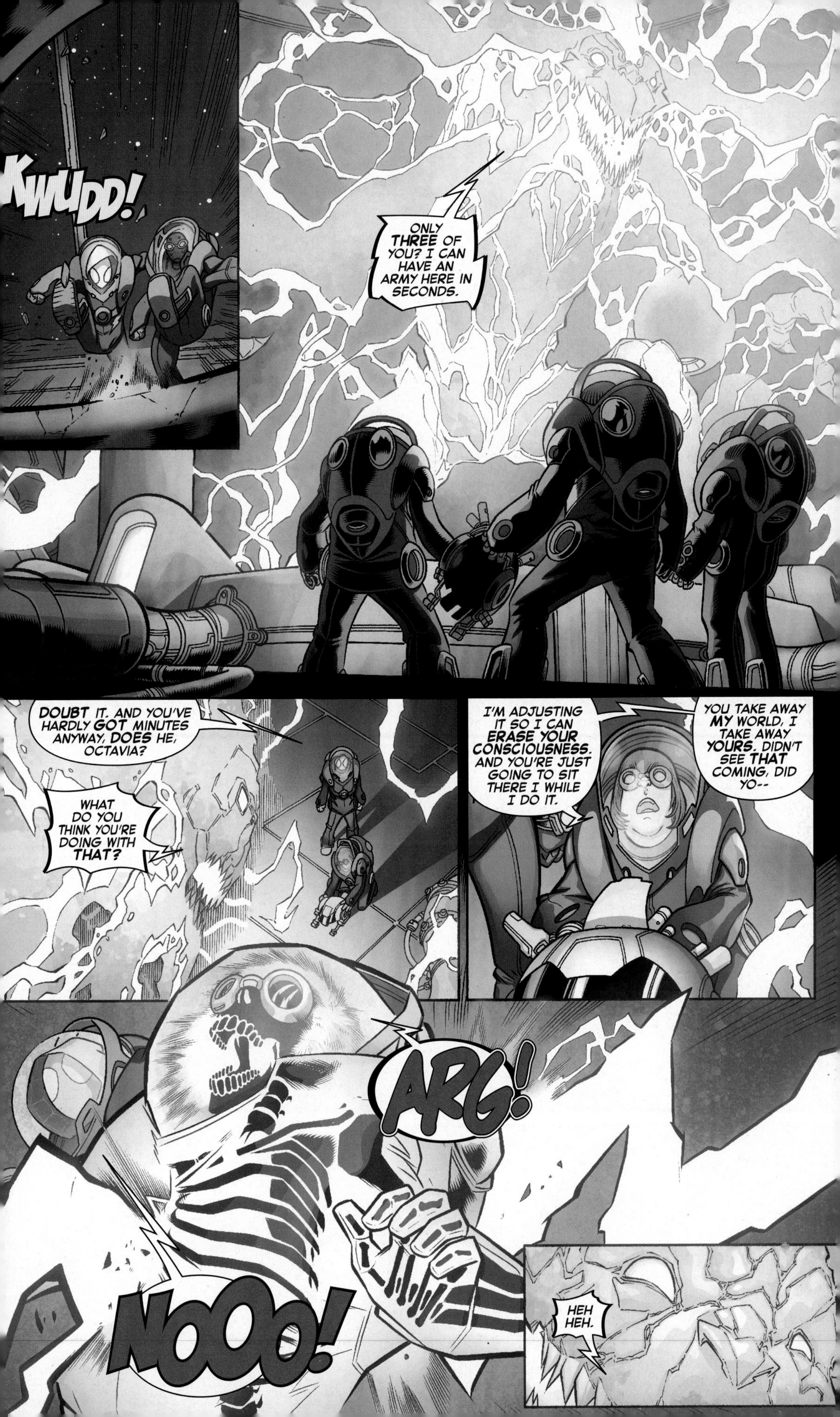
KWUDD!
ONLY THREE OF YOU? I CAN HAVE AN ARMY HERE IN SECONDS.
DOUBT IT. AND YOU'VE HARDLY GOT MINUTES ANYWAY, DOES HE, OCTAVIA?
WHAT DO YOU THINK YOU'RE DOING WITH THAT?
I'M ADJUSTING IT SO I CAN ERASE YOUR CONSCIOUSNESS. AND YOU'RE JUST GOING TO SIT THERE I WHILE I DO IT.
YOU TAKE AWAY MY WORLD, I TAKE AWAY YOURS. DIDN'T SEE THAT COMING, DID YO--
ARG!
NOOOO!
HEH HEH.

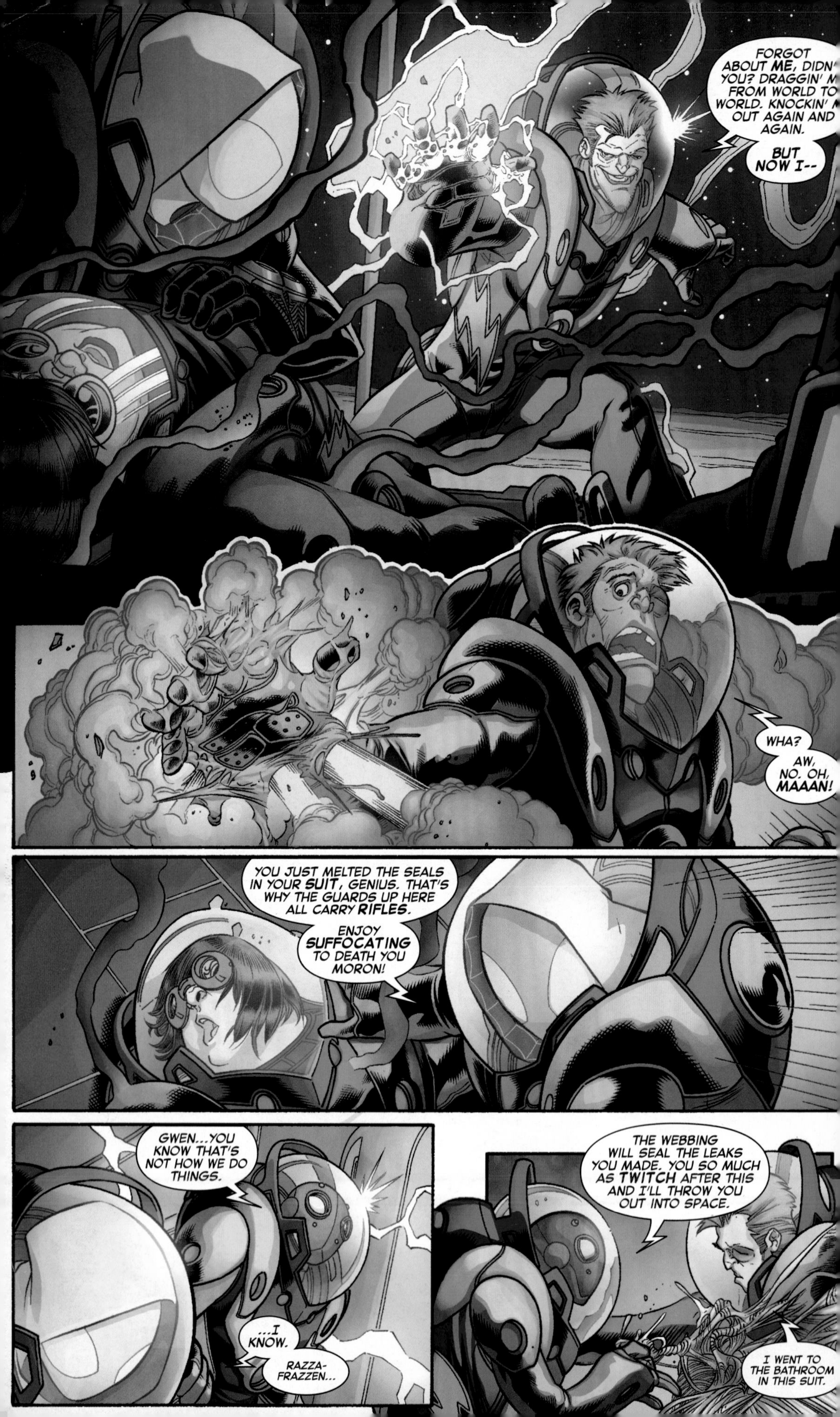

FORGOT ABOUT ME, DIDN' YOU? DRAGGIN' M FROM WORLD TO WORLD. KNOCKIN' M OUT AGAIN AND AGAIN.
BUT NOW I--
WHA?
AW, NO. OH, MAAAN!
YOU JUST MELTED THE SEALS IN YOUR SUIT, GENIUS. THAT'S WHY THE GUARDS UP HERE ALL CARRY RIFLES.
ENJOY SUFFOCATING TO DEATH YOU MORON!
GWEN...YOU KNOW THAT'S NOT HOW WE DO THINGS.
...I KNOW.
RAZZA-FRAZZEN...
THE WEBBING WILL SEAL THE LEAKS YOU MADE. YOU SO MUCH AS TWITCH AFTER THIS AND I'LL THROW YOU OUT INTO SPACE.
I WENT TO THE BATHROOM IN THIS SUIT.

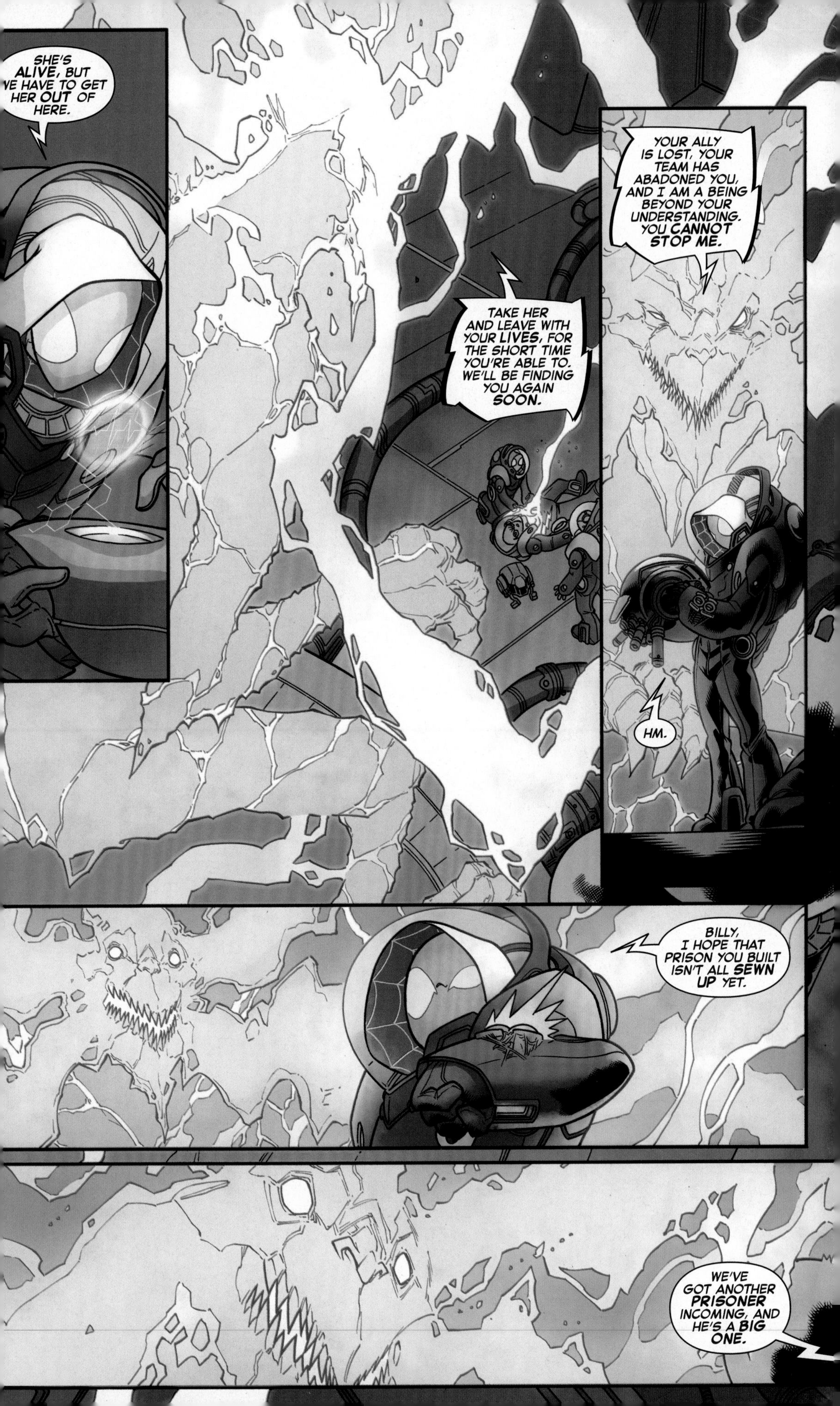

SHE'S ALIVE, BUT WE HAVE TO GET HER OUT OF HERE.
TAKE HER AND LEAVE WITH YOUR LIVES, FOR THE SHORT TIME YOU'RE ABLE TO. WE'LL BE FINDING YOU AGAIN SOON.
YOUR ALLY IS LOST, YOUR TEAM HAS ABADONED YOU, AND I AM A BEING BEYOND YOUR UNDERSTANDING. YOU CANNOT STOP ME.
HM.
BILLY, I HOPE THAT PRISON YOU BUILT ISN'T ALL SEWN UP YET.
WE'VE GOT ANOTHER PRISONER INCOMING, AND HE'S A BIG ONE.

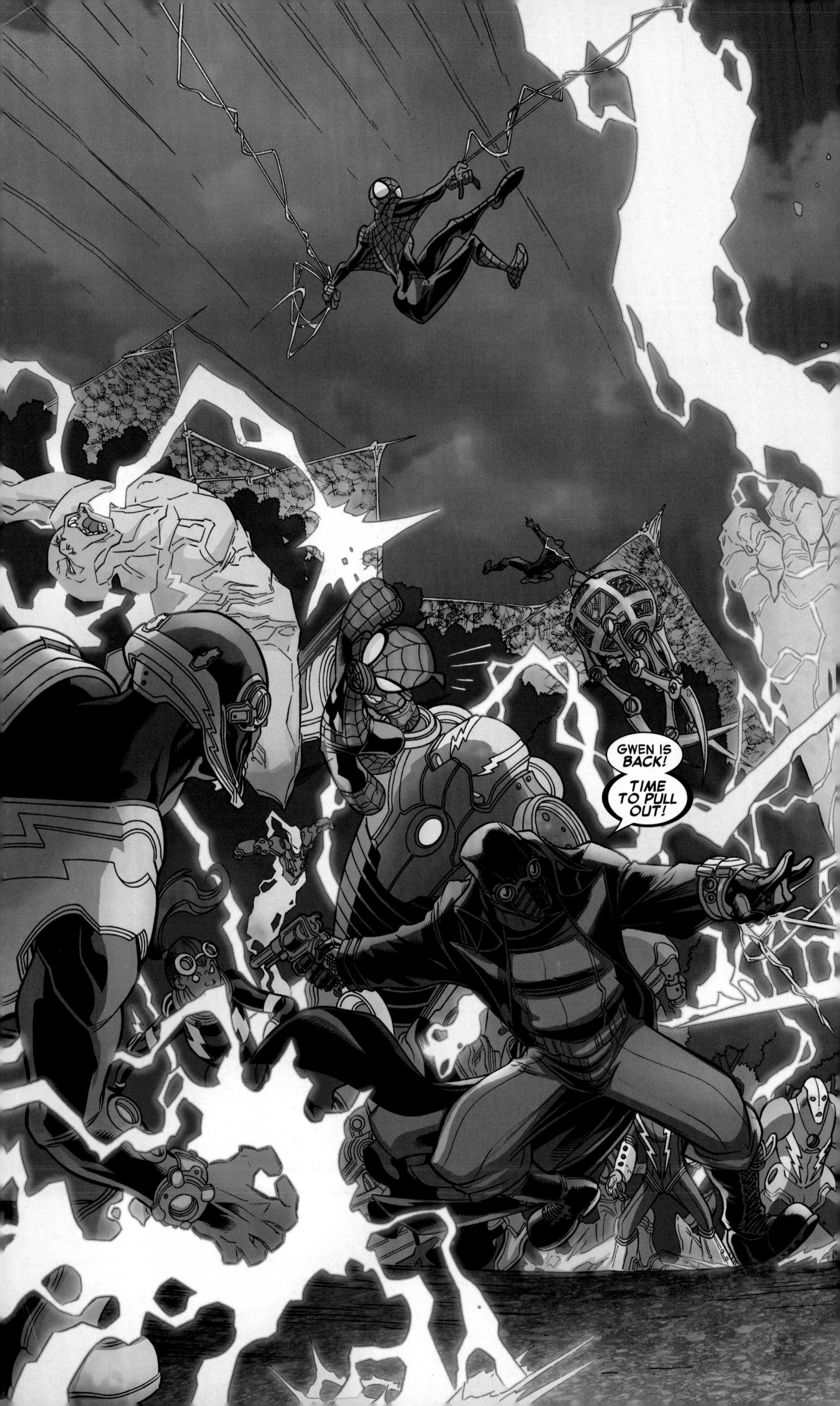
GWEN IS BACK!
TIME TO PULL OUT!

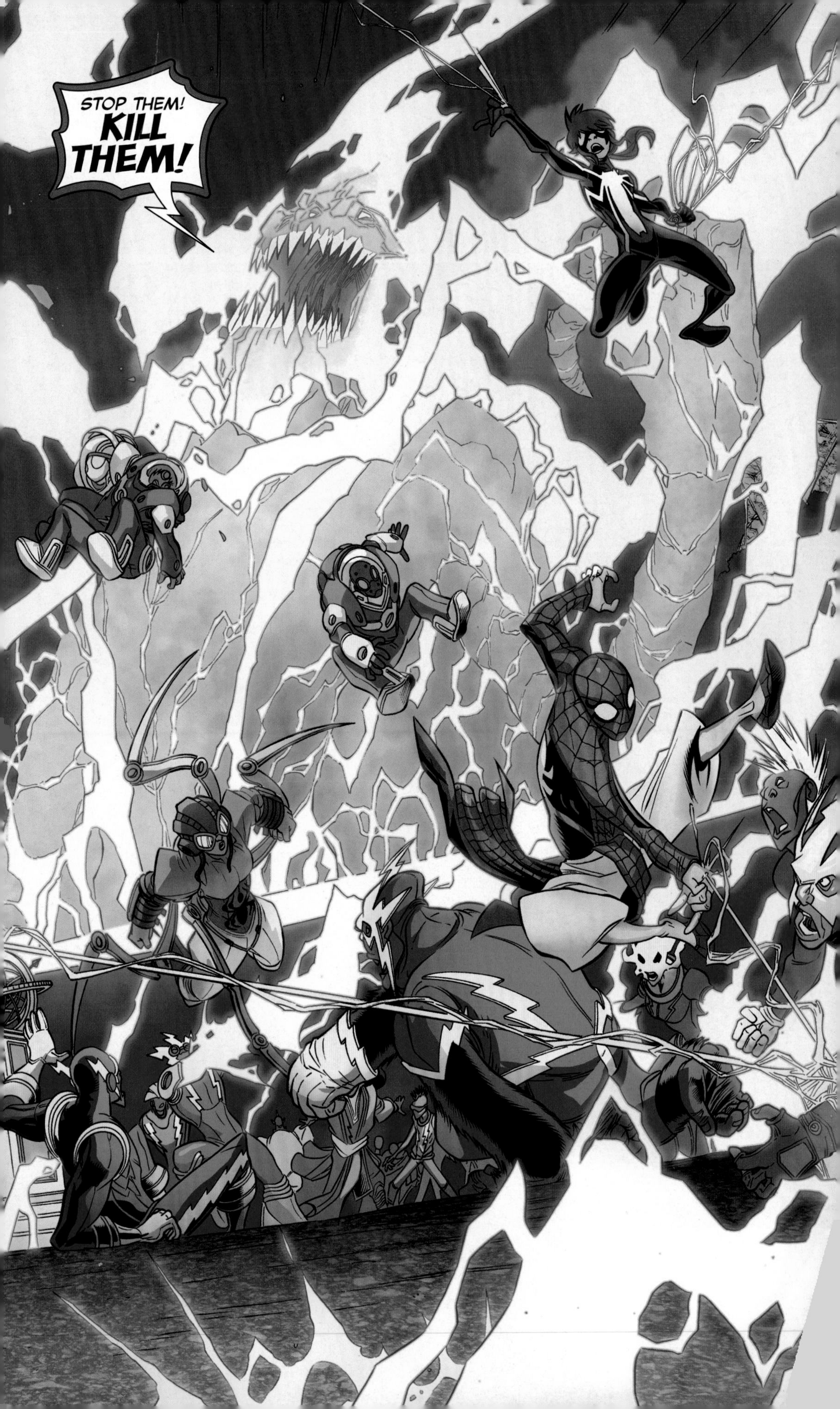
STOP THEM! KILL THEM!

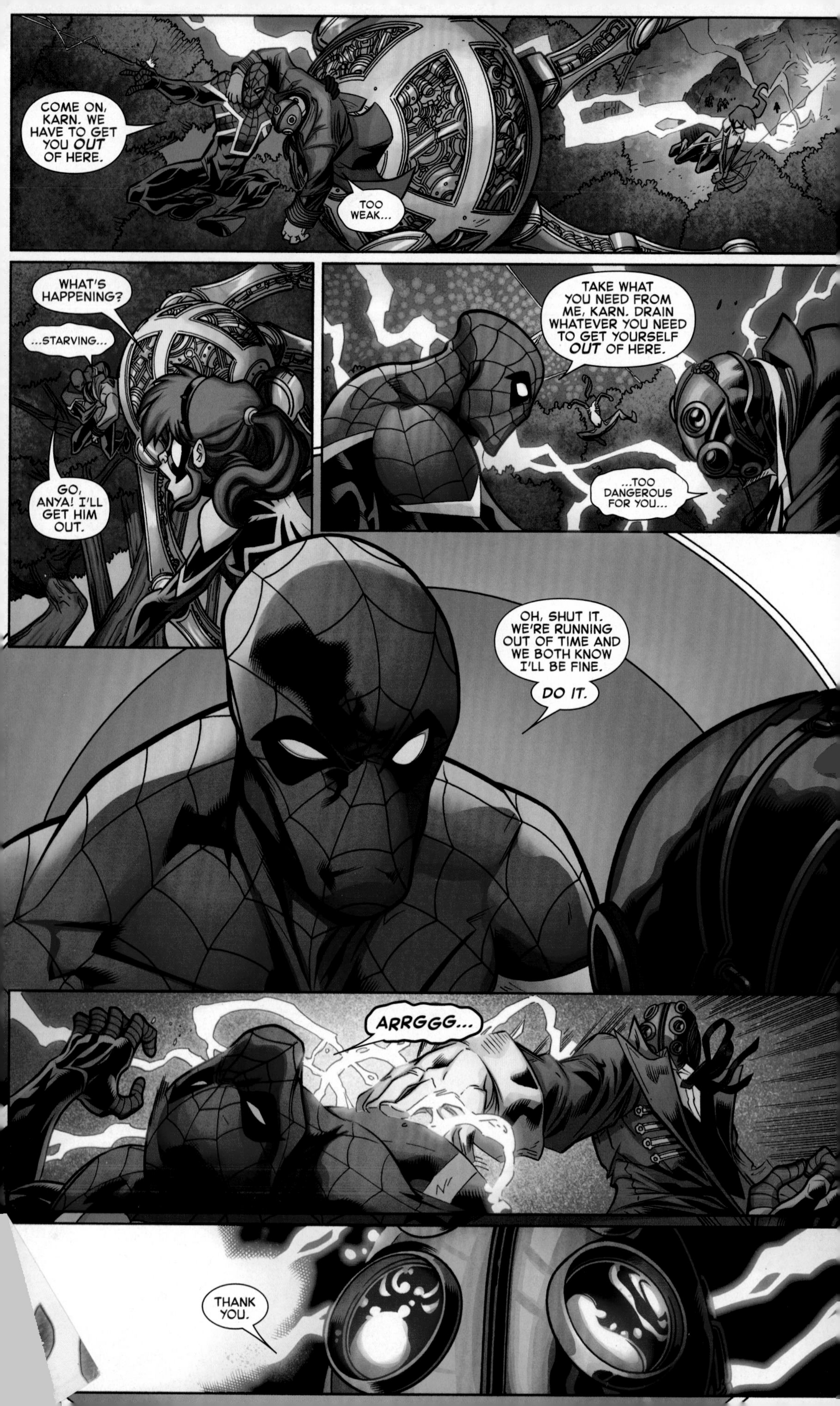
COME ON, KARN. WE HAVE TO GET YOU OUT OF HERE.
TOO WEAK...
WHAT'S HAPPENING?
...STARVING...
GO, ANYA! I'LL GET HIM OUT.
TAKE WHAT YOU NEED FROM ME, KARN. DRAIN WHATEVER YOU NEED TO GET YOURSELF OUT OF HERE.
...TOO DANGEROUS FOR YOU...
OH, SHUT IT. WE'RE RUNNING OUT OF TIME AND WE BOTH KNOW I'LL BE FINE.
DO IT.
ARRGGG...
THANK YOU.

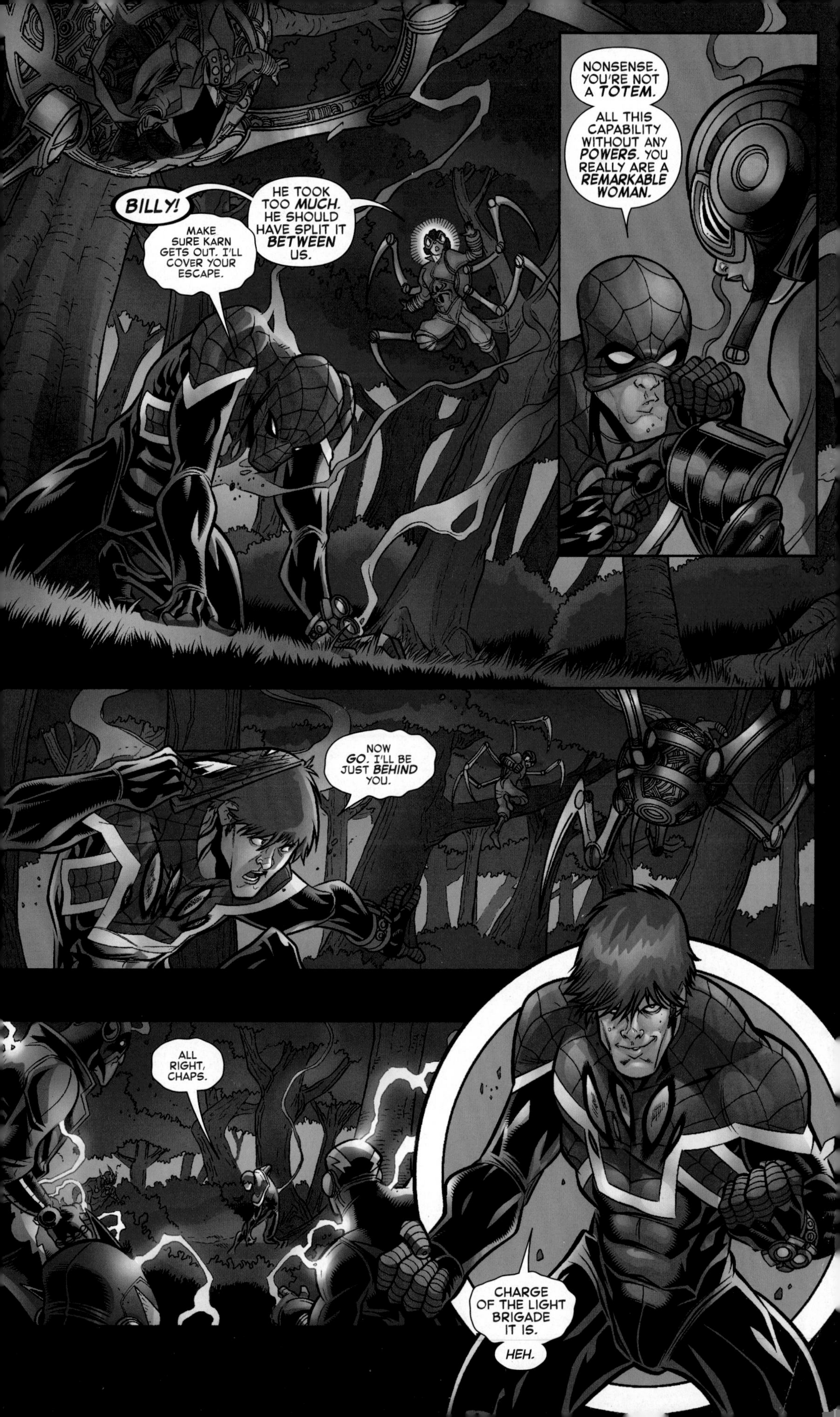
BILLY!
MAKE SURE KARN GETS OUT. I'LL COVER YOUR ESCAPE.
HE TOOK TOO MUCH. HE SHOULD HAVE SPLIT IT BETWEEN US.
NONSENSE. YOU'RE NOT A TOTEM.
ALL THIS CAPABILITY WITHOUT ANY POWERS. YOU REALLY ARE A REMARKABLE WOMAN.
NOW GO. I'LL BE JUST BEHIND YOU.
ALL RIGHT, CHAPS.
CHARGE OF THE LIGHT BRIGADE IT IS.
HEH.

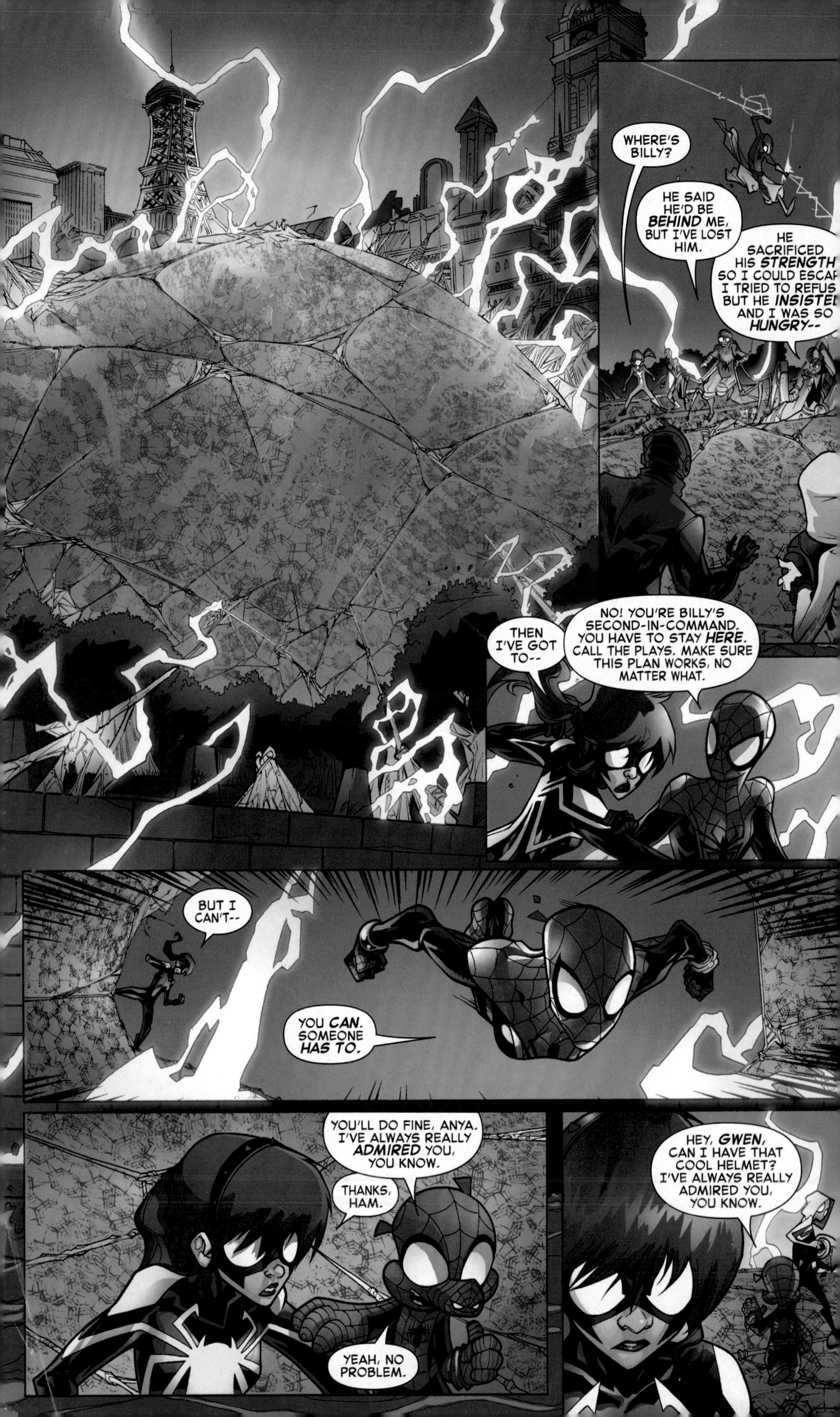
WHERE'S BILLY?
HE SAID HE'D BE BEHIND ME, BUT I'VE LOST HIM.
HE SACRIFICED HIS STRENGTH SO I COULD ESCAP I TRIED TO REFUS BUT HE INSISTE AND I WAS SO HUNGRY--
THEN I'VE GOT TO--
NO! YOU'RE BILLY'S SECOND-IN-COMMAND. YOU HAVE TO STAY HERE. CALL THE PLAYS. MAKE SURE THIS PLAN WORKS, NO MATTER WHAT.
BUT I CAN'T--
YOU CAN. SOMEONE HAS TO.
YOU'LL DO FINE, ANYA. I'VE ALWAYS REALLY ADMIRED YOU, YOU KNOW.
THANKS, HAM.
YEAH, NO PROBLEM.
HEY, GWEN, CAN I HAVE THAT COOL HELMET? I'VE ALWAYS REALLY ADMIRED YOU, YOU KNOW.

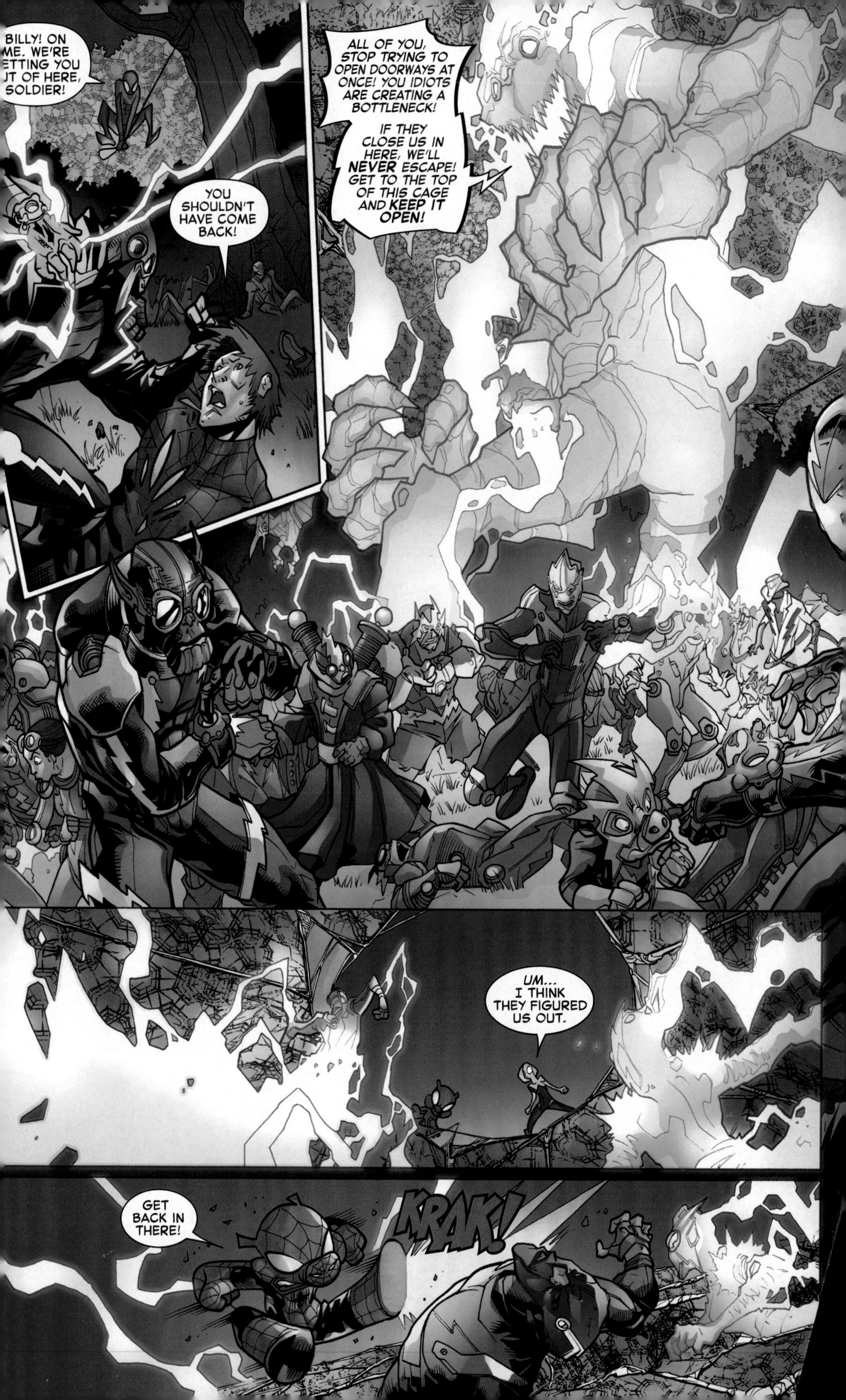
BILLY! ON ME. WE'RE ETTING YOU UT OF HERE, SOLDIER!
YOU SHOULDN'T HAVE COME BACK!
ALL OF YOU, STOP TRYING TO OPEN DOORWAYS AT ONCE! YOU IDIOTS ARE CREATING A BOTTLENECK!
IF THEY CLOSE US IN HERE, WE'LL NEVER ESCAPE! GET TO THE TOP OF THIS CAGE AND KEEP IT OPEN!
UM... I THINK THEY FIGURED US OUT.
GET BACK IN THERE!
KRAK!

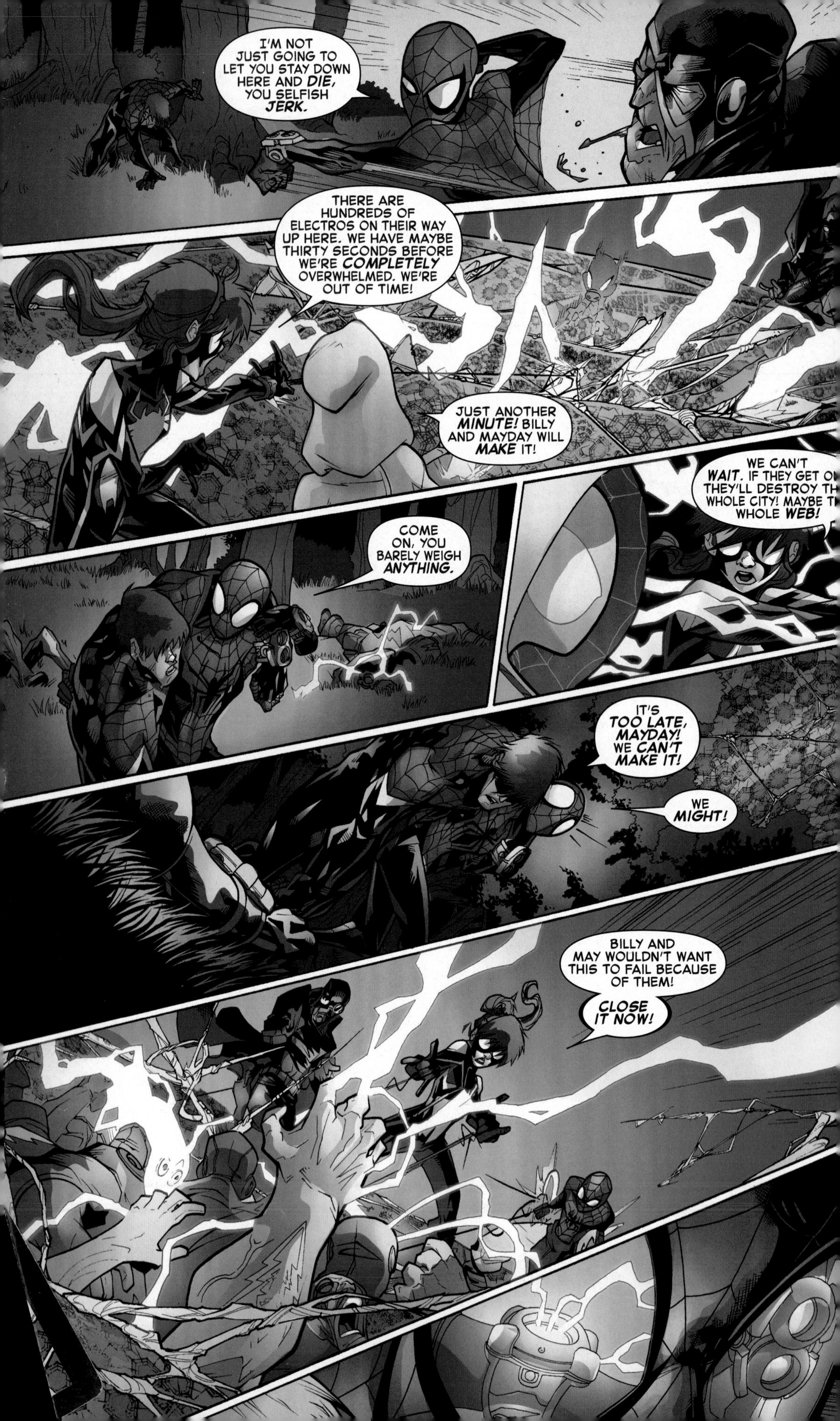
I'M NOT JUST GOING TO LET YOU STAY DOWN HERE AND DIE, YOU SELFISH JERK.
THERE ARE HUNDREDS OF ELECTROS ON THEIR WAY UP HERE. WE HAVE MAYBE THIRTY SECONDS BEFORE WE'RE COMPLETELY OVERWHELMED. WE'RE OUT OF TIME!
JUST ANOTHER MINUTE! BILLY AND MAYDAY WILL MAKE IT!
COME ON, YOU BARELY WEIGH ANYTHING.
IT'S TOO LATE, MAYDAY! WE CAN'T MAKE IT!
WE MIGHT!
BILLY AND MAY WOULDN'T WANT THIS TO FAIL BECAUSE OF THEM!
CLOSE IT NOW!

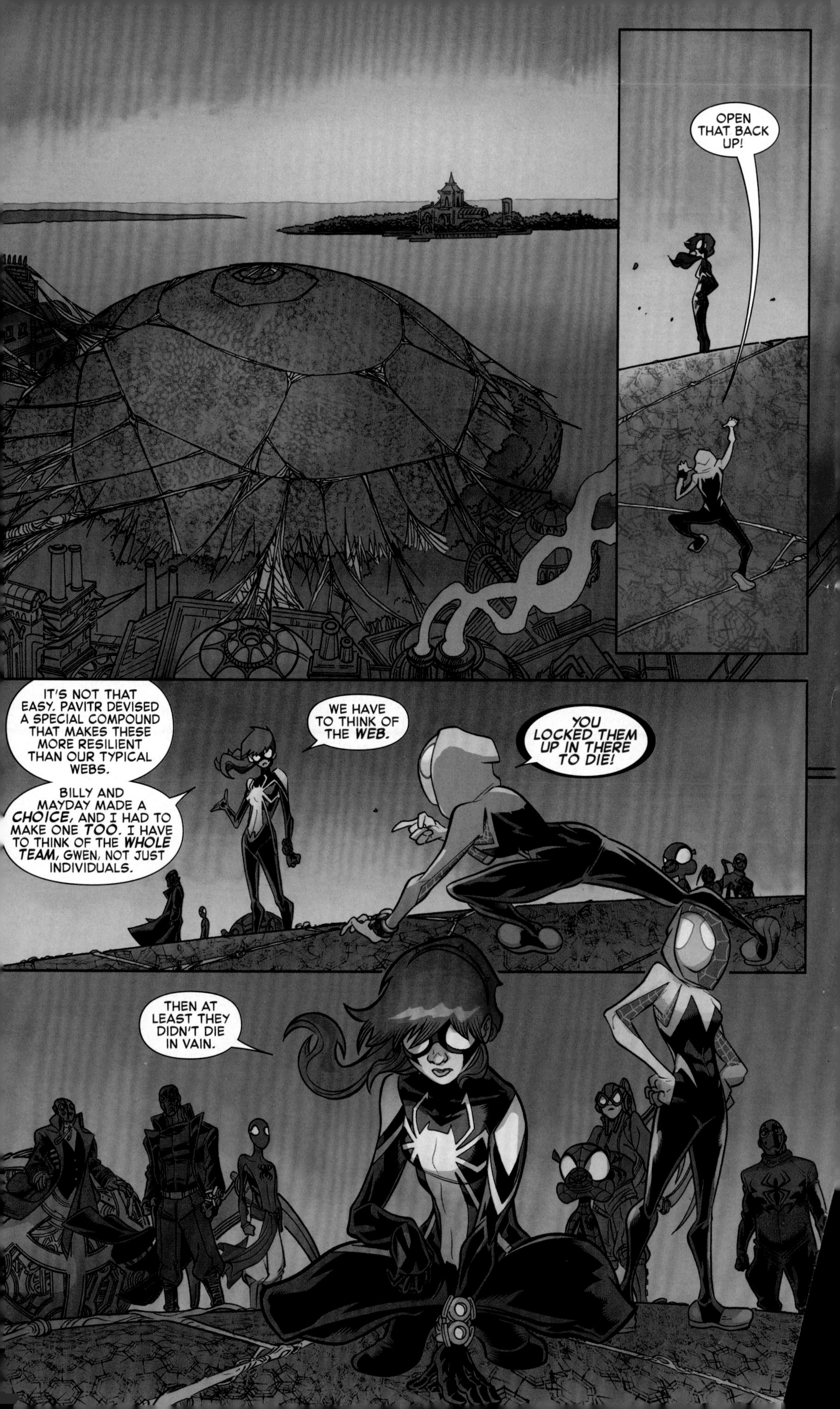

OPEN THAT BACK UP!
IT'S NOT THAT EASY. PAVITR DEVISED A SPECIAL COMPOUND THAT MAKES THESE MORE RESILIENT THAN OUR TYPICAL WEBS.
BILLY AND MAYDAY MADE A CHOICE, AND I HAD TO MAKE ONE TOO. I HAVE TO THINK OF THE WHOLE TEAM, GWEN, NOT JUST INDIVIDUALS.
WE HAVE TO THINK OF THE WEB.
YOU LOCKED THEM UP IN THERE TO DIE!
THEN AT LEAST THEY DIDN'T DIE IN VAIN.

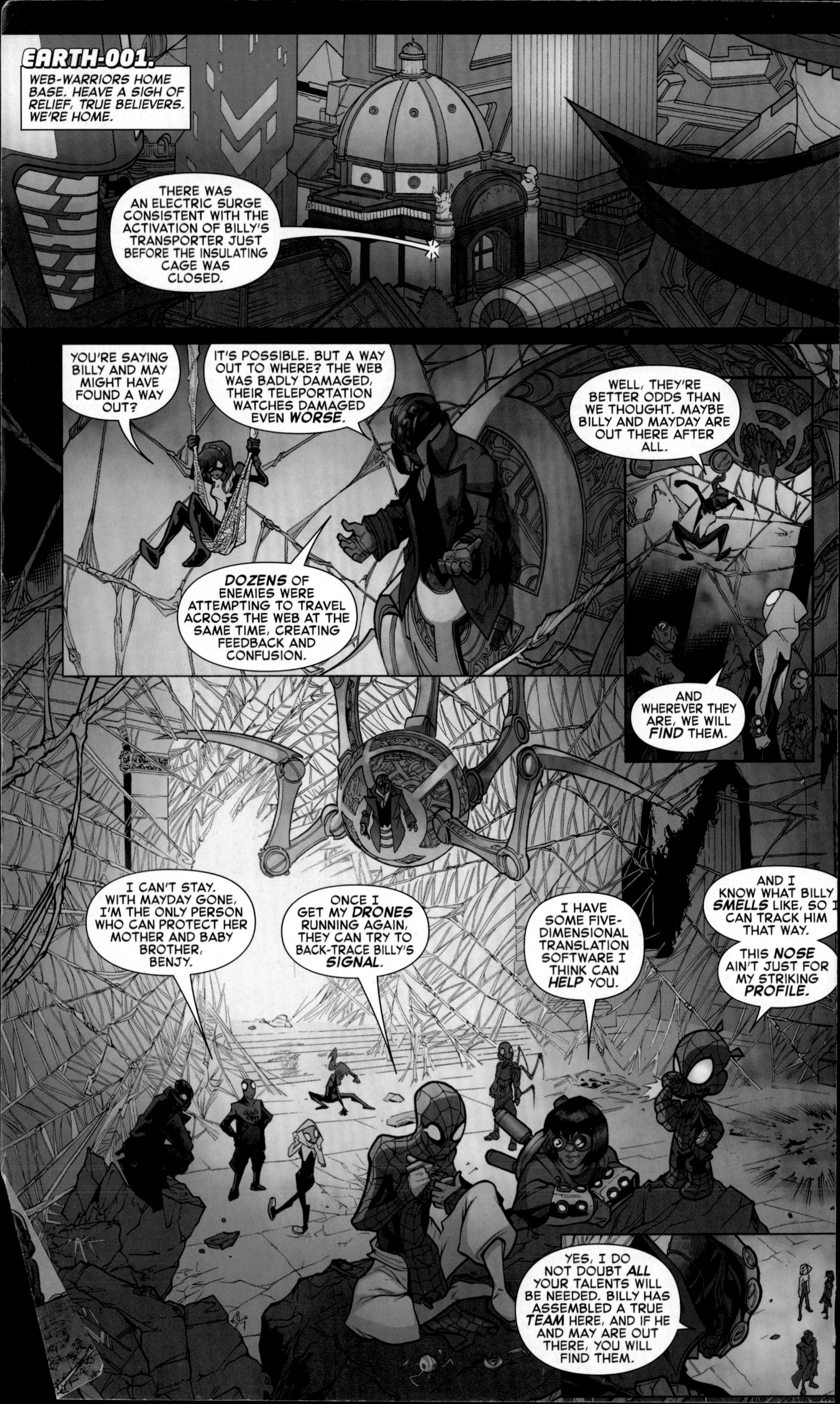
EARTH-001.
WEB-WARRIORS HOME BASE. HEAVE A SIGH OF RELIEF, TRUE BELIEVERS. WE'RE HOME.
THERE WAS AN ELECTRIC SURGE CONSISTENT WITH THE ACTIVATION OF BILLY'S TRANSPORTER JUST BEFORE THE INSULATING CAGE WAS CLOSED.
YOU'RE SAYING BILLY AND MAY MIGHT HAVE FOUND A WAY OUT?
IT'S POSSIBLE. BUT A WAY OUT TO WHERE? THE WEB WAS BADLY DAMAGED, THEIR TELEPORTATION WATCHES DAMAGED EVEN WORSE.
DOZENS OF ENEMIES WERE ATTEMPTING TO TRAVEL ACROSS THE WEB AT THE SAME TIME, CREATING FEEDBACK AND CONFUSION.
WELL, THEY'RE BETTER ODDS THAN WE THOUGHT. MAYBE BILLY AND MAYDAY ARE OUT THERE AFTER ALL.
AND WHEREVER THEY ARE, WE WILL FIND THEM.
I CAN'T STAY. WITH MAYDAY GONE, I'M THE ONLY PERSON WHO CAN PROTECT HER MOTHER AND BABY BROTHER, BENJY.
ONCE I GET MY DRONES RUNNING AGAIN, THEY CAN TRY TO BACK-TRACE BILLY'S SIGNAL.
I HAVE SOME FIVE-DIMENSIONAL TRANSLATION SOFTWARE I THINK CAN HELP YOU.
AND I KNOW WHAT BILLY SMELLS LIKE, SO I CAN TRACK HIM THAT WAY.
THIS NOSE AIN'T JUST FOR MY STRIKING PROFILE.
YES, I DO NOT DOUBT ALL YOUR TALENTS WILL BE NEEDED. BILLY HAS ASSEMBLED A TRUE TEAM HERE, AND IF HE AND MAY ARE OUT THERE, YOU WILL FIND THEM.

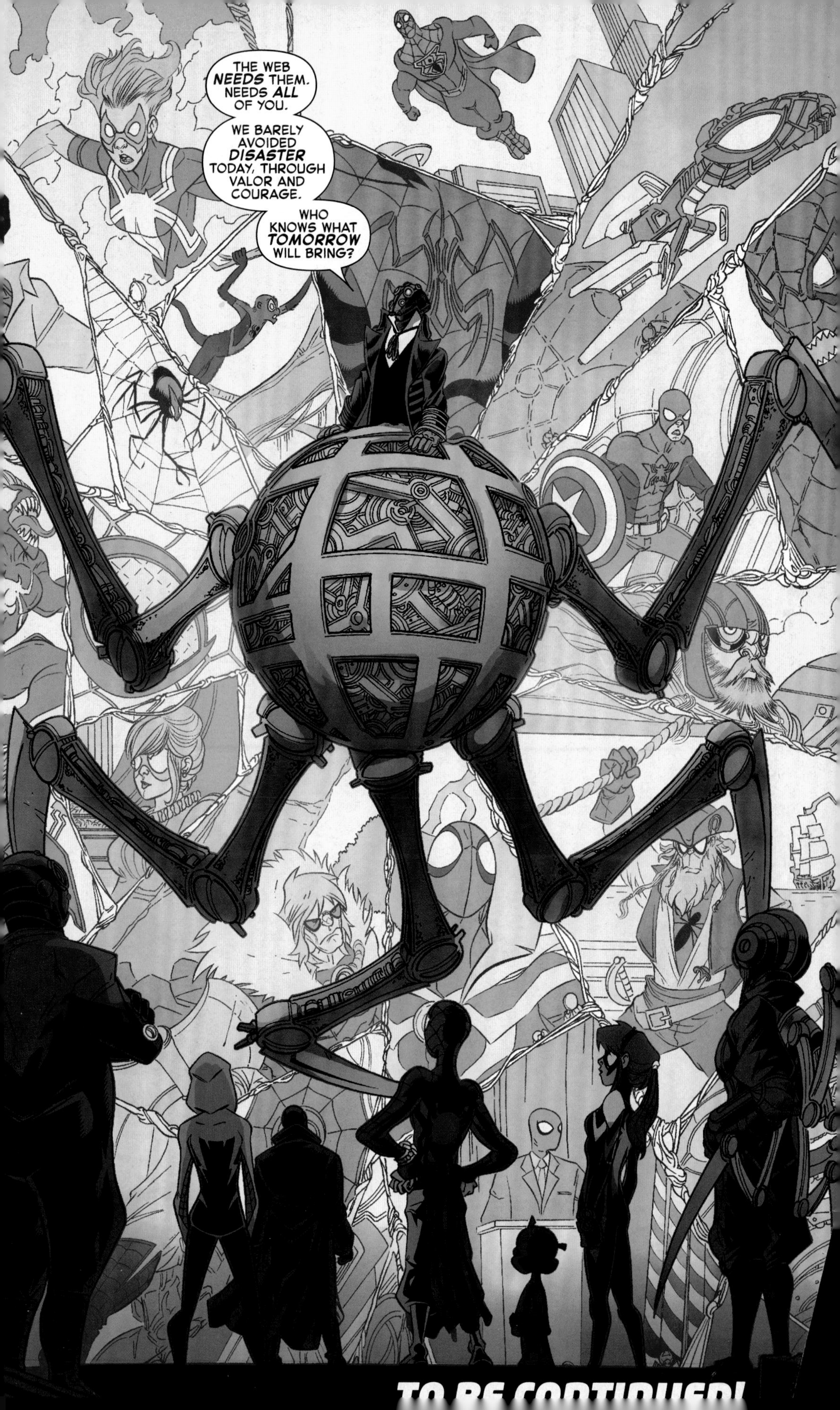
THE WEB NEEDS THEM. NEEDS ALL OF YOU.
WE BARELY AVOIDED DISASTER TODAY, THROUGH VALOR AND COURAGE.
WHO KNOWS WHAT TOMORROW WILL BRING?
TO BE CONTINUED!

#1 VARIANT BY
**TRADD MOORE &
MATT WILSON**

#2 MARVEL '92 VARIANT BY
**MARK BAGLEY,
ANDREW HENNESSY &
RACHELLE ROSENBERG**